how europe underdeveloped AFRICA

how europe underdeveloped AFRICA

Walter Rodney

Black Classic Press

Baltimore

THE WALTER RODNEY FOUNDATION

The Rodney Family formed The Walter Rodney Foundation in 2006 in order to share the life and works of Walter Rodney with students, scholars and community activists around the world. The Foundation is a non-profit organization working to advance education, health and development by promoting human rights, social justice and sustainable development from a Pan-African perspective.

The Principal Objectives of the Foundation are to:
- Contribute to a more equitable society;
- Promote and facilitate literacy and education;
- Promote and facilitate health and development initiatives;
- Promote and facilitate civic involvement and leadership skills;
- Provide resources for the marginalized, especially women and youth;
- Promote scholarly use of the Walter Rodney Papers housed at the Robert W. Woodruff Library of the Atlanta University Center;
- Consolidate the intellectual property of Dr. Walter Rodney, and;
- Promote his legacy by holding seminars, conferences and symposia in schools, colleges and universities and communities.

Annual Symposium
An annual symposium is held in Atlanta, Georgia during the week of Walter Rodney's birthday (March 23rd). The goal is to bring together scholars, researchers, activists, students and the community to discuss contemporary issues from a Rodney perspective. The first symposium was held in 2003 - the Tenth Annual Walter Rodney Symposium will be held in 2012.

The Walter Rodney Papers
In 2003, the Walter Rodney Papers were donated to the Robert W. Woodruff Library of the Atlanta University Center. The Walter Rodney collection is the largest and most comprehensive collection of writings, speeches, correspondence, photographs and documents created by or about Walter Rodney anywhere in the world. They are available for viewing and research in the Archives and Special Collections of the Woodruff Library.

Programs
The Foundation continues Rodney's legacy and is currently by supporting programs in Guyana, Ghana, Tanzania.

For more information and to contribute to the Foundation and its activities, please visit www.walterrodneyfoundation.org. The Walter Rodney Foundation, Inc. is a non-profit 501(c)(3) charitable organization.

To
Pat, Muthoni, Mashaka
and
the extended family

PREFACE

This book derives from a concern with the contemporary African situation. It delves into the past only because otherwise it would be impossible to understand how the present came into being and what the trends are for the near future. In the search for an understanding of what is now called "underdevelopment" in Africa, the limits of inquiry have had to be fixed as far apart as the fifteenth century, on the one hand, and the end of the colonial period, on the other hand.

Ideally, an analysis of underdevelopment should come even closer to the present than the end of the colonial period in the 1960s. The phenomenon of neo-colonialism cries out for extensive investigation in order to formulate the strategy and tactics of African emancipation and development. This study does not go that far, but at least certain solutions are implicit in a correct historical evaluation, just as given medical remedies are indicated or contraindicated by a correct diagnosis of a patient's condition and an accurate case history. Hopefully, the facts and interpretation that follow will make a small contribution towards reinforcing the conclusion that African development is possible only on the basis of a radical break with the international capitalist system, which has been the principal agency of underdevelopment of Africa over the last five centuries.

As the reader will observe, the question of development strategy is tackled briefly in the final section by A. M. Babu, former Minister of Economic Affairs and Development Planning, who has been actively involved in fashioning policy along those lines in the Tanzanian context. It is no accident that the text as a whole has been written within Tanzania, where expressions of concern for development have been accompanied by considerably more positive action than in several parts of the continent.

Many colleagues and comrades shared in the preparation of this work. Special thanks must go to comrades Karim Hirji and Henry Mapolu of the University of Dar es Salaam, who read the manuscript in a spirit of constructive criticism. But, contrary to the fashion in most prefaces, I will not add that "all mistakes and shortcomings are entirely my responsibility." That is sheer bourgeois subjectivism. Responsibility in matters of these sorts is always collective, especially with regard to the remedying of shortcomings. The purpose has been to try and reach Africans who wish to explore further the nature of their exploitation, rather than to satisfy the "standards" set by our oppressors and their spokesmen in the academic world.

WALTER RODNEY
Dar es Salaam

CONTENTS

INTRODUCTION

At the outset, before anything else is written, we need openly to acknowledge how difficult it has been for us to come to terms with the undeniable fact that Walter Rodney, our brother, friend and comrade, is dead. On June 13, 1980, the author of this unparalleled work of historical analysis became the best-known victim of a systematic campaign of assasination and other forms of ruthless repression carried out by the governing authorities of his native land, Guyana.

The end was predictable, for Walter had determined that the only path to true human development and liberation for the majority of the people of his country was through the transformation of their own lives in a struggle to replace and reshape the neo-colonialist government that dominated their society and prescribed their existence. However, Forbes Burnham, the President of Guyana, had made it clear on many occasions that, in this struggle for the minds and hearts of the people, he knew no limits in the determination to "exterminate the forces of opposition." In the opinion of many, there is no doubt that the bomb that tore away the life of Walter Rodney was the result of Burnham's deadly pledge.

Hard as his death is to accept and absorb, we must begin here, not primarily for purposes of sentiment or political invective, but because no new introduction to *How Europe Underveloped Africa* is possible without a serious and direct encounter with Walter Rodney, the revolutionary scholar, the scholar-revolutionary, the man of great integrity and hope. For, more so than most books of its genre, this work is clearly imbued with the spirit, the intellect and the commitment of its author—both the man who produced the audacious and wide-ranging study before he was thirty, and the man who moved with an unswerving integrity to live out its implications in his relatively brief years.

With Rodney the life and the work were one, and the life drives us back to recall the essential themes of the work. In spite of its title, this is not simply a work about European oppressors and African victims, serving primarily as a weapon to flay the exploiters and beat them at their own intellectual games. (Of course, it has done yeoman service in that limited role.) Rather, there is much more to this masterly survey, and at its deepest levels it offers no easy comfort to any of us.

At one point, early in the book, Rodney summarizes its basic message:

> The question as to who, and what, is responsible for African underdevelopment can be answered at two levels. Firstly, the answer is that the operation of the imperialist system bears major responsibility for African economic retardation by draining African wealth and by making it impossible to develop more rapidly the resources of the continent. Secondly, one has to deal with those who manipulated the system and those who are either agents or unwitting accomplices of the said system. The capitalists of Western Europe were the ones who actively extended their exploitation from inside Europe to cover the whole of Africa. In recent times, they were joined, and to some extent replaced, by the capitalists from the United States; and for many years now even the workers of those metropolitan countries have benefited from the exploitaiton and underdevelopment of Africa. (27–28)

All this Walter supported with a profuse and creative set of precise examples from many sources, periods and places. Yet, he was not satisfied to pour well-documented blows upon the oppressors—though he was a master at this activity. Nor did it suffice to remind many of us who live in the United States that our blackness provides no exemption from our willing participation in the benefits of our country's exploitation of Africa. Rather, his summary of the book's central themes concluded with words that moved beyond accusation or guilt. He said,

> None of these remarks are intended to remove the ultimate responsibility for development from the shoulders of Africans. Not only are there African accomplices inside the imperialist system, but every African has a responsibility to understand the system and work for its overthrow. (28)

Unlike many of us who read and write such words, Walter took them seriously. He knew that they were meant for him, for the children of Africa in the Caribbean and the United States of America; for Indians, Asians and many other sufferers at the hands of European-fueled underdevelopment. Indeed, he knew they were meant, too, for all those Europeans and Americans who claimed solidarity with the Third World struggle for development and liberation.

Rodney envisioned and worked on the assumption that the new development of Africans and other dependent peoples of the "periphery" would require what he called "a radical break with the international capitalist system," a courageous challenge to the failing "center" of the current world order. Of course, he also knew that any such break or serious contestation would participate in and precipitate profound revolutionary changes at the center itself. Thus, from his perspective, what was ultimately at stake, what was absolutely necessary was a fundamental transformation in the ordering of the political, cultural and economic forces that have dominated the world for almost half a millenium.

This was an awesome vision, especially since Walter dared to say and believe that such a stupendous transformation must be initiated by Africans and other dwellers in the nether regions of exploitation and subordination. Nevertheless, he did not flinch from the implications of his own analysis. Instead, he continued—especially by his example—to encourage all of us to move toward a radically transformed vision of ourselves and of our capacities for changing our lives and our objective conditions. Quietly, insistently, he urged us to claim our full responsibility for engaging in the struggle for a new world order.

No one could ignore Walter's work, nor question his call, for he set the example by assuming his own part of the awesome responsibility. That is why he was in Guyana in June 1980. That is why he had been there since 1974, developing the leadership of what was called the Working People's Alliance (WPA), struggling to support his family, somehow finding time to carry on research and writing on the history of the working people of his country and other parts of the Caribbean. That is why he was murdered.

In the midst of our sorrow and indignation none of us who knew Walter could honestly say that we were surprised by the news of his death. For his life carried a certain consistency and integrity that could not be ignored or denied. Indeed, in his relatively brief time certain patterns were established early. Born on March 13, 1942, Rodney grew up in Georgetown, the capital of what was then British Guiana. From the outset, he was part of a family that took transformational politics with great seriousness. His parents, especially his father, were deeply involved in the development of the Peoples Progressive Party (PPP). A multi-racial party, it was at the time the only mass political organization in the Caribbean that was opening the common people to the world of Marxist/Socialist thought, as well as raising the possibilities of alternative futures that might go beyond the mere establishment of independence within the British Commonwealth.

So, even before he entered his teens, Walter was already engaged in leafletting, attending party meetings and absorbing the thousands of hours of political discussions that went on in his home. Then, when he entered Queens College, the highly regarded secondary school in Georgetown, the young political activist also became one of the "scholarship boys" so familiar to West Indian life at the time. Bright, energetic and articulate, he excelled in academics and sports (he broke his school record for the high jump), and when he won the coveted Guyana scholarship to the University College of the West Indies at Mona, Jamaica, the traditional path to academic prestige and distinction was open to him.

In 1963, Rodney graduated with first class honors in history from UCWI, and was awarded a scholarship to the University of London where he entered the School of Oriental and African Studies to work on his doctorate in African History. Walter's political instincts and early nurturing would not allow him to settle into the safety of conventional academic life. Instead, the years in London (1963–1966) were among the most important of his continuing political and intellectual development. He immediately became part of a study group of younger West Indians who met regularly under the guidance of the man who was then the exemplar of the revolutionary intellectual, C. L. R. James, the Trinidadian Marxist scholar, best known for his history of the Haitian revolution, *Black Jacobins.*

The experience with James and the study group was a crucial supplement to Rodney's earlier exposure to the day-to-day life of radical Caribbean politics, and it was also an important source of grounding in intellectual reality as he moved through the sometimes surreal world of the academic community. By the time he left London for Tanzania in 1966, Rodney was prepared to write history from what he later described as "a revolutionary, socialist and people-centered perspective." (Within the boundaries of an academic thesis, his excellent dissertation: "A History of the Upper Guinea Coast, 1545–1800," addressed itself to the subject from that perspective.)*

During the 1966–67 academic year, Walter taught history at the University College in Dar es Salaam, Tanzania. In 1968, he returned to Jamaica to take a post in History at his alma mater and to develop what he planned to be a major program in African and Caribbean studies. More importantly, he wanted to test his convictions about the need for revolutionary intellectuals to remain grounded in the ongoing life of the people. Walter met with initial success in both of these endeavors, but it was precisely this success, especially in his work among the common people of the Jamaican streets, hills and gullies, that led to a drastic foreshortening of his stay in that country. In less than a year Rodney had come in touch with and helped articulate the profound discontent and

---

* The dissertation was published by Clarendon Press in 1970, and recently reprinted in paperback by *Monthly Review Press.*

unrest that filled the lives of the ordinary people of Jamaica, as well as many of the university students. As they began seriously to talk and listen together—to ground with one another—about the ways to organize for change, as they heard and pondered the implications of the powerful calls for Black Power rising in this country, it was obvious that a deep and unpredictable ferment was at work, and the conservative Jamaican government readily identified Walter as an undesirable foreign element. Thus, in October, 1968, while attending a Black Writer's Conference in Montreal, Walter Rodney was officially expelled from Jamaica. The government action led to several days of protest in Kingston, but Rodney was kept out.

It was this political activity, combined with his powerful participation in the Montreal conference, that first brought the twenty-six-year old Caribbean historian to the attention of many of us in the United States. Then, following the Jamaican government's action, Walter's fellow members of the C. L. R. James study group and other Caribbean activists based in London, pressed Walter for the opportunity to publish some of the lectures that he had delivered in Jamaica. With that purpose in mind they formed the Bogle-L'Ouverture Publishing House, and in 1969 brought out Walter's first widely-read book, *Groundings With My Brothers.** Walter returned to Dar es Salaam, teaching again at the University (1969–1972), while *Groundings* was making a profound impression on many people in this country, especially among those of us who were involved in the struggle for hegemony over the definitions of the black (and white) experience in the United States, a struggle temporarily crystallized in the Black Studies movement.

Not surprisingly, it was at one of the many conferences spawned by that movement that Walter Rodney was first introduced to a major audience of Afro-Americans. In May, 1970, he participated in the second annual gathering of the African Heritage Studies Association at Howard University. While one of the contributors to this introduction (Robert Hill) had already met and worked with Walter at the University of the West Indies, the Howard conference provided the first opportunity for the other two of us.

Like many persons at the conference, my first impression of this slightly built, soft-spoken, dark-skinned brother from Guyana was his capacity to

---

* The new press was named after Paul Bogle, the leader of the 1865 Morant Bay rebellion in Jamaica and Toussaint L'Ouverture, the Haitian leader. Among those most actively involved in the endeavor were Andrew Salkey, Jessica and Eric Huntley, Richard Small, John LaRose, Selma James, Earl Greenwood and Chris Le Maitre. Not long after Rodney's assassination, Bogle-L'Ouverture Book Store was renamed the Walter Rodney Book Store.

speak without notes—and largely without rhetorical flourish—for more than an hour, and yet have his highly informative material so carefully and cogently organized that it would have been possible to take it directly from a transcript and publish it. Eventually, we discovered that this tremendous intellectual discipline (and political instinct) was matched by a disciplined force of spirit, a mastery of—but not slavery to—dialectical materialism, and an unflinching commitment to collective work on behalf of the wretched of the earth. All this was insulated from self-righteousness by a dry and ready sense of humor. In other words, it was clear to us that Walter Rodney was a moral, political and intellectual force to be reckoned with, one of Africa's most beautiful children.

From the point of our first encounter, we knew that we had met a brother, teacher and comrade. At the time of the Howard conference, Robert Hill, Bill Strickland and I were working with others in the development of the Institute of the Black World (IBW), an Atlanta-based center for research, publication and advocacy. Immediately, we began to explore with Walter some of the ways in which he might share with us in this experiment in collective intellectual work. As a result, in a series of visits he spent quiet, unhurried time among us. In our homes we also shared the company of his wife, Pat, and their lively children, Shaka, Knini and Asha.

As our ties were being developed and cemented, the first edition of *How Europe Underdeveloped Africa* was jointly published by Bogle-L'Ouverture and the Tanzanian Publishing House in 1972. For all of those who could obtain copies of the work, it was like a mighty, uplifting gust of fresh air. Without romanticising pre-colonial Africa, Walter had placed it in the context of human development across the globe, traced its real historical relationships to the colonizing forces of Europe and suggested the path for Africa's movement toward a new life for its people and a new role in the re-shaping of the world.

The book immediately struck an exciting and responsive chord among many in this country. Among politically-oriented black people it played something of the same formative role as Frantz Fanon's *Wretched of the Earth* almost a decade before. Indeed, both men were dealing with the ravages of colonialism and neo-colonialism; both were calling for a break with the exploiting, ravaging system in order to move forward and create a new order. Both were living examples of the transformation they demanded.

Like Fanon's seminal work, Rodney's also began from an African/ Caribbean perspective, but we in the United States of America immediately recognized the global connection. Although Walter ended his primary historical analysis with the close of the 1950s, he nevertheless offered a brief, cogent and powerful treatment of the contemporary role of the United States in the exploitation of Africa, implicitly warning us against our own active or passive participation in that damaging work. But there were also connections perhaps even more directly related to the Afro-American struggles in the early 1970s, especially in his treatment of colonial and neo-colonial education and its effects on the African mind and spirit. For instance, Walter wrote, "In the final analysis, perhaps the most important principle of colonial education was that of capitalist individualism. . . . In Africa, both the formal school system and the informal value system of colonialism destroyed social solidarity and promoted the worst form of alienated individualism without social responsibility." (254–255)

We Afro-Americans immediately recognized that condition. Indeed, one of the central themes of the movement for Black Studies and Black Power had been the call for social solidarity among black people and resistance to the destructive individualism of the mainstream American way of life. For we were painfully aware of the rising alienation among our young people as they moved ever more fully into the cultural flow of mass American society with its powerful networks of formal and informal mis-education. Thus, it was natural that those of us at the Institute of the Black World (IBW) invited Walter Rodney to participate with us in two projects directly related to those concerns. The first was as a contributor to a book-length monograph, *Education and Black Struggle,* that we organized and edited for *Harvard Educational Review* in 1974. His paper was on "Education in Africa and Contemporary Tanzania."

The second project was of a different nature. Early in 1974 Walter had received an appointment as professor and chairman of History at the University of Guyana. The appointment was considered a clear victory for Walter and his supporters, a vindication of his vision. We invited him to spend part of the summer in Atlanta with us before his return to Guyana. He spent more than a month at IBW, primarily in the development and leadership of a Summer Research Symposium. Colleagues from other parts of the nation and from the Caribbean joined us in the venture as we experimented with models for an educational program that would provide broader scope and new alternatives for young black people in colleges and universities across the country.* At the same time, in an act of vision and

---

* Among the colleagues who participated in the Summer Research Symposium (SRS) were C. L. R. James, St. Clair Drake, Katherine Dunham, George Beckford, Edward Braithwaite, Lerone Bennett, Mary Berry, Tran Van Dinh, Mack Jones and Frank Smith.

courage, the Howard University Press was publishing the first American edition of *How Europe Underdeveloped Africa.*

The extended time that Walter spent at IBW that summer was critical to us all. It helped to crystallize much of our thinking about the role of black intellectuals in our own society, and the role that IBW might play in that development. Concurrently, it provided Walter with an opportunity to explore more deeply the implications of the unique black-American experience. Moreover, it brought us all into community with an exciting group of students and co-workers, and we looked forward to the many ways in which we could continue to work together with Walter in his new post at the University of Guyana.

However, even before Walter left Atlanta, we had begun to receive signals that all was not well with the university appointment. By the time he arrived home the official word was given. At the last moment, in an unprecedented move, the appointment had been cancelled, apparently the result of pressure from the highest levels of government. From that point on, Walter Rodney, revolutionary-scholar, began once more to dig deeply into the soil of his native land. In spite of invitations and appeals from many places, he steadfastly refused to leave Guyana on any permanent basis.

He had set himself two major tasks, both consistent with his definition of his role as a black intellectual who was committed to the liberation and development of his people. Both required his presence in Guyana. The first was to develop a major, multi-volume work on the history of the working people of his country. The second task (and this was all-encompassing) was to immerse himself in the contemporary life of those same people and search with them to find a way to resist the power of a government that had clearly betrayed their hopes and their trust, a government that now stood in the way of their development. In other words, Walter was still trying to deal with the neo-colonial implications of *How Europe Underdeveloped Africa,* dauntlessly carrying the search for solutions to the center of his own life and the life of his nation. All the while, especially since Pat, his wife, had also been denied an opportunity to work at her profession of social welfare, Walter had to find ways to feed, clothe and house his family.

Even though it was hard for some of us to imagine how he did it in spite of a situation of constantly heightening tension and danger, Walter managed to find time and energy to spend long hours in the Guyana National Archives and in the Caribbean Research Library at the University in Georgetown. In addition to a number of monographs, the ultimate fruit of that disciplined and sacrificial work will appear when the Johns Hopkins University Press publishes Walter's *History of the Guyanese Working People, 1881–1905.* He also published during this period of intensified struggle an important text, *Guyanese Sugar Plantations in the Late Nineteenth Century.*

Meanwhile, he continued to organize. Before 1974 was over Walter had helped to centralize the Working Peoples Alliance. This became his political base in the relentless struggle to build a force that would bring about the revolutionary transformation of the Guyanese society.

With the help of many persons in the United States and other parts of the world, Walter found opportunities to lecture and teach in an attempt to keep in touch with his comrades outside of Guyana and to earn the funds his family needed. (James Turner, Director of the Africana Studies and Research Center at Cornell and Immanuel Wallerstein of the State University of New York at Binghamton, were especially helpful to those of us who were trying to organize these activities.)

Whenever Walter travelled abroad, especially as the government's repression increased, many friends urged him to leave Guyana and bring himself and his family to some place of relative safety. Walter's response to us generally had two parts. First was his sense of the responsibility he had to his comrades and the people of Guyana. He said that he was working among them to encourage them in a fearless struggle for the transformation of themselves and their society, and that he could not leave simply because he happened to have ready access to the means of escape. Second, Rodney said he felt he had been singularly privileged in the broad set of contacts he had been able to establish in the course of his work and travels throughout the Third World. For him, this privilege carried with it a responsibility to continue to share with his people the content and spirit of that international network of women and men involved in liberation struggles. Thus, without any trace of a desire for martyrdom, but with a clear recognition of the situation he faced, Walter's response was always the same: *"It is imperative that I stay here."*

Toward the end, all these dangers, hopes and tensions were concentrated in the events of one last, year-long outpouring of life and death. In June, 1979, the WPA formally announced that it had transformed itself into a political party, one that would work untiringly for the overthrow of the strong-hold that Burnham's Peoples National Congress had established in the country. In the following month, a government building in Georgetown was set afire and Walter and four other WPA members were among the eight persons arrested and charged with arson.* Because

---

* Known as the "Referendum Five," they included Walter Rodney, Rupert Roopnarine, Maurice Omawale, Kwame Apata and Karen De Souza. All five were denied trial by jury.

it was a government bulding, the charge was very serious. But it was also clear to many observers that the action was entirely set up as part of the measures for breaking the force of Rodney's small but influential organization. On the day of the arraignment, Father Bernard Danke, a priest who was a reporter for the *Catholic Standard,* was fatally stabbed in the back as he stood observing a pro-WPA demonstration outside the court building. From that point on, a repressive situation deteriorated into what might be called a long night of official terrorism, including bombings, police beatings and escalating threats of "extermination" by Burnham against Walter and other leaders of the opposition WPA.

By the end of February 1980, two of Walter's close associates in the WPA, Ohene Koama and Edward Lublin, had been killed by the police, others shot and beaten; still others jailed, their houses raided, ransacked and bombed. By then, some of the leading members of the WPA were actually being held as political prisoners in Guyana, for their government refused them permission to leave the country. However, Rodney managed to get out in May 1980, accepting an invitation from the Patriotic Front to attend the independence ceremonies in Zimbabwe. Then Walter returned to Guyana, continuing to work in the Archives, to organize among the people. He had ominously told some of us in this country that we might not see him again.

On June 2, the trial for arson began, witnesssed by concerned observers from the Caribbean, the United States and England. Within a few days it was clear that the government had no case and could not prosecute Rodney and his co-workers. As a result, on June 6, at the request of the government, the trial was adjourned until August 20.

One week after the adjournment, on Friday evening, June 13, Walter was sitting in his brother's car, waiting for Donald Rodney at the driver's seat. They had stopped at the house of a man who we now know had infiltrated the ranks of the WPA. Donald Rodney went in to pick up what the man said was a walkie-talkie that Walter wanted. As they stood in the infiltrator's yard around 7:30 p.m., he told Rodney to drive off and wait for a test signal at 8:00. Donald returned to the car and drove away. When the signal came, it turned out to be the explosion that ended Walter Rodney's life.

A few weeks before his death, Rodney had been persistently interviewed about the dangers that he faced and his plans for defending himself against them. He said,

> As to my own safety and the safety of a number of other persons within the WPA, we will try to guarantee our safety by the level of political

mobilization and political action inside and outside of the country. Ultimately, it is this rather than any kind of physical defense which will guarantee our safety. None of us are unmindful of the threat that is constantly posed. We don't regard ourselves as adventurers, as martyrs or potential martyrs, but we think there is a job which needs to be done and at a certain point in time we have to do what has to be done.

Again, Walter's courageous sense of commitment and integrity evokes sharp memories of Fanon. He too sacrificed his life for the liberation of his people and died before he was forty. He too called the children of Africa and all those damned by Europe to seize the initiative and change our ways. He too asked us to resist all temptations to live out our lives as permanent victims, angry accusers or fawning imitators of Europe. It was he who said,

> Come, then, comrades, the European game has finally ended. . . . Look at them today swaying between atomic and spiritual disintegration. . . . we must find something different. We today can do everything, so long as we do not imitate Europe, so long as we are not obsessed by the desire to catch up with Europe we have taken the liberty at this point of changing "Europe" to Europe/America—we think Fanon would permit that.
>
> The Third World faces Europe/America like a colossal mass whose aim should be to try to resolve the problems to which Europe/America has not been able to find the answers.
>
> So comrades, let us not pay tribute to Europe/America by creating states, institutions, and societies which draw their inspiration from her.
>
> . . . If we want humanity to advance a step further, if we want to bring it up to a different level than that which Europe/America has shown it, then we must invent and we must make discoveries.
>
> If we wish to live up to our people's expectations, we must seek the response elsewhere than in Europe/America. For Europe/America, for ourselves and for humanity, comrades, we must turn over a new leaf, we must work out new concepts, and we must try to set afoot a new man. (*Wretched of the Earth*, 252–255)

From Walter's perspective, that was the "job that needs to be done," the challenge that he and his comrades had determined to take on; experimenting, inventing, risking, trying to work out new forms of organization, new modes of struggle, new visions and concepts to guide and undergird them, starting on their own home ground. For Walter Rodney, the WPA was one element of the job and his research and writing was another. He saw no contradiction between them. All elements of the task were held firmly together by the righteous integrity of his life, the disciplined power of his visions and his undying love for the people and their possibilities.

Thus, he went about doing the job that needed to be done. But, as it was said of Malcolm X, so it could be said of Walter: "He became much more than there was time for him to be."

Now we are starkly aware of the fact that the time he no longer has is really ours, that the job he took on is in our hands, to continue, to re-define, wherever we are, whoever we are. The call that he tried to answer is here for us all: "if we want humanity to advance a step further . . . we must invent and we must make discoveries . . . we must turn over a new leaf, we must work out new concepts, and we must try to set afoot a new [humanity]." (255, *Wretched of the Earth*)

Walter's Legacy

It is our courageous, creative attempts to respond to such a magnificent summons that we begin to break the chains of our underdevelopment and shake the foundations of all human exploitation. And is it not clear by now that the process of exploitation leads to an underdeveloped humanity both at the "center" and at the "periphery"? Do we not see that the underdevelopment of the center, in the homeland of the exploiters, is simply covered over with material possessions and deadly weaponry, but that the nakedness and human retardation are nevertheless there? So who among us does not need to break the coils of the past, to transcend and re-create our history?

Perhaps it is only as we take up the challenge of Walter and Fanon that we will be prepared to give up all the deadly games of the last half-millenia, seeking out new means of defense, new forms of struggle, new pathways toward revolution, new visions of what truly humane society demands of us. Only as we begin to entertain such thoughts, consider such inventions, will we be prepared to carefully examine again and then move beyond the marvelous limits of *How Europe Underdeveloped Africa,* pressing on—in the spirit of Rodney and Fanon—to ask a new question: *how shall we re-develop the world?*

Beginning with ourselves, beginning where we are, what must we tear down, what must we build up, what foundations must we lay? Who shall we work with, what visions can we create, what hopes shall possess us? How shall we organize? How shall we be related to those who raise the same questions in South Africa, in El Salvadore, in Guyana? How shall we communicate with others the urgency of our time? How shall we en-vision and work for the revolutionary transformation of our own country? What are the inventions, the discoveries, the new concepts that will help us move toward the revolution we need in this land?

Neither rhetoric nor coercion will serve us now. We must decide whether we shall remain crippled and underdeveloped, or move to participate in our own healing by taking on the challenge to re-develop ourselves, our people, our endangered nation and the earth. No one can force us toward this. By conventional measurements, there are no guarantees of success—as the blood of our martyrs and heroes, known and less known, like Walter Rodney and Frantz Fanon, Ruby Doris and Fanny Lou, Malcolm and Martin, fully testify.

But there is a world waiting for us; indeed, many worlds await us. One is the world of our children, not yet born, or just beginning, but wanting to live, to grow, to become their best possible selves. This will not happen unless, as Walter suggests, the center is transformed and fundamentally changed. That will not happen unless *we* are transformed, re-developed and renewed. The future of our children depends upon these rigorous transformations.

The Afro-American Challenge

Then there is another more difficult world that awaits us: the world of the sons and daughters of Europe/America who have begun to discover their own underdevelopment, who recognize the warping and desensitizing of their spirits. Without rehearsing all the old political arguments about coalitions and alliances, neither forgetting the past nor being bound by it, we must find some way to respond to them and to allow them to come in touch with us. This is no passing luxury, in the old "race relations" style. Rather, we now realize that the children of the oppressed and the children of the oppressors are involved in a dialectical relationship that is deeper than most of us choose to recognize, and that there is no fundamental re-development for one without the other. This is a heavy burden, but it represents a great possibility as well. In this country, with our peculiar history, it is also an undeniable reality.

So, it is by the way of these difficult issues that we return to Walter and his great work. Now, what seems demanded of us as we re-visit *How Europe Underdeveloped Africa,* is that we read it this time in the light of Walter Rodney's life and death; this time in the consciousness of the dangerous, explosive American center; this time in the company of our children; this time in the presence of Fanon's insistent call to us all.

Then we shall likely see more clearly than ever before that Europe's underdevelopment of Africa, and other worlds, required Europe's ravaging of itself and everyone—and everything—that came under its sway. So the wounded are all around us and within us. Now, opening ourselves to all those who recognize the brutal dialectics of underdevelopment, who acknowledge the cohesive powers of our common needs, our common dangers and our common possibilities, we can begin to stand in a newly grounded solidarity and reach out toward each other, facing the harsh but beautiful fact that we must either re-develop ourselves and our world or be pushed together into some terrible, explosive closing of the light.

Of course, if we choose to go the way of our essential community, we cannot go far by responding primarily to the urgency of fear (for that would repeat history rather than transform it—and that would be unfaithful to a courageous brother like Walter). Instead, we must be drawn by the fact that there is much to attract us. For instance, one of the hopeful elements on the other side of the patterns of domination/subordination of the past 500 years has been the drawing of humankind into networks of communication and interrelatedness that hold great possibilities for the establishment of new communities beyond the traditional, national barriers. Reshaped and re-directed, the mechanisms of exploitation may actually place some vital means of re-development within our grasp.

Now it is in our hands—to overcome our history, to break the shackles of the past, to re-develop ourselves, our people, our nation and our world—to find humane, creative and fearless ways of dealing with those who presently oppose such development. These are audacious visions, and truly awesome responsibilities. But we must go forward. Indeed, it seems clear to us that even without any guarantees of success, we must move in the flow of humankind's best, most creative imagination, in the direction of our most profoundly renewing dreams.

Anything less is inadequate for the perilous times. Anything less would be unworthy of the memory of our brother, the needs of our children, or the magnificent, untapped capacities of our own best selves.

March 1981

VINCENT HARDING
ROBERT HILL
WILLIAM STRICKLAND

CHAPTER
I

Some Questions on Development

· What Is Development?   · What Is Underdevelopment?

IN CONTRAST WITH THE SURGING GROWTH OF THE COUNTRIES IN THE socialist camp and the development taking place, albeit much more slowly, in the majority of the capitalist countries, is the unquestionable fact that a large proportion of the so-called underdeveloped countries are in total stagnation, and that in some of them the rate of economic growth is lower than that of population increase.

These characteristics are not fortuitous; they correspond strictly to the nature of the capitalist system in full expansion, which transfers to the dependent countries the most abusive and barefaced forms of exploitation. It must be clearly understood that the only way to solve the questions now besetting mankind is to eliminate completely the exploitation of dependent countries by developed capitalist countries, with all the consequences that this implies.

—CHÉ GUEVARA, 1964

What Is Development?

Development in human society is a many-sided process. At the level of the individual, it implies increased skill and capacity, greater freedom, creativity, self-discipline, responsibility, and material well-being. Some of these are virtually moral categories and are difficult to evaluate—depending as they do on the age in which one lives, one's class origins, and one's personal code of what is wrong. However, what is indisputable is that the achievement of any of those aspects of personal development is very much tied in with the state of the society as a whole. From earliest times, man found it convenient and necessary to come together in groups to hunt and for the sake of survival. The relations which develop within any given social group are crucial to an understanding of the society as a whole. Freedom, responsibility, skill, have real meaning only in terms of the relations of men in society.

Of course, each social group comes into contact with others. The relations between individuals in any two societies are regulated by the form of the two societies. Their respective political structures are important because the ruling elements within each group are the ones that begin to have dialogue, trade, or fight, as the case may be. At the level of social groups, therefore, development implies an increasing capacity to regulate both internal and external relationships. Much of human history has been a fight for survival against natural hazards and against real and imagined

3

human enemies. Development in the past has always meant the increase in the ability to guard the independence of the social group and indeed to infringe upon the freedom of others—something that often came about irrespective of the will of the persons within the societies involved.

Men are not the only beings that operate in groups, but the human species embarked upon a unique line of development because man had the capacity to make and use tools. The very act of making tools was a stimulus to increasing rationality rather than the consequence of a fully matured intellect. In historical terms, man the worker was every bit as important as man the thinker, because the work with tools liberated men from sheer physical necessity, so that he could impose himself upon other more powerful species and upon nature itself. The tools with which men work and the manner in which they organize their labor are both important indices of social development.

More often than not, the term "development" is used in an exclusive economic sense—the justification being that the type of economy is itself an index of other social features. What then is economic development? A society develops economically as its members increase jointly their capacity for dealing with the environment. This capacity for dealing with the environment is dependent on the extent to which they understand the laws of nature (science), on the extent to which they put that understanding into practice by devising tools (technology), and on the manner in which work is organized. Taking a long-term view, it can be said that there has been constant economic development within human society since the origins of man, because man has multiplied enormously his capacity to win a living from nature. The magnitude of man's achievement is best understood by reflecting on the early history of human society and noting the following: firstly, the progress from crude stone tools to the use of metals; secondly, the changeover from hunting and gathering wild fruit to the domestication of animals and the growing of food crops; and thirdly, the improvement in organization of work from being an individualistic activity towards being an activity which assumes a social character through the participation of many.

Every people have shown a capacity for independently increasing their ability to live a more satisfactory life through exploiting the resources of nature. Every continent independently participated in the early epochs of the extension of man's control over his environment—which means in effect that every continent can point to a period of economic development. Africa, being the original home of man, was obviously a major participant in the processes in which human groups displayed an ever increasing capacity to extract a living from the natural environment. Indeed, in the early period, Africa was the focus of the physical development of man as such, as distinct from other living beings.

Development was universal because the conditions leading to economic expansion were universal. Everywhere, man was faced with the task of survival by meeting fundamental material needs; and better tools were a consequence of the interplay between human beings and nature as part of the struggle for survival. Of course, human history is not a record of advances and nothing else. There were periods in every part of the world when there were temporary setbacks and actual reduction of the capacity to produce basic necessities and other services for the population. But the overall tendency was towards increased production, and at given points of time the increase in the quantity of goods was associated with a change in the quality or character of society. This will be shown later with reference to Africa, but to indicate the universal application of the principle of quantitative/qualitative change an example will be drawn from China.

Early man in China lived at the mercy of nature, and slowly discovered such basic things as the fact that fire can be man-made and that seeds of some grasses could be planted in the soil to meet food requirements. Those discoveries helped inhabitants of China to have simple farming communities using stone tools and producing enough for bare subsistence. That was achieved several thousand years before the birth of Christ or the flight of the Prophet Mohammed. The goods produced at that stage were divided more or less equally among the members of society, who lived and worked in families. By the time of the T'ang dynasty of the seventh century A.D., China had expanded its economic capacity not only to grow more food but also to manufacture a wide variety of items such as silks, porcelain, ships, and scientific devices. This, of course, represented a quantitative increase in the goods produced, and it was interrelated with qualitative changes in Chinese society. By the later date, there was a political state, where before there were only self-governing units. Instead of every family and every individual performing the tasks of agriculturalists, housebuilders, tailors, there had arisen specialization of function. Most of the population still tilled the land, but there were skilled artisans who made silk and porcelain, bureaucrats who administered the state, and Buddhist and Confucian religious philosophers who specialized in trying to explain those things that lay outside of immediate understanding.

Specialization and division of labor led to more production as well as inequality in distribution. A small section of Chinese society came to take a disproportionate share of the proceeds of human labor, and that was the section which did least to actually generate wealth by working in agriculture or industry. They could afford to do so because grave inequalities had emerged in the ownership of the basic means of production, which was the land. Family land became smaller as far as most peasants were concerned, and a minority took over the greater portion of the land. Those changes in land tenure were part and parcel of development in its broadest sense. That is why development cannot be seen purely as an economic affair, but rather as an overall social process which is dependent upon the outcome of man's efforts to deal with his natural environment.

Through careful study, it is possible to comprehend some of the very complicated links between the changes in the economic base and changes in the rest of the superstructure of the society—including the sphere of ideology and social beliefs. The changeover from communalism in Asia and Europe led for instance to codes of behavior peculiar to feudalism. The conduct of the European knights in armor had much in common with that of the Japanese Samurai, or warriors. They developed notions of so-called chivalry—conduct becoming a gentleman knight on horseback; while in contrast the peasant had to learn extreme humility, deference, and obsequiousness—symbolized by doffing his cap and standing bareheaded before his superiors. In Africa, too, it was to be found that the rise of the state and superior classes led to the practice whereby common subjects prostrated themselves in the presence of the monarchs and aristocrats. When that point had been reached, it became clear that the rough equality of the family had given way to a new state of society.

In the natural sciences, it is well known that in many instances quantitative change becomes qualitative after a certain period. The common example is the way that water can absorb heat (a quantitative process) until at $100°$ C. it changes to steam (a qualitative change of form). Similarly, in human society it has always been the case that the expansion of the economy leads eventually to a change in the form of social relations. Karl Marx, writing in the nineteenth century, was the first writer to appreciate this, and he distinguished within European history several stages of development. The first major stage following after simple bands of hunters was Communalism, where property was collectively owned, work was done in common, and goods were shared equally. The second was Slavery, caused by the extension of domineering elements within the family and by some groups being physically overwhelmed by others. Slaves did a variety of tasks, but their main job was to produce food. The next stage was Feudalism, where agriculture remained the principal means of making a livelihood, but the land which was necessary for that purpose was in the hands of the few, and they took the lion's share of the wealth. The workers on the land (now called serfs) were no longer the personal property of the masters, but were tied to the land of a particular manor or estate.

When the manor changed hands, the serfs had to remain there and provide goods for the landlord—just keeping enough to feed themselves. Just as the child of a slave was a slave, so the children of serfs were also serfs. Then came Capitalism, under which the greatest wealth in the society was produced not in agriculture but by machines—in factories and in mines. Like the preceding phase of feudalism, capitalism was characterized by the concentration in a few hands of ownership of the means of producing wealth and by unequal distribution of the products of human labor. The few who dominated were the bourgeoisie who had originated in the merchants and craftsmen of the feudal epoch, and who rose to be industrialists and financiers. Meanwhile, the serfs were declared legally free to leave the land and go in search of employment in capitalist enterprises. Their labor thereby became a commodity—something to be bought and sold.

It was predicted that there would be a further stage—that of Socialism —in which the principle of economic equality would be restored, as in communalism. In the present century, the phase of socialism has indeed emerged in some countries. Economically, each succeeding stage represented development in the strict sense that there was increased capacity to control the material environment and thereby to create more goods and services for the community. The greater quantity of goods and services were based on greater skills and human inventiveness. Man was liberated in the sense of having more opportunities to display and develop his talents. Whether man uplifted himself in a moral sense is open to dispute. The advance in production increased the range of powers which sections of society had over other sections, and it multiplied the violence which was part of the competition for survival and growth among social groups. It is not at all clear that a soldier serving capitalism in the last World War was less "primitive" in the elemental sense of the word than a soldier serving in one of Japan's feudal armies in the sixteenth century, or for that matter than a hunter living in the first phase of human organization in the forests of Brazil. Nevertheless, we do know that in those three respective epochs—hunting band, feudalism, capitalism—the quality of life improved. It became less hazardous and less uncertain, and members of society potentially had greater choice over their destinies. All of that is involved when the word "development" is used.

In the history of those societies which have passed through several modes of production, the opportunity is presented of seeing how quantitative changes give rise ultimately to an entirely different society. The key feature is that at given junctures the social relations in the society were no longer effective in promoting advance. Indeed, they began to act as brakes on the productive forces and therefore had to be discarded. Take for instance the epoch of slavery in Europe. However morally indefensible slavery may have been, it did serve for a while to open up the mines and agricultural plantations in large parts of Europe and notably within the Roman Empire. But then those peasants who remained free had their labor depressed and underutilized because of the presence of slaves. The slaves were not disposed to work at any tasks requiring skills, so the technological evolution of society threatened to come to a halt. Furthermore, the slaves were restless, and slave revolts were expensive to put down. The landowners, seeing their estates going to ruin, decided that it would be best to grant the legal freedom for which slaves were clamoring, and to keep exploiting the labor of these free serfs by insuring that they had no lands to plow other than those of the landlords. Thereby, a new set of social relations—that of landlord and serf—replaced the old relations of slavemaster and slave.

In some instances, the changeover to a new mode was accompanied by violence at a critical point. This occurred when the ruling classes involved were being threatened with removal by the process of change. The feudal landlords remained in power for centuries during which the merchant and manufacturing interests grew wealthy and sought to achieve political power and social pre-eminence. When classes are so well defined, their consciousness is at a high level. Both the landlord class and the capitalists recognized what was at stake. The former fought to hold on to the social relations which no longer corresponded to the new technology of machine production and the organization of work by means of purchasing labor power. The capitalists flung themselves into revolutions in Europe in the eighteenth and nineteenth centuries to break the old relations of production.

The notions of revolution and class consciousness must be borne in mind when it comes to examining the situation of the modern worker and peasant classes in Africa. However, for the greater part of Africa's history, the existing classes have been incompletely crystallized and the changes have been gradual rather than revolutionary. What is probably of more relevance for early African development is the principle that development over the world's territories has always been uneven.

While all societies have experienced development, it is equally true that the rate of development differed from continent to continent, and within each continent different parts increased their command over nature at different rates. Inside Africa, Egyptians were capable of producing wealth in abundance twenty-five centuries ago, because of mastery of many scientific natural laws and their invention of technology to irrigate, grow food, and extract minerals from the subsoil. At that time, hunting with bows and even wooden clubs was what people depended on for survival in most parts of the African continent—and in various other places such as the British Isles.

One of the most difficult questions to answer is exactly why different peoples developed at different rates when left on their own. Part of the answer lies in the environment in which human groups evolved and part of it lies in the "superstructure" of human society. That is to say, as human beings battled with the material environment, they created forms of social relations, forms of government, patterns of behavior, and systems of belief which together constituted the superstructure—which was never the same in any two societies. Each element in the superstructure interacted with other elements in the superstructure as well as with the material base. For instance, the political and religious patterns affected each other and were often intertwined. The religious belief that a certain forest was sacred was the kind of element in the superstructure that affected economic activity, since that forest would not be cleared for cultivation. While in the final analysis the breakthrough to a new stage of human development is dependent upon man's technical capacity to deal with the environment, it is also to be borne in mind that peculiarities in the superstructure of any given society have a marked impact on the rate of development.

Many observers have been puzzled by the fact that China never became capitalist. It entered the feudal phase of development virtually 1,000 years before the birth of Christ; it had developed many aspects of technology; and it had many craftsmen and artisans. Yet the mode of production was never transformed to one where machines were the main means of producing wealth and where the owners of capital would be the dominant class. The explanation is very complex, but in general terms the main differences between feudal Europe and feudal China lay in the superstructure—i.e., in the body of beliefs, motivations, and socio-political institutions which derived from the material base but in turn affected it. In China, religious, educational, and bureaucratic qualifications were of utmost importance, and government was in the hands of state officials rather than being run by the landlords on their own feudal estates. Besides, there were greater egalitarian tendencies in Chinese land distribution than in European land distribution, and the Chinese state owned a great deal of land. The consequence was that the landowners had greater powers as bureaucrats than as men of property, and they used that to keep social relations in the same mold. It would have been impossible for them to have done that indefinitely, but they slowed down the movement of history. In Europe, the elements of change were not stifled by the weight of a state bureaucracy.

As soon as the first capitalists appeared in European society, an incentive was created for further development through the attitude of this class. Never before in any human society had a group of people seen themselves consciously functioning in order to make the maximum profit out of production. To fulfill their objective of acquiring more and more capital, capitalists took a greater interest in the laws of science which could be harnessed in the form of machinery to work and make profit on their behalf. At the political level, capitalism was also responsible for most of the features which today are referred to as Western Democracy. In abolishing feudalism, the capitalists insisted on parliaments, constitutions, freedom of the press. These too can be considered as development. However, the peasants and workers of Europe (and eventually the inhabitants of the whole world) paid a huge price so that the capitalists could make their profits from the human labor that always lies behind the machines. That contradicts other facets of development, especially viewed from the standpoint of those who suffered and still suffer to make capitalist achievements possible. This latter group are the majority of mankind. To advance, they must overthrow capitalism; and that is why at the moment capitalism stands in the path of further human social development. To put it another way, the social (class) relations of capitalism are now outmoded, just as slave and feudal relations became outmoded in their time.

There was a period when the capitalist system increased the well-being of significant numbers of people as a by-product of seeking out profits for a few, but today the quest for profits comes into sharp conflict with people's demands that their material and social needs should be fulfilled. The capitalist or bourgeois class is no longer capable of guiding the un-inhibited development of science and technology—again because these objectives now clash with the profit motive. Capitalism has proved incapable of transcending fundamental weaknesses such as underutilization of productive capacity, the persistence of a permanent sector of unemployed, and periodic economic crises related to the concept of "market"— which is concerned with people's ability to pay rather than their need for commodities. Capitalism has created its own irrationalities such as a vicious white racism, the tremendous waste associated with advertising, and the irrationality of incredible poverty in the midst of wealth and wastage even inside the biggest capitalist economies, such as that of the United States of America. Above all, capitalism has intensified its own political contradictions in trying to subjugate nations and continents outside of Europe, so that workers and peasants in every part of the globe have become self-conscious and are determined to take their destiny into their own hands. Such a determination is also an integral part of the process of development.

It can be offered as a generalization that all phases of development are temporary or transient and are destined sooner or later to give way to something else. It is particularly important to stress this with reference to capitalism because the capitalist epoch is not quite over and those who live at a particular point in time often fail to see that their way of life is in the process of transformation and elimination. Indeed, it is one of the functions of those bourgeois writers who justify capitalism to try and pretend that capitalism is here to stay. A glance at the remarkable advance of socialism over the last fifty-odd years will show that the apologists for capitalism are spokesmen of a social system that is rapidly expiring.

The fact that capitalism today is still around alongside socialism should warn us that the modes of production cannot simply be viewed as a question of successive stages. Uneven development has always insured that societies have come into contact when they were at different levels—for example, one that was communal and one that was capitalist.

When two societies of different sorts come into prolonged and effective contact, the rate and character of change taking place in both is seriously affected to the extent that entirely new patterns are created. Two general rules can be observed to apply in such cases. First, the weaker of the two societies (i.e., the one with less economic capacity) is bound to be adversely affected—and the bigger the gap between the two societies concerned the more detrimental are the consequences. For example, when European capitalism came into contact with the indigenous hunting societies of America and the Caribbean, the latter were virtually exterminated. Second, assuming that the weaker society does survive, then ultimately it can resume its own independent development only if it proceeds to a level higher than that of the economy which had previously dominated it. The concrete instances of the operation of this second rule are found in the experience of the Soviet Union, China, and Korea.

China and Korea were both at a stage approximating feudalism when they were colonized by the capitalist powers of Europe and Japan. Russia was never legally colonized, but while in the feudal stage and before its own indigenous capitalism could get very far, the Russian economy was subjugated by the more mature capitalism of Western Europe. In all three cases, it took a socialist revolution to break the domination of capitalism, and only the rapid tempo of socialist development could make amends for the period of subjugation when growth was misdirected and retarded. Indeed, as far as the two biggest socialist states are concerned (the Soviet Union and China), socialist development has already catapulted them beyond states such as Britain and France, which have been following the capitalist path for centuries.

Up to the end of the 1950s (the point at which this study terminates),

Russia, China, Korea, and certain nations in Eastern Europe were the only countries which had decisively broken with capitalism and imperialism. Imperialism is itself a phase of capitalist development in which Western European capitalist countries, the U.S.A., and Japan established political, economic, military, and cultural hegemony over other parts of the world which were initially at a lower level and therefore could not resist domination. Imperialism was in effect the extended capitalist system, which for many years embraced the whole world—one part being the exploiters and the other the exploited, one part being dominated and the other acting as overlords, one part making policy and the other being dependent.

Socialism has advanced on imperialism's weakest flanks—in the sector that is exploited, oppressed, and reduced to dependency. In Asia and Eastern Europe, socialism released the nationalist energies of colonized peoples; it turned the goal of production away from the money market and towards the satisfaction of human needs; it has eradicated bottlenecks such as permanent unemployment and periodic crises; and it has realized some of the promise implicit in Western or bourgeois democracy by providing the equality of economic condition which is necessary before one can make use of political equality and equality before the law.

Socialism has reinstated the economic equality of communalism, but communalism fell apart because of low economic productivity and scarcity. Socialism aims at and has significantly achieved the creation of plenty, so that the principle of egalitarian distribution becomes consistent with the satisfaction of the wants of all members of society.

One of the most crucial factors leading to more rapid and consistent expansion of economic capacity under socialism has been the implementation of planned development. Most of the historical processes so far described relate to involuntary and unplanned development. No one planned that at a given stage human beings should cease using stone axes and use iron implements instead; and (to come to more recent times) while individual capitalist firms plan their own expansion, their system is not geared to overall planning of the economy and the society. The capitalist state intervened only fitfully and partially to supervise capitalist development. The socialist state has as its prime function the control of the economy on behalf of the working classes. The latter—i.e., workers and peasants— have now become the most dynamic force in world history and human development.

To conclude this brief introduction to the extremely complex problem of social development, it is useful to recognize how inadequate are the explanations of that phenomenon which are provided by bourgeois scholars. They very seldom try to grapple with the issue in its totality, but rather concentrate attention narrowly on "economic development." As defined by the average bourgeois economist, development becomes simply a matter of the combination of given "factors of production": namely, land, population, capital, technology, specialization, and large-scale production. Those factors are indeed relevant, as is implied in the analysis so far; but omissions from the list of what bourgeois scholars think relevant are really overwhelming. No mention is made of the exploitation of the majority which underlay all development prior to socialism. No mention is made of the social relations of production or of classes. No mention is made of the way that the factors and relations of production combine to form a distinctive system or mode of production, varying from one historical epoch to another. No mention is made of imperialism as a logical phase of capitalism.

In contrast, any approach which tries to base itself on socialist and revolutionary principles must certainly introduce into the discussion at the earliest possible point the concepts of class, imperialism, and socialism, as well as the role of the workers and oppressed peoples. Each new concept bristles with its own complications, and it is not to be imagined that the mere resort to certain terminology is the answer to anything. However, one has at least to recognize the full human, historical, and social dimensions of development, before it is feasible to consider "underdevelopment" or the strategies for escaping from underdevelopment.

What Is Underdevelopment?

Having discussed development, it is easier to comprehend the concept of underdevelopment. Obviously, underdevelopment is not absence of development, because every people have developed in one way or another and to a greater or lesser extent. Underdevelopment makes sense only as a means of comparing levels of development. It is very much tied to the fact that human social development has been uneven and from a strictly economic viewpoint some human groups have advanced further by producing more and becoming more wealthy.

The moment that one group appears to be wealthier than others, some inquiry is bound to take place as to the reason for the difference. After Britain had begun to move ahead of the rest of Europe in the eighteenth century, the famous British economist Adam Smith felt it necessary to look into the causes behind the "Wealth of Nations." At the same time, many Russians were very concerned about the fact that their country was "backward" in comparison with England, France, and Germany in the eighteenth century and subsequently in the nineteenth century. Today, our main preoccupation is with the differences in wealth between, on the one hand Europe and North America, and on the other hand Africa, Asia, and Latin America. In comparison with the first, the second group can be said to be backward or underdeveloped. At all times, therefore, one of the ideas behind underdevelopment is a comparative one. It is possible to compare the economic conditions at two different periods for the same country and determine whether or not it had developed; and (more importantly) it is possible to compare the economics of any two countries at any given period in time.

A second and even more indispensable component of modern underdevelopment is that it expresses a particular relationship of exploitation: namely, the exploitation of one country by another. All of the countries named as "underdeveloped" in the world are exploited by others; and the underdevelopment with which the world is now preoccupied is a product of capitalist, imperialist, and colonialist exploitation. African and Asian societies were developing independently until they were taken over directly or indirectly by the capitalist powers. When that happened, exploitation increased and the export of surplus ensued, depriving the societies of the benefit of their natural resources and labor. That is an integral part of underdevelopment in the contemporary sense.

In some quarters, it has often been thought wise to substitute the term "developing" for "underdeveloped." One of the reasons for so doing is to avoid any unpleasantness which may be attached to the second term, which might be interpreted as meaning underdeveloped mentally, physically, morally, or in any other respect. Actually, if "underdevelopment" were related to anything other than comparing economies, then the most underdeveloped country in the world would be the U.S.A., which practices external oppression on a massive scale, while internally there is a blend of exploitation, brutality, and psychiatric disorder. However, on the economic level, it is best to remain with the word "underdeveloped" rather than "developing," because the latter creates the impression that all the countries of Africa, Asia, and Latin America are escaping from a state of economic backwardness relative to the industrial nations of the world, and that they are emancipating themselves from the relationship of exploitation. That is certainly not true, and many underdeveloped countries in Africa and elsewhere are becoming more underdeveloped in comparison with the world's great powers, because their exploitation by the metropoles is being intensified in new ways.

Economic comparisons can be made by looking at statistical tables or indices of what goods and services are produced and used in the societies under discussion. Professional economists speak of the national income of countries and the national income per capita. These phrases have already become part of the layman's language, by way of the newspapers, and no detailed explanation will be offered here. It is enough to note that the national income is a measurement of the total wealth of the country, while the per capita income is a figure obtained by dividing the national income by the number of inhabitants in order to get an idea of the "average" wealth of each inhabitant. This "average" can be misleading where there are great extremes of wealth. A young Ugandan put it in a very personal form when he said that the per capita income of his country camouflaged the fantastic difference between what was earned by his poor peasant father and what was earned by the biggest local capitalist, Madhvani. In considering the question of development away from the state of underdevelopment, it is of supreme importance to realize that such a process demands the removal of the gross inequalities of land distribution, property holding, and income, which are camouflaged behind national income figures. At one stage in history, advance was made at the cost of entrenching privileged groups. In our times, development has to mean advance which liquidates present privileged groups with their corresponding unprivileged groups. Nevertheless, the per capita income is a useful statistic for comparing one country with another; and the developed countries all have per capita incomes several times higher than any one of the recently independent African nations.

The following table gives a clear picture of the gap between Africa and certain nations measured in per capita incomes. It is the gap that allows one group to be called "developed" and another "underdeveloped." (The information was obtained from United Nations statistical publications, and applies to the year 1968 unless otherwise stated.)

The gap that can be seen from the evidence is not only great, but it is also increasing. Many people have come to realize that the developed countries are growing richer quite rapidly, while underdeveloped countries for the most part show stagnancy or slow rates of growth. In each country, a figure can be calculated to represent the rate at which the economy grows. The growth rate is highest in socialist countries, followed by the big capitalist countries, and with the colonies and ex-colonies trailing far behind. The proportion of international trade which is in the hands of the underdeveloped countries is declining. That proportion was roughly 30 per cent in 1938 and went down to less than 20 per cent in the 1960s. This is an important indicator because trade is both a reflection of the quantity of goods produced and a way of obtaining goods not locally produced.

Countries	Per Capita Income in U.S. Dollars
Canada	2,247
U.S.A.	3,578
France	1,738 (1967)
United Kingdom	1,560 (1967)
AFRICA as a whole	140 (1965)
Congo	52
Ghana	198
Kenya	107
Malawi	52
Morocco	185
South Africa	543
Tanzania	62
U.A.R.	156
Zambia	225

Developed economies have certain characteristics which contrast with underdeveloped ones. The developed countries are all industrialized. That is to say, the greater part of their working population is engaged in industry rather than agriculture, and most of their wealth comes out of mines, factories, and other industries. They have a high output of labor per man in industry because of their advanced technology and skills. This is well known, but it is also striking that the developed countries have a much more advanced agriculture than the rest of the world. Their agriculture has already become an industry, and the agricultural part of the economy produces more even though it is small. The countries of Africa, Asia, and Latin America are called agricultural countries because they rely on agriculture and have little or no industry; but their agriculture is unscientific and the yields are far less than those of the developed countries. In several of the largest underdeveloped nations, there was stagnation and fall in agricultural output in and after 1966. In Africa, the output of food per person has been falling in recent years. Because the developed countries have a stronger industrial and agricultural economy than the rest of the world, they produce far more goods than the poor nations—in the category of necessities as well as luxuries. It is possible to draw up statistical tables showing the production of grain, milk, steel, electric power, paper, and a wide range of other goods; and showing at the same time how much of each commodity is made available to each citizen (on the average). Once again, the figures are highly favorable to a few privileged countries in the world.

The amount of steel used in a country is an excellent indicator of the level of industrialization. At one extreme, one finds that the U.S.A. consumes 685 kilograms of steel per person, Sweden 623, and East Germany 437. At the other extreme, one finds that Zambia consumes 10 kilograms, East Africa 8, and Ethiopia 2. When the same kind of calculation is made for sugar, a sample of the results shows Australia with 57 kilograms and North America and the Soviet Union with 45 to 50 on the average. Africa, however, consumes only 10 kilograms of sugar per person per year, and this is better than Asia with 7.

An even more gloomy set of statistics relates to basic food requirements. Each individual needs a certain quantity of food per day, measured in calories. The desirable amount is 3,000 calories per day; but no African country comes anywhere near that figure. Algerians consume on average only 1,870 calories per day, while Ivory Coast can consider itself very well off within an African context with 2,290 calories as the national average. Furthermore, one also has to judge the protein content of the food; and many parts of Africa suffer from "protein famine"—which means that even when calories are available from starchy foods, little protein is to be found. Persons in developed capitalist and socialist countries consume twice as much protein food as those in underdeveloped countries. Such differences help to make it clear which countries are developed and which are underdeveloped.

The social services provided by a country are of importance equal to that of its material production in bringing about human well-being and happiness. It is universally accepted that the state has the responsibility to establish schools and hospitals, but whether these are provided by the government or by private agencies, their numbers can be established in relation to the size of the population. The extent to which basic goods and social services are available in a country can also be measured indirectly by looking at the life expectancy, the frequency of deaths among children, the amount of malnutrition, the occurrence of diseases which could be prevented by inoculation and public health services, and the proportion of illiterates. In all these respects, the comparison between the developed and underdeveloped countries shows huge and even frightening differences. For every 1,000 children who are born alive in Cameroon, 100 never live to see their first birthday, and out of every 1,000 African children born alive in rural Sierra Leone, 160 die before reaching one year. Yet the comparable figures for the United Kingdom and Holland are only 12 and 18 respectively. Besides, many more African children die before they reach the age of five. Lack of doctors is a major drawback. In Italy, there is one doctor for every 580 Italians, and in Czechoslovakia, there is one doctor for every 510 citizens. In Niger, one doctor must do for 56,140 persons; in Tunisia, one doctor for every 8,320 Tunisians; and in Chad, one doctor for 73,460 persons.

It takes a large number of skilled people to make an industrial economy function; while the countries of Africa have a woefully insufficient number of highly qualified personnel. The figures on doctors just given confirm this, and the same problem exists with engineers, technicians, agriculturalists, and even administrators and lawyers in some places. Middle-level skills in fields such as welding are also lacking. To make matters worse, there is at present a "brain drain" from Africa, Asia, Latin America, and Western Europe. This is to say, professionals, technicians, high-level administrators, and skilled workers emigrate from their homes, and the small number of skilled people available to the underdeveloped world is further depleted by the lure of better pay and opportunities in the developed world.

This lopsided nature of the present international economy is strikingly brought home by the fact that the underdeveloped countries must in turn recruit foreign experts at fantastic cost.

Most of the data presented so far can be described as "quantitative." It gives us measurements of the quantity of goods and services produced in various economies. In addition, certain qualitative assessments have to be made concerning the way that a given economy is put together. For economic development it is not enough to produce more goods and services. The country has to produce more of those goods and services which in turn will give rise spontaneously to future growth in the economy. For example, the food-producing sector must be flourishing so that workers would be healthy, and agriculture on the whole must be efficient so that the profits (or savings) from agriculture would stimulate industry. Heavy industry, such as the steel industry and the production of electrical power, must be present so that one is capable of making machinery for other types of industry and for agriculture. Lack of heavy industry, inadequate production of food, unscientific agriculture—those are all characteristics of the underdeveloped economies.

It is typical of underdeveloped economies that they do not (or are not allowed to) concentrate on those sectors of the economy which in turn will generate growth and raise production to a new level altogether, and there are very few ties between one sector and another so that (say) agriculture and industry could react beneficially on each other.

Furthermore, whatever savings are made within the economy are mainly sent abroad or are frittered away in consumption rather than being redirected to productive purposes. Much of the national income which remains within the country goes to pay individuals who are not directly involved in producing wealth but only in rendering auxiliary services—civil servants, merchants, soldiers, entertainers. What aggravates the situation is that more people are employed in those jobs than are really necessary to give efficient service; and to crown it all, these people do not reinvest in agriculture or industry. They squander the wealth created by the peasants and workers by purchasing cars, whisky, and perfume.

It has been noted with irony that the principal "industry" of many underdeveloped countries is administration. Not long ago, 60 per cent of the internal revenue of Dahomey went into paying salaries of civil servants and government leaders. The salaries given to the elected politicians are higher than those given to a British Member of Parliament, and the number of parliamentarians in the underdeveloped African countries is also relatively high. In Gabon, there is one parliamentary representative for every six thousand inhabitants, compared to one French parliamentary representative for every hundred thousand Frenchmen. Many more figures of that sort indicate that in describing a typical underdeveloped economy it is essential to point out the high disproportion of the locally distributed wealth that goes into the pockets of a privileged few.

Members of the privileged groups inside Africa always defend themselves by saying that they pay the taxes which keep the government going. At face value this statement sounds reasonable, but on close examination it is really the most absurd argument and shows total ignorance of how the economy functions. Taxes do not produce national wealth and development. Wealth has to be produced out of nature—from tilling the land or mining metals or felling trees or turning raw materials into finished products for human consumption. These things are done by the vast majority of the population who are peasants and workers.

There would be no incomes to tax if the laboring population did not work.

The incomes given to civil servants, professionals, merchants, come from the store of wealth produced by the community. Quite apart from the injustices in the distribution of wealth, one has to dismiss the argument that "the taxpayers' " money is what develops a country. In pursuing the goal of development, one must start with the producers and move on from there to see whether the products of their labor are being rationally utilized to bring greater independence and well-being to the nation.

By paying attention to the wealth created by human labor out of nature, one can immediately appreciate that very few underdeveloped countries are lacking in the natural resources which could go into making a better life, and in those cases it is usually possible for two or three territories to combine together for their mutual benefit. In fact, it can be shown that the underdeveloped countries are the ones with the greatest wealth of natural resources and yet the poorest in terms of goods and services presently provided by and for their citizens.

The United Nations *Survey of Economic Conditions in Africa* up to 1964 had this to say about the continent's natural resources:

> Africa is well endowed with mineral and primary energy resources. With an estimated 9 per cent of the world's population the region accounts for approximately 28 per cent of the total value of world mineral production and 6 per cent of its crude petroleum output. In recent years, its share of the latter is increasing. Of sixteen important metallic and non-metallic minerals the share of Africa in ten varies from 22 to 95 per cent of the world production.

Actually, African potential is shown to be greater every day with new discoveries of mineral wealth. On the agricultural side, African soil is not as rich as the picture of tropical forests might lead one to believe; but there are other climatic advantages so that with proper irrigation crops can be grown all the year round in most parts of the continent.

The situation is that Africa has not yet come anywhere close to making the most of its natural wealth, and most of the wealth now being produced is not being retained within Africa for the benefit of Africans. Zambia and Congo produce vast quantities of copper, but that is for the benefit of Europe, North America, and Japan. Even the goods and services which are produced inside of Africa and which remain in Africa nevertheless fall into the hands of non-Africans. Thus, South Africa boasts of having the highest per capita income in Africa; but as an indication of how this is shared out, one should note that while the apartheid regime assures that only 24 white babies die out of every 1,000 live births, they are quite happy to allow 128 African babies to die out of every 1,000 live births. In order to understand present economic conditions in Africa, one needs to know why it is that Africa has realized so little of its natural potential, and one also needs to know why so much of its present wealth goes to non-Africans who reside for the most part outside of the continent.

In a way, underdevelopment is a paradox. Many parts of the world that are naturally rich are actually poor and parts that are not so well off in wealth of soil and sub-soil are enjoying the highest standards of living. When the capitalists from the developed parts of the world try to explain this paradox, they often make it sound as though there is something "God-given" about the situation. One bourgeois economist, in a book on development, accepted that the comparative statistics of the world today show a gap that is much larger than it was before. By his own admission, the gap between the developed and the underdeveloped countries has increased by at least 15 to 20 times over the last 150 years. However, the bourgeois economist in question does not give a historical explanation, nor does he consider that there is a relationship of exploitation which allowed capitalist parasites to grow fat and impoverished the dependencies. Instead, he puts forward a biblical explanation! He says:

It is all told in the Bible:

> For unto every one that hath shall be given, and he shall have abundance; but from him that hath not shall be taken away even that which he hath. (St. Matthew, xxv, 29)

The story of the "hath nots" is the story of the modern underdeveloped countries.

Presumably, the only comment which one can make on that is "Amen." The interpretation that underdevelopment is somehow ordained by God is emphasized because of the racist trend in European scholarship. It is in line with racist prejudice to say openly or to imply that their countries are more developed because their people are innately superior, and that the responsibility for the economic backwardness of Africa lies in the generic backwardness of the race of black Africans. An even bigger problem is that the people of Africa and other parts of the colonized world have gone through a cultural and psychological crisis and have accepted, at least partially, the European version of things. That means that the African himself has doubts about his capacity to transform and develop his natural environment. With such doubts, he even challenges those of his brothers who say that Africa can and will develop through the efforts of its own people. If we can determine when underdevelopment came about, it would dismiss the lingering suspicion that it is racially or otherwise predetermined and that we can do little about it.

When the "experts" from capitalist countries do not give a racist explanation, they nevertheless confuse the issue by giving as causes of underdevelopment the things which really are consequences. For example, they would argue that Africa is in a state of backwardness as a result of lacking skilled personnel to develop. It is true that because of lack of engineers Africa cannot on its own build more roads, bridges, and hydroelectric stations. But that is not a cause of underdevelopment, except in the sense that causes and effects come together and reinforce each other. The fact of the matter is that the most profound reasons for the economic back-wardness of a given African nation are not to be found inside that nation. All that we can find inside are the symptoms of underdevelopment and the secondary factors that make for poverty.

Mistaken interpretations of the causes of underdevelopment usually stem either from prejudiced thinking or from the error of believing that one can learn the answers by looking inside the underdeveloped economy. The true explanation lies in seeking out the relationship between Africa and certain developed countries and in recognizing that it is a relationship of exploitation.

Man has always exploited his natural environment in order to make a living. At a certain point in time, there also arose the exploitation of man by man, in that a few people grew rich and lived well through the labor of others. Then a stage was reached by which people in one community called a nation exploited the natural resources and the labor of another nation and its people. Since underdevelopment deals with the comparative economics of nations, it is the last kind of exploitation that is of greatest interest here—i.e., the exploitation of nation by nation. One of the common means by which one nation exploits another and one that is relevant to Africa's external relations is exploitation through trade. When the terms of trade are set by one country in a manner entirely advantageous to itself, then the trade is usually detrimental to the trading partner. To be specific, one can take the export of agricultural produce from Africa and the import of manufactured goods into Africa from Europe, North America, and Japan. The big nations establish the price of the agricultural products and subject these prices to frequent reductions. At the same time the price of manufactured goods is also set by them, along with the freight rates necessary for trade in the ships of those nations. The minerals of Africa also fall into the same category as agricultural produce as far as pricing is concerned. The whole import-export relationship between Africa and its trading partners is one of unequal exchange and of exploitation.

More far-reaching than just trade is the actual ownership of the means of production in one country by the citizens of another. When citizens of Europe own the land and the mines of Africa, this is the most direct way of sucking the African continent. Under colonialism the ownership was complete and backed by military domination. Today, in many African countries the foreign ownership is still present, although the armies and flags of foreign powers have been removed. So long as foreigners own land, mines, factories, banks, insurance companies, means of transporta-tion, newspapers, power stations, then for so long will the wealth of Africa flow outwards into the hands of those elements. In other words, in the absence of direct political control, foreign investment insures that the natural resources and the labor of Africa produce economic value which is lost to the continent.

Foreign investment often takes the form of loans to African governments. Naturally, these loans have to be repaid; and in the 1960s the rate of repayment (amortization) on official loans in underdeveloped countries rose from $400 million per year to about $700 million per year, and it is constantly on the increase. Besides, there is interest to be paid on these loans as well as profits which come from the direct investment in the economy. These two sources accounted for the fact that over $500 million flowed outwards from the underdeveloped countries in 1965. The information on these matters is seldom complete, for the obvious reason that those making the profit are trying to keep things quiet, so the figures given above are likely to be underestimates. They are meant to give some idea of the extent to which the wealth of Africa is being drained off by those who invest in, and thereby own, a large part of the means of production of wealth in Africa. Furthermore, in more recent times the forms of investment have become more subtle and more dangerous. They include so-called aid and the management of local African companies by international capitalist experts.

Africa trades mainly with the countries of Western Europe, North America, and Japan. Africa is also diversifying its trade by dealing with socialist countries, and if that trade proves disadvantageous to the African economy, then the developed socialist countries will also have joined the ranks of the exploiters of Africa. However, it is very essential at this stage to draw a clear distinction between the capitalist countries and the socialist ones, because socialist countries have never at any time owned any part of the African continent nor do they invest in African economies in such a way as to expatriate profits from Africa. Therefore, socialist countries are not involved in the robbery of Africa.

Most of the people who write about underdevelopment and who are read in the continents of Africa, Asia, and Latin America are spokesmen for the capitalist or bourgeois world. They seek to justify capitalist exploitation both inside and outside their own countries. One of the things which they do to confuse the issue is to place all underdeveloped countries in one camp and all developed countries in another camp irrespective of different social systems; so that the terms capitalist and socialist never enter the discussion. Instead, one is faced with a simple division between the industrialized nations and those that are not industrialized. It is true that both the United States and the Soviet Union are industrialized and it is true that when one looks at the statistics, countries such as France,

Norway, Czechoslovakia, and Rumania are much closer together than any one of them is to an African country. But it is absolutely necessary to determine whether the standard of living in a given industrialized country is a product of its own internal resources or whether it stems from exploiting other countries. The United States has a small proportion of the world's population and exploitable natural wealth but it enjoys a huge percentage of the wealth which comes from exploiting the labor and natural resources of the whole world.

The erroneous views about underdevelopment and the oversimplified distinction between rich and poor nations are opposed by socialist scholars both inside and outside the socialist countries. Those erroneous views are also being exposed by economists in underdeveloped countries who are discovering that the explanations offered by bourgeois scholars are explanations which suit the interests of those countries which exploit the rest of the world through trade and investment. One French socialist writer, Pierre Jalée, proposes that to obtain a proper perspective of relations between developed countries and underdeveloped ones, two categories should be set up, namely, imperialist and socialist. The socialist camp includes all countries big and small which have decided to break away from international capitalism. The imperialist camp contains not only the capitalist giants like the U.S.A., France, West Germany, and Japan but also the weak nations in which those industrial nations have investments. Therefore, the imperialist camp can be subdivided into exploiting and exploited countries. For the most part, the nations of Africa fall into the group of exploited countries inside the capitalist/imperialist system. Roughly one-third of the world's peoples are already living under some form of socialism. The other two-thirds constitute the capitalist/imperialist camp, with the majority being in the exploited section.

It is interesting to notice that in spite of their efforts to confuse the situation, the bourgeois writers often touch on the truth. For example, the United Nations (which is dominated by Western capitalist powers) would never stress the exploitation by capitalist nations, but their economic reviews refer on the one hand to "the centrally planned economies," which means the socialist countries, and on the other hand they speak of "the market economies," which means in effect the imperialist sector of the world. The latter is subdivided into "the developed market economies" and "the developing market economies," disguising the fact that the market means capitalist market. This study is concerned with analyzing the relations between those countries which are together within the capitalist market system.

The things which bring Africa into the capitalist market system are trade, colonial domination, and capitalist investment. Trade has existed for several centuries; colonial rule began in the late nineteenth century and has almost disappeared; and the investment in the African economy has been increasing steadily in the present century. Throughout the period that Africa has participated in the capitalist economy, two factors have brought about underdevelopment. In the first place, the wealth created by African labor and from African resources was grabbed by the capitalist countries of Europe; and in the second place, restrictions were placed upon African capacity to make the maximum use of its economic potential—which is what development is all about. Those two processes represent the answer to the two questions raised above as to why Africa has realized so little of its potential and why so much of its present wealth goes outside of the continent.

African economies are integrated into the very structure of the developed capitalist economies; and they are integrated in a manner that is unfavorable to Africa and insures that Africa is dependent on the big capitalist countries. Indeed, structural dependence is one of the characteristics of underdevelopment. Most progressive writers divide the capitalist/imperialist system into two parts. The first is the dominant or metropolitan section, and the countries in the second group are often called satellites because they are in the orbit of the metropolitan economies. The same idea is conveyed by simply saying that the underdeveloped countries are dependencies of the metropolitan capitalist economies.

When a child or the young of any animal species ceases to be dependent upon its mother for food and protection, it can be said to have developed in the direction of maturity. Dependent nations can never be considered developed. It is true that modern conditions force all countries to be mutually interdependent in order to satisfy the needs of their citizens; but that is not incompatible with economic independence because economic independence does not mean isolation. It does, however, require a capacity to exercise choice in external relations, and above all it requires that a nation's growth at some point must become self-reliant and self-sustaining. Such things are obviously in direct contradiction to the economic dependence of numerous countries on the metropoles of Western Europe, North America, and Japan.

It is also true that metropoles are dependent on the wealth of the exploited portions of the world. This is a source of their strength and a potential weakness within the capitalist/imperialist system, since the peasants and workers of the dependencies are awakening to a realization that it is possible to cut the tentacles which imperialism has extended into their countries. However, there is a substantial difference between the dependence of the metropoles on the colonies and the subjugation of the colonies under a foreign capitalist yoke. The capitalist countries are technologically more advanced and are therefore the sector of the imperialist system which determined the direction of change. A striking example of this effect is the fact that synthetic fabrics manufactured in the capitalist metropoles have begun to replace fabrics made from raw material grown in the colonies. In other words, (within certain limits) it is the technologically advanced metropoles who can decide when to end their dependence on the colonies in a particular sphere. When that happens, it is the colony or neo-colony which goes begging cap in hand for a reprieve and a new quota. It is for this reason that a formerly colonized nation has no hope of developing until it breaks effectively with the vicious circle of dependence and exploitation which characterizes imperialism.

At the social and cultural level, there are many features which aid in keeping underdeveloped countries integrated into the capitalist system and at the same time hanging on to the apron strings of the metropoles. The Christian church has always been a major instrument for cultural penetration and cultural dominance, in spite of the fact that in many instances Africans sought to set up independent churches. Equally important has been the role of education in producing Africans to service the capitalist system and to subscribe to its values. Recently, the imperialists have been using new universities in Africa to keep themselves entrenched at the highest academic level.

Something as basic as language has come to serve as one of the mechanisms of integration and dependence. The French and English that are so widely used in Africa are more for the purpose of African communication with the exploiters than for African with African. Actually, it would be difficult to find a sphere which did not reflect the economic dependence and structural integration. At a glance, nothing could be less harmful and more entertaining than music, and yet this too is used as a weapon of cultural domination. The American imperialists go so far as to take the folk music, jazz, and soul music of oppressed black people and transform this into American propaganda over the Voice of America beamed at Africa.

During the colonial period, the forms of political subordination in Africa were obvious. There were governors, colonial officials, and police. In politically independent African states, the metropolitan capitalists have to insure favorable political decisions by remote control. So they set up their political puppets in many parts of Africa, who shamelessly agree to compromise with the vicious apartheid regime of South Africa when their masters tell them to do so. The revolutionary writer, Frantz Fanon, has dealt scorchingly and at length with the question of the minority in Africa which serves as the transmission line between the metropolitan capitalists and the dependencies in Africa. The importance of this group cannot be underestimated. The presence of a group of African sell-outs is part of the definition of underdevelopment. Any diagnosis of underdevelopment in Africa will reveal not just low per capita income and protein deficiencies, but also the gentlemen who dance in Abidjan, Accra, and Kinshasa when music is played in Paris, London, and New York.

Political instability is manifesting itself in Africa as a chronic symptom of the underdevelopment of political life within the imperialist context. Military coups have followed one after the other, usually meaning nothing to the mass of the people, and sometimes representing a reactionary reversal of the efforts at national liberation. This trend was well exemplified in Latin American history, so that its appearance in neo-colonial South Vietnam or in neo-colonial Africa is not at all surprising. If economic power is centered outside national African boundaries, then political and military power in any real sense is also centered outside until, and unless, the masses of peasants and workers are mobilized to offer an alternative to the system of sham political independence. All of those features are ramifications of underdevelopment and of the exploitation of the imperialist system. In most analyses of this question, they are either left out entirely or the whole concept of imperialism and neo-colonialism is dismissed as mere rhetoric—especially by "academics" who claim to be removed from "politics." During the remainder of this study, a great deal of detail will be presented to indicate the grim reality behind the so-called slogans of capitalism, imperialism, colonialism, neo-colonialism, and the like. For the present moment, the position to be adopted can be stated briefly in the following terms:

The question as to who, and what, is responsible for African underdevelopment can be answered at two levels. First, the answer is that the operation of the imperialist system bears major responsibility for African economic retardation by draining African wealth and by making it impossible to develop more rapidly the resources of the continent. Second, one has to deal with those who manipulate the system and those who are either agents or unwitting accomplices of the said system. The capitalists of Western Europe were the ones who actively extended their exploitation from inside Europe to cover the whole of Africa.

In recent times, they were joined, and to some extent replaced, by capitalists from the United States; and for many years now even the workers of those metropolitan countries have benefited from the exploitation and underdevelopment of Africa. None of these remarks are intended to remove the ultimate responsibility for development from the shoulders of Africans. Not only are there African accomplices inside the imperialist system, but every African has a responsibility to understand the system and work for its overthrow.

Brief Guide to Reading

There is a great deal of literature on "development" and "underdevelopment," although less than one would expect in view of the importance of the subjects. Most of that which is available seeks to justify capitalism. Hence, there is a narrow concentration on "economic development," and particularly on capitalist economies, rather than any analysis of human social development. That approach is challenged by Marxist writers in the metropoles and increasingly by scholars from the underdeveloped world.

FREDERICK ENGELS, *Origins of the Family, Private Property and the State.* Chicago: C. H. Kerr and Co., 1902.
KARL MARX, *Preface to a Contribution to a Critique of Political Economy.*
KARL MARX, *Pre-Capitalist Economic Formations*, edited by E. J. Hobsbawm. New York: International Publishers, 1964.
These three works are samples of writing by the founders of what is now called Marxism. Most of the publications of Marx and Engels have a relevance to the theme of development, with particular emphasis on feudal and capitalist times.

RICHARD T. GILL, *Economic Development: Past and Present.* Englewood Cliffs, N.J.: Prentice-Hall, 1967.
RAGNAR NURKSE, *Problems of Capital Formation in Underdeveloped Countries.* Oxford University Press, 1953.
These are typical examples of bourgeois metropolitan views on development and underdevelopment—the first being a text for North American college students by a Canadian economist and the second being a frequently reprinted work of one of the most prominent bourgeois advocates of the "vicious circle of poverty" theory. Unfortunately, these are also examples of the kind of book which dominates the shelves of any university or public library in Africa. The reader is invited to test this generalization.

J. D. BERNAL, *Science in History.* (4 vol.) Cambridge: MIT Press, 1972.
JOSEPH NEEDHAM, *Science and Civilization in China.* Cambridge University Press, 1954.
Both of these are lengthy, but they should be tackled. Science and technology derive from the effort to understand and control the natural environment. Familiarity with the history of science is essential to an awareness of the development of society. Needham's book is cited here as a corrective to the fairly common view that science is something peculiarly European.

CELSO FURTADO, *Development and Underdevelopment*. Berkeley: U. of California Press, 1964.

A. GUNDER FRANK, *Capitalism and Underdevelopment in Latin America*. New York: Monthly Review Press, 1967.

TAMÁS SZENTES, *The Political Economy of Underdevelopment*. Budapest: Center for Afro-Asian Research of the Hungarian Academy of Sciences, 1971.

The first writer is from Brazil, a country with a long history of dependence on and exploitation by the metropoles of Europe and North America. Frank's book reflects the thinking of many progressive Latin American intellectuals and it has now become well entrenched as a view of Marxists inside the metropoles. Szentes is a Hungarian economist systematically applying Marxist insights to the actual data and processes of the underdeveloped world and imperialism as a whole.

SAMIR AMIN, *The Class Struggle in Africa*. Cambridge, Mass.: Africa Research Group, n.d.

Samir Amin is a North African. He stands out with regard both to the volume of his productions and the quality of his insights. The text cited above is very general—covering in outline the period of the roots of development in ancient Africa right up to the present and the projected socialist future. It is likely that more of his work will be translated into English (French being his working language).

CHAPTER
II

How Africa Developed before the Coming of the Europeans—Up to the Fifteenth Century

· A General Overview   · Some Concrete Examples   · Conclusion

BEFORE EVEN THE BRITISH CAME INTO RELATIONS WITH OUR PEOPLE, WE were a developed people, having our own institutions, having our own ideas of government.

—J. E. CASELY-HAYFORD, 1922
African (Gold Coast) Nationalist

A General Overview

It has been shown that, using comparative standards, Africa today is underdeveloped in relation to Western Europe and a few other parts of the world; and that the present position has been arrived at, not by the separate evolution of Africa on the one hand and Europe on the other, but through exploitation. As is well known, Africa has had prolonged and extensive contact with Europe, and one has to bear in mind that contact between different societies changes their respective rates of development. To set the record straight, four operations are required:

(1) Reconstruction of the nature of development in Africa before the coming of Europeans.

(2) Reconstruction of the nature of development which took place in Europe before expansion abroad.

(3) Analysis of Africa's contribution to Europe's present "developed" state.

(4) Analysis of Europe's contribution to Africa's present "under-developed" state.

The second task has already been extensively carried out in European literature, and only passing references need be made; but the others are all deserving of further attention.

The African continent reveals very fully the workings of the law of uneven development of societies. There are marked contrasts between the Ethiopian empire and the hunting groups of pygmies in the Congo forest or between the empires of the Western Sudan and the Khoisan hunter-gatherers of the Kalahari Desert. Indeed, there were striking contrasts within any given geographical area. The Ethiopian empire embraced literate feudal Amharic noblemen as well as simple Kaffa cultivators and Galla pastoralists. The empires of the Western Sudan had sophisticated, educated Mandinga townsmen, small communities of Bozo fishermen, and nomadic Fulani herdsmen. Even among clans and lineages that appear

33

roughly similar, there were considerable differences. However, it is possible to distinguish between what was uniquely "African" and what was universal in the sense of being characteristic of all human societies at a given stage of development. It is also essential to recognize the process of dialectical evolution from lower to higher forms of social organization; and, in looking at the most advanced social formations, one would appreciate the potential of the continent as a whole and the direction of change.

The moment that the topic of the pre-European African past is raised, many individuals are concerned for various reasons to know about the existence of African "civilizations." Mainly, this stems from a desire to make comparisons with European "civilizations." This is not the context in which to evaluate the so-called civilizations of Europe. It is enough to note the behavior of European capitalists from the epoch of slavery through colonialism, fascism, and genocidal wars in Asia and Africa. Such barbarism causes suspicion to attach to the use of the word "civilization" to describe Western Europe and North America. As far as Africa is concerned during the period of early development, it is preferable to speak in terms of "cultures" rather than civilizations.

A culture is a total way of life. It embraces what people ate and what they wore; the way they walked and the way they talked; the manner in which they treated death and greeted the newborn. Obviously, unique features came into existence in virtually every locality with regard to all social details. In addition, the continent of Africa south of the great Sahara desert formed a broad community where resemblances were clearly discernible. For example, music and dance had key roles in "uncontaminated" African society. They were ever present at birth, initiation, marriage, death, as well as at times of recreation. Africa is the continent of drums and percussion. African peoples reached the pinnacle of achievement in that sphere.

Because of the impact of colonialism and cultural imperialism (which will be discussed later), Europeans and Africans themselves in the colonial period lacked due regard for the unique features of African culture. Those features have a value of their own that cannot be eclipsed by European culture either in the comparable period before 1500 or in the subsequent centuries. They cannot be eclipsed because they are not really comparable phenomena. Who in this world is competent to judge whether an Austrian waltz is better than a Makonde Ngoma? Furthermore, even in those spheres of culture that are more readily comparable, such as "the fine arts," it is known that African achievements of the pre-European period stand as contributions to man's heritage of beautiful creations. The art of

Egypt, the Sudan, and Ethiopia was known to the rest of the world at an early date. That of the rest of Africa is still being "discovered" and rediscovered by Europeans and present-day Africans. The verdict of art historians on the Ife and Benin bronzes is well known. Since they date from the fourteenth and fifteenth centuries, they are very relevant to any discussion of African development in the epoch before the contacts with Europe. Nor should they be regarded as unusual, except with regard to the material in which the sculptures were executed. The same skill and feeling obviously went into sculpture and art-work in non-durable materials, especially wood.

African dance and art were almost invariably linked with a religious world-outlook in one way or another. As is well known, traditional African religious practices exist in great variety, and it should also be remembered that both Islam and Christianity found homes on the African continent almost from their very inception. The features of the traditional African religions help to set African cultures apart from those in other continents; but in this present context it is more important to note how much African religion had in common with religion elsewhere and how this can be used as an index to the level of development in Africa before European impact in the fifteenth century.

Religion is an aspect of the superstructure of a society, deriving ultimately from the degree of control and understanding of the material world. However, when man thinks in religious terms, he starts from the ideal rather than with the material world (which is beyond his comprehension). This creates a non-scientific and metaphysical way of viewing the world, which often conflicts with the scientific materialist outlook and with the development of society. African ancestral religions were no better or worse than other religions as such. But by the end of feudalism, Europeans began to narrow the area of human life in which religion and the church played a part. Religion ceased to dominate politics, geography, medicine. To free those things from religious restraints, it had to be argued that religion had its own sphere and the things of this world had their own secular sphere. This secularization of life speeded up the development of capitalism and later socialism. In contrast, in the period before the coming of the whites, religion pervaded African life just as it pervaded life in other pre-feudal societies, such as those of the Maoris of Australia or the Afghans of Afghanistan or the Vikings of Scandinavia.

Religion can play both a positive and a negative role as an aspect of the superstructure. In most instances in early Africa, religious beliefs were associated with the mobilization and discipline of large numbers of people to form states. In a few instances, religion also provided concepts in the struggle for social justice. The negative aspects usually arose out of the tendency of religion to persist unchanged for extremely long periods, especially when the technology of earning a living changes very slowly. This was the case in African societies, as in all other pre-capitalist societies. At the same time, the religious beliefs themselves react upon the mode of production, further slowing up progress in that respect. For instance, belief in prayer and in the intervention of ancestors and various gods could easily be a substitute for innovations designed to control the impact of weather and environment.

The same kind of two-sided relationship also exists between the means of earning a living and the social patterns that arise in the process of work. In Africa, before the fifteenth century, the predominant principle of social relations was that of family and kinship associated with communalism. Every member of an African society had his position defined in terms of relatives on his mother's side and on his father's side. Some societies placed greater importance on matrilineal ties and others on patrilineal ties. Those things were crucial to the daily existence of a member of an African society, because land (the major means of production) was owned by groups such as the family or clan—the head of which were parents and those yet unborn. In theory, this pattern was explained by saying that the residents in any community were all direct descendants of the first person who settled the land. When a new group arrived, they often made a pretense that they too had ancestry dating back to the settling of the land or else they insured that members of the earliest kin groups continued to perform the ceremonies related to the land and water of the region.

Similarly, the labor that worked the land was generally recruited on a family basis. A single family or household would till its own plots and it would also be available to share certain joint farming activities with other members of the extended family or clan. Annual hunts and river fishing were also organized by a whole extended family or village community. In a matrilineal society such as that of the Bemba (Zambia), the bridegroom spent a number of years working for the father of his bride; and many young men who had married daughters of the same household often formed work teams to help each other. In Dahomey, a young man did not go to live with his wife's family, but the *dokpwe*, or work team, allowed a son to participate in carrying out a task of some magnitude for the father of his wife. In both of those examples, the right of the father-in-law to acquire labor and the obligations of the son-in-law to give labor were based on kinship. This can be contrasted with capitalism where money buys labor, and with feudalism where the serf provides labor in order to have access to a portion of land which belongs to the landlord.

Having been produced on land that was family property and through family labor, the resultant crops and other goods were distributed on the basis of kinship ties. If a man's crops were destroyed by some sudden calamity, relatives in his own village helped him. If the whole community was in distress, people moved to live with their kinsmen in another area where food was not scarce. In Akan country (Ghana), the clan system was highly organized, so that a man from Brong could visit Fante many hundreds of miles away and receive food and hospitality from a complete stranger who happened to be of his own clan.

Numerous examples could be brought forward to show the dominance of the family principle in the communal phase of African development. It affected the two principal factors of production—land and labor—as well as the system of distributing goods. European anthropologists who have studied African societies have done so mainly from a very prejudiced and racist position, but their researchers can nevertheless provide abundant facts relating to family homesteads and compounds, to the extended family (including affinal members who join by association rather than by birth), and to lineages and clans which carried the principles of kinship alliances over large areas. However, while the exact details might have differed, similar social institutions were to be found among the Gauls of eleventh-century France, among the Viet of Indochina at the same date, and virtually everywhere else in the world at one time or another—because communalism is one phase through which all human society passed.

In all African societies during the early epoch, the individual at every stage of life had a series of duties and obligations to others in the society as well as a set of rights: namely, things that he or she could expect or demand from other individuals. Age was a most important factor determining the extent of rights and obligations. The oldest members of the society were highly respected and usually in authority; and the idea of seniority through age was reflected in the presence of age-grades and age-sets in a great many African societies. Circumcision meant initiation into the society and into adulthood. From that moment, a man was placed with others in his own age-group and a woman likewise. Usually, there were at least three age-grades, corresponding roughly to the young, the middle-aged, and the old.

In large parts of Europe, when communalism broke down it gave way to widespread slavery as the new form in which labor was mobilized. This slavery continued throughout the European Middle Ages, with the Crusades between Christians and Moslems giving an added excuse for enslaving people. Slavery in turn gave way to serfdom, whereby the laborer was tied to the land and could no longer be sold and transported. Because it took many years for the transition from slavery to feudalism to take place in Europe, it was common to find that feudal society still retained numbers of slaves. Parts of China, Burma, and India also had considerable numbers of slaves as the society moved away from elementary communalism, but there was never any time-span when slavery was the dominant mode of production in Asia. In Africa, there were few slaves and certainly no epoch of slavery. Most of the slaves were in North African and other Moslem societies, and in those instances a man and his family could have the same slave status for generations, within the overall feudal structure of the society. Elsewhere in Africa, communal societies were introduced to the concept of owning alien human beings when they took captives in war. At first, those captives were in a very disadvantaged position, comparable to that of slaves, but very rapidly captives or their offspring became ordinary members of the society, because there was no scope for the perpetual exploitation of man by man in a context that was neither feudal nor capitalist.

Both Marxists and non-Marxists alike (with different motivations) have pointed out that the sequence of modes of production noted in Europe were not reproduced in Africa. In Africa, after the communal stage there was no epoch of slavery arising out of internal evolution. Nor was there a mode of production which was the replica of European feudalism. Marx himself recognized that the stages of development in Asia had produced a form of society which could not easily be fitted into a European slot. That he called "the Asian mode of production." Following along those lines, a number of Marxists have recently been discussing whether Africa was in the same category as Asia or whether Africa had its own "African mode of production." The implications of the arguments are very progressive, because they are concerned with the concrete conditions of Africa rather than with preconceptions brought from Europe. But the scholars concerned seem to be bent on finding a single term to cover a variety of social formations which were existing in Africa from about the fifth century A.D. to the coming of colonialism. The assumption that will underlie this study is that most African societies before 1500 were in a transitional stage between the practice of agriculture (plus fishing and herding) in family communities and the practice of the same activities within states and societies comparable to feudalism.

In a sense, all history is transition from one stage to another, but some historical situations along the line have more clearly distinguishable characteristics than others. Thus under communalism there were no classes, and there was equal access to land, and equality in distribution—at a low level of technology and production. Feudalism involved great inequality in distribution of land and social products. The landlord class and its bureaucracy controlled the state and used it as an instrument for oppressing peasants, serfs, slaves, and even craftsmen and merchants. The movement from communalism to feudalism in every continent took several centuries, and in some instances the interruption of internal evolution never allowed the process to mature. In Africa, there is no doubt that the societies which eventually reached feudalism were extremely few. So long as the feudal state was still in the making, elements that were communal coexisted with elements that were feudal and with some peculiarities due to African conditions. The transition was also characterized by a variety of social formations: There were pastoralists and cultivators, fishing societies and trading societies, raiders and nomads. They were all being progressively drawn into a relationship with the land, with each other, and with the state, through the expansion of productive forces and the network of distribution.

In feudal societies, there were clashes between the landlord and peasant classes and later on between the landlord and merchant classes. Under capitalism, the principal class contradiction inside Europe was between the proletariat and the bourgeoisie. Those hostile class relations provided the motive force within the respective societies. African communal societies had differences such as age-grades and differences between ordinary members and religious leaders such as rainmakers. However, those were not exploitative or antagonistic relations. The concept of class as a motive force in social development had not yet come about; and in the communal phase one must look at the fundamental forces of production to understand the process of change.

Using a number of methods and concepts, it is possible to reconstruct the most likely manner in which isolated family living was broken down and production increased. For instance, the rise of age-grades can be seen as responding to the need for greater solidarity, because age-grades included and cut across many families. Similarly, communal labor was entered into by cross sections of the community to make work more efficient. The *dokpwe* work group of Dahomey mentioned above had a wider application in serving the whole community to perform such heavy tasks as clearing land and housebuilding. With the offer of some food and beer or palm wine, a work team or "work bee" could be mobilized in a short time in most African communities, including those of the light-skinned Berbers of North Africa.

Of course, while the organization of labor might have helped to produce more, the principal change in the productive forces was that which comprised new techniques—using the word in its broadest sense to include both tools and skills in dealing with the environment and new plant and animal species. The first prerequisite for mastery of the environment is knowledge of that environment. By the fifteenth century, Africans everywhere had arrived at a considerable understanding of the total ecology— of the soils, climate, animals, plants, and their multiple interrelationships. The practical application of this lay in the need to trap animals, to build houses, to make utensils, to find medicines, and above all to devise systems of agriculture.

In the centuries before the contact with Europeans, the overwhelmingly dominant activity in Africa was agriculture. In all the settled agricultural communities, people observed the peculiarities of their own environment and tried to find techniques for dealing with it in a rational manner. Advanced methods were used in some areas, such as terracing, crop rotation, green manuring, mixed farming, and regulated swamp farming. The single most important technological change underlying African agricultural development was the introduction of iron tools, notably the ax and the hoe, replacing wooden and stone tools. It was on the basis of the iron tools that new skills were elaborated in agriculture as well as in other spheres of economic activity.

The coming of iron, the rise of cereal growing, and the making of pottery were all closely related phenomena. In most parts of Africa, it was in the period after the birth of Christ that those things came about. The rate of change over a few centuries was quite impressive. Millet and rice had been domesticated from wild grasses just as yams were made to evolve from selected wild roots. Most African societies raised the cultivation of their own particular staple to a fine art. Even the widespread resort to shifting cultivation with burning and light hoeing was not as childish as the first European colonialists supposed. That simple form of agriculture was based on a correct evaluation of the soil potential, which was not as great as initially appears from the heavy vegetation; and when the colonialists started upsetting the thin topsoil the result was disastrous.

The above remarks show that when an outsider comes into a new ecological system, even if he is more skilled he does not necessarily function as effectively as those who have familiarized themselves with the environment over centuries; and the newcomer is likely to look more ridiculous if he is too arrogant to realize that he has something to learn from the "natives." However, it is not being suggested that African agriculture in the early period was superior to that of other continents. On the contrary, African standards of husbandry on the land and with livestock were not as high as those independently evolved in most parts of Asia and Europe. The weakness in Africa seemed to have been the lack of a professional interest in acquiring more scientific knowledge and in devising tools to lighten the load of labor as well as to transform hostile environments into areas suitable for human activity. As far as agriculture in Europe was concerned, this professionalism was undertaken by the class with a vested interest in the land—namely, the feudalist landowners and later the capitalist farmers.

It has previously been stated that development is very much determined by the social relations of production (i.e., those which have to do with people's functions in producing wealth). Where a few people owned the land and the majority were tenants, this injustice at a particular stage of history allowed the few to concentrate on improving their land. In contrast, under communalism every African was assured of sufficient land to meet his own needs by virtue of being a member of a family or community. For that reason, and because land was relatively abundant, there were few social pressures or incentives for technical changes to increase productivity.

In Asia, where much of the land was communally owned, there were tremendous advances in some types of farming, especially irrigated farming. This was because the state in India, China, Ceylon, and other places intervened and engaged in irrigation and other hydraulic works on a large scale. This was also true of North Africa, which in most respects followed a pattern of evolution similar to that of Asia. The African land tenure pattern was closer to that of Asia than to that of Europe, but even the most politically developed African states did not play the role of initiators and supervisors of agricultural development. One reason may have been the lack of population pressure and hence the scattered nature of settlements. Another may have been state concentration on trading non-agricultural products to the exclusion of other things. Certainly, when African societies became linked up with other social systems outside the continent on the basis of trade, little attention was paid to agriculture.

When it comes to the question of manufacturing in Africa before the time of the white man, it is also essential to recognize where achievements have been underestimated. African manufacturers have been contemptuously treated or overlooked by European writers, because the modern conception of the word brings to mind factories and machines. However, "manufactures" means literally "things made by hand," and African manufacture in this sense had advanced appreciably. Most African societies fulfilled their own needs for a wide range of articles of domestic use, as well as for farming tools and weapons.

One way of judging the level of economic development in Africa five centuries ago is through the quality of the products. Here a few examples will be given of articles which came to the notice of the outside world.

Through North Africa, Europeans became familiar with a superior brand of red leather from Africa which was termed "Moroccan leather." In fact, it was tanned and dyed by Hausa and Mandinga specialists in northern Nigeria and Mali. When direct contact was established between Europeans and Africans on the East and West coasts, many more impressive items were displayed. As soon as the Portuguese reached the old kingdom of Kongo, they sent back word on the superb local cloths made from bark and palm fiber—and having a finish comparable to velvet. The Baganda were also expert barkcloth makers. Yet, Africa had even better to offer in the form of cotton cloth, which was widely manufactured before the coming of the Europeans. Well into the present century, local cottons from the Guinea coast were stronger than Manchester cottons. Once European products reached Africa, Africans too were in a position to make comparisons between their commodities and those from outside. In Katanga and Zambia, the local copper continued to be preferred to the imported items, while the same held true for iron in a place like Sierra Leone.

It was at the level of scale that African manufactures had not made a breakthrough. That is to say, the cotton looms were small, the iron smelters were small, the pottery was turned slowly by hand and not on a wheel. Yet some changes were taking place in this context. Under communalism, each household met its own needs by making its own clothes, pots, mats, and such. That was true of every continent. However, economic expansion from there on was associated with specialization and localization of industry—people's needs being met by exchange. This trend was displayed in the principal African manufactures, and notably in the cloth industry. Cotton fiber had to be ginned (separated from the seed), then carded and spun into yarn, before being woven. Either the yarn or the woven cloth had to be dyed, and the making of the dye itself was a complex process. There was a time when all these stages would be performed by a single family or rather by the women in a single family, as in Yorubaland. But economic development was reflected in the separation of dyeing from cloth-making, and the separation of spinning from weaving. Each separation marked greater specialization and quantitative and qualitative changes in output.

European industry has been intensively studied, and it is generally recognized that in addition to new machinery a most decisive factor in the growth of industry was the changeover from domestic production to the factory system, with the guild marking an intermediary stage. The guild was an association of specialists, passing on their skills by training apprentices and working in buildings set aside for that purpose. Africa, too, had elements of the guild system. At Timbuktu, there were tailoring guilds, while in Benin guilds of a very restricted caste type controlled the famous brass and bronze industry. In Nupe (now northern Nigeria) the glass and bead industry operated on a guild basis. Each Nupe guild had a common workshop and a master. The master obtained contracts, financed the guild, and disposed of the product. Both his own relatives as well as strangers were free to enter the guild and learn the various specialized tasks within the glass industry. What this amounted to was simply that there was increasing specialization and division of labor.

Traditional African economies are usually called "subsistence" economies. Often, small villages farmed, hunted, fished, and looked after themselves independently with little reference to the rest of the continent. Yet, at the same time, the vast majority of African communities fulfilled at least a few of their needs by trade. Africa was a continent of innumerable trade routes. Some extended for long distances, like the routes across the Sahara or the routes connected with Katanga copper. But in the main, it was trade between neighboring or not too far distant societies. Such trade was always a function of production. Various communities were producing surpluses of given commodities which could be exchanged for items which they lacked. In that way, the salt industry of one locality would be stimulated while the iron industry would be encouraged in another. In a coastal, lake, or river area, dried fish could become profitable, while yams and millet would be grown in abundance elsewhere to provide a basis for exchange. The trade so readily distinguishable in every part of the continent between the tenth and fifteenth centuries was an excellent indicator of economic expansion and other forms of development which accompanied increasing mastery over the environment.

As part of the extension of trade, it was noticeable that barter was giving way to some forms of money exchange. Barter was generally practiced when the volume of trade was small and when only a few commodities were involved. However, as trade became more complicated, some items began to be used as the standards for measuring other goods. Those items could be kept as a form of wealth easily transformed into other commodities when the need arose. For example, salt, cloth, iron hoes, and cowry shells were popular forms of money in Africa—apart from gold and copper, which were much rarer and therefore restricted to measuring things of great value. In a few places, such as North Africa, Ethiopia, and the Kongo, the monetary systems were quite sophisticated, indicating that the economy was far removed from simple barter and subsistence.

There were many other changes of a socio-political nature accompanying the expansion of the productive forces. Indeed, things such as agricultural practices, industry, trade, money, and political structures were inseparable—each interacting with the others. The most developed areas of Africa were those where all the elements converged, and the two sociopolitical features which were the outstanding indices to development were the increase of stratification and the consolidation of states.

The principles of family and deferment to age were slowly breaking down throughout the centuries preceding the arrival of Europeans in their sailing ships. Changes in technology and in the division of labor made that inevitable. The introduction of iron, for example, gave economic and military strength to those who could make and acquire it. Better tools meant more food and a greater population, but the latter tended to outrun the supplies of material goods, and the possibilities of wealth opened up by the possession of iron were seized upon by a few to their own advantage. Skilled workers in iron, cloth, pottery, leather, or salt-making tended to pass on their skills in closed groups known as castes. That insured that the division of labor operated in their favor, because their position was privileged and strategic. Ironworkers were particularly favored in some African societies in which they either became the ruling groups or were very close to the top of the social hierarchy. The division of labor also carried over into non-material spheres, producing professional minstrels and historians. They too had certain special rights and privileges, notably the ability to criticize freely without fear of reprisal. In some circumstances, skilled castes were reduced to very low status. But that was rare, and in any case it does not contradict the general assertion that the tendency was for communalism to give rise to more and more stratification.

Social stratification was the basis for the rise of classes and for social antagonisms. To some extent, this was a logical follow-up of the previous non-antagonistic differences in communal society. For instance, old men could use their control over land allocation, over bride-price, and over other traditional exchanges to try to establish themselves as a privileged economic stratum. Secret societies arose in the area that is now Liberia, Sierra Leone, and Guinea, and they permitted knowledge, power, and wealth to pass into the hands of the elders and ultimately to the elders of particular lineages.

The contradiction between young men and their elders was not the type that caused violent revolution. But young men clearly had reasons for resenting their dependence on elders, especially when it came to such vital personal matters as the acquisition of wives. When disgruntled, they could either leave their communities and set up for themselves or they could challenge the principles within the society. In either case, the trend was that some individuals and families were more successful than others, and those families established themselves as permanent rulers. Then age ceased to matter as much because even a junior could succeed to his father, once the notion of royal blood or royal lineage was established.

In the period of transition, while African society retained many features that were undisputably communal, it also accepted the principle that some families or clans or lineages were destined to rule and others were not. This was true not only of cultivators but of pastoralists as well. In fact, livestock became unevenly distributed much more readily than land; and those families with the largest herds became socially and politically dominant.

An even more important aspect of the process of social stratification was that brought about by contact between different social formations. Fishermen had to relate to cultivators and the latter to pastoralists. There were even social formations such as bands of hunters and food-gatherers who had not yet entered the phase of communal cooperation. Often the relationship was peaceful. In many parts of the African continent, there arose what is known as "symbiosis" between groups earning their living in different ways—which really means that they agreed to exchange goods and coexist to their mutual advantage. However, there was also room for considerable conflict; and when one group imposed itself by force on another, the result was invariably the rise of social classes with the conquerors on top and the conquered at the bottom.

The most common clashes between different social formations were those between pastoralists and cultivators. In some instances, the cultivators had the upper hand, as for instance in West Africa where cultivators like the Mandinga and Hausa were the overlords of the Fulani cattlemen right up to the eighteenth and nineteenth centuries. The reverse situation was found in the Horn of Africa and most of East Africa. Another type of clash was that in which raiding peoples took power over agriculturalists, as happened in Angola and in and around the Sahara, where the Moors and Tuareg exacted tribute from and even enslaved more peaceful and sedentary peoples. The result in each case was that a relatively small faction held control of the land and (where relevant) cattle, mines, and long-distance trade. It meant also that the minority group could make demands on the labor of their subjects—not on the basis of kinship but because a relationship of domination and subordination existed.

In truly communal societies, the leadership was based on religion and family ties. The senior members of the society shared the work with others and received more or less the same share of the total product. Certainly, no one starved while others stuffed themselves and threw away the excess.

However, once African societies began to expand by internal evolution, conquest, or trade, the style of life of the ruling group became noticeably different. They consumed the most and the best that the society offered. Yet, they were least directly involved in the production of wealth by farming, cattle herding, or fishing. The ruling class and the kings in particular had the right to call upon the labor of the common man for certain projects and for a given number of days per year. This is known as *corvée* labor, from a similar procedure followed in feudal France. Such a system meant greater exploitation and at the same time greater development of productive resources.

Social stratification as outlined above went hand in hand with the rise of the state. The notion of royal lineages and commoner clans could not have any meaning except in a political state with a concrete geographical existence. It is significant that the great dynasties of the world ruled over feudal states. To the European or European-trained ear, the names of the Tudors, Bourbons, Hohenzollerns, and Romanovs would already be familiar. Japan had its Kamakuras and its Tokugawas; China had its T'ang and its Ming; India had its Guptas and its Marathas; and so on. All of those were feudal dynasties existing in a period some centuries after the birth of Christ, but in addition there were dynasties which ruled in each of those countries before feudal land tenure and class relations had fully crystalized. It means that the transition to feudalism in Europe* and Asia saw the rise of ruling groups and the state as interdependent parts of the same process. In that respect, Africa was no different.

From a political perspective, the period of transition from communalism to feudalism in Africa was one of state formation. At the beginning (and for many centuries), the state remained weak and immature. It acquired definite territorial boundaries, but inside those boundaries subjects lived in their own communities with scarcely any contact with the ruling class until the time came to pay an annual tax or tribute. Only when a group within the state refused to pay the tribute did the early African states mobilize their repressive machinery in the form of an army to demand what it considered as its rights from subjects. Slowly, various states acquired greater power over their many communities of citizens. They exacted *corvée* labor, they enlisted soldiers, and they appointed regular tax collectors and local administrators. The areas of Africa in which labor relations were breaking out of communal restrictions corresponded to areas in which sophisticated political states were emerging. The rise of states

---

* In Europe, communalism gave way to slavery, and therefore dynasties and strong states were present on the eve of the slavery epoch.

was itself a form of development, which increased the scale of African politics and merged small ethnic groups into wider identities suggestive of nations.

In some ways, too much importance is attached to the growth of political states. It was in Europe that the nation-state reached an advanced stage, and Europeans tended to use the presence or absence of well-organized polities as a measure of "civilization." That is not entirely justified, because in Africa there were small political units which had relatively advanced material and non-material cultures. For instance, neither the Ibo people of Nigeria nor the Kikuyu of Kenya ever produced large centralized governments in their traditional setting. But both had sophisticated systems of political rule based on clans and (in the case of the Ibo) on religious oracles and "Secret Societies." Both of them were efficient agriculturalists and ironworkers, and the Ibo had been manufacturing brass and bronze items ever since the ninth century A.D., if not earlier.

However, after making the above qualification, it can be conceded that on the whole the larger states in Africa had the most effective political structures and greater capacity for producing food, clothing, minerals, and other material artifacts. It can readily be understood that those societies which had ruling classes were concerned with acquiring luxury and prestige items. The privileged groups in control of the state were keen to stimulate manufactures as well as to acquire them through trade. They were the ones that mobilized labor to produce a greater surplus above subsistence needs, and in the process they encouraged specialization and the division of labor.

Scholars often distinguish between groups in Africa which had states and those which were "stateless." Sometimes, the word "stateless" is carelessly or even abusively used; but it does describe those peoples who had no machinery of government coercion and no concept of a political unit wider than the family or the village. After all, if there is no class stratification in a society, it follows that there is no state, because the state arose as an instrument to be used by a particular class to control the rest of society in its own interests. Generally speaking, one can consider the stateless societies as among the older forms of socio-political organization in Africa, while the large states represented an evolution away from communalism—sometimes to the point of feudalism.

Again, it must be emphasized that a survey of the scene in Africa before the coming of Europeans would reveal considerable unevenness of development. There were social formations representing hunting bands, communalism, feudalism, and many positions intermediate between the last two. The remainder of this section will be devoted to a review of the principal features of several of the most developed societies and states of Africa in the last thousand years or so before Africa came into permanent contact with Europe. The areas to be considered are Egypt, Ethiopia, Nubia, Morocco, the Western Sudan, the interlacustrine zone of East Africa, and Zimbabwe. Each serves as an example of what development meant in early Africa and what the direction of social movement was. To a greater or lesser extent, each was also a leading force on the continent in the sense of carrying neighbors along the same path, either by absorbing them or influencing them more indirectly.

Some Concrete Examples

Egypt

It is logical to start with Egypt as the oldest culture in Africa which rose to eminence. The glories of Egypt under the Pharaohs are well known and do not need recounting. At one time, it used to be said or assumed that ancient Egypt was not "African"—a curious view which is no longer seriously propounded. However, for the present purposes, it is more relevant to refer to Egypt under Arab and Turkish rule from the seventh century onwards. During that latter period, the ruling class was foreign, and that meant that Egypt's internal development was tied up with other countries, notably Arabia and Turkey. Colonized Egypt sent abroad great amounts of wealth in the form of food and revenue, and that was a very negative factor. But the tendency was for the ruling foreigners to break with their own imperial masters and to act simply as a ruling elite within Egypt, which became an independent feudal state.

One of the first features of feudalism to arrive in Egypt was the military aspect. The Arab, Turk, and Circassian invaders were all militarily inclined. This was particularly true of the Mameluks who held power from the thirteenth century onwards. Political power in Egypt from the seventh century lay in the hands of a military oligarchy which delegated the actual government to bureaucrats, thereby creating a situation similar to that in places like China and Indochina. Even more fundamental was the fact that land tenure relations were undergoing change in such a way that a true feudal class came on the scene. All the conquerors made land grants to their followers and military captains. Initially, the land in Egypt was the property of the state to be rented out to cultivators. The state then had the right to reappropriate the land and allocate it once more, somewhat like the head of a village community acting as the guardian of the lands of related families. However, the ruling military elements also became a new class of landowners. By the fifteenth century, most of the land in Egypt was the property of the sultan and his military lords.

If there was a small class which monopolized most of the land, it followed that there was a large class of landless. Peasant cultivators were soon converted into mere agricultural laborers, tied to the soil as tenants or vassals of the feudal landlords. These peasants with little or no land were known as the *fellahin*. In Europe, there are legends about the exploitation and suffering of the Russian serfs, or *muzhik*, under feudalism. In Egypt, the exploitation of the *fellahin* was carried out even more thoroughly. The feudalists had no interest in the *fellahin* beyond seeing that they produced revenue. Most of what the peasants produced was taken from them in the form of tax, and the tax collectors were asked to perform the miracle of taking from the peasants even that which they did not have! When their demands were not met, the peasants were brutalized.

The antagonistic nature of the contradiction between the feudal warrior landlords and the *fellahin* was revealed by a number of peasant revolts, notably in the early part of the eighth century. In no continent was feudalism an epoch of romance for the laboring classes, but the elements of development were seen in the technology and the increase in productive capacity. Under the patronage of the Fatimid dynasty (969 A.D. to 1170 A.D.), science flourished and industry reached a new level in Egypt. Windmills and waterwheels were introduced from Persia in the tenth century. New industries were introduced—papermaking, sugar refining, porcelain, and the distillation of gasoline. The older industries of textiles, leather, and metal were improved upon. The succeeding dynasties of the Ayyubids and the Mameluks also achieved a great deal, especially in the building of canals, dams, bridges, and aqueducts, and in stimulating commerce with Europe. Egypt at that time was still able to teach Europe many things and was flexible enough to receive new techniques in return.

Although feudalism was based on the land, it usually developed towns at the expense of the countryside. The high points of Egyptian feudal culture were associated with the towns. The Fatimids founded the city of Cairo, which became one of the most famous and most cultured in the world. At the same time, they established the Azhar University which exists today as one of the oldest in the world. The feudalists and the rich merchants were the ones who benefited most, but the craftsmen and other city dwellers of Cairo and Alexandria were able to participate to some extent in the leisured lives of the towns.

Ethiopia

Ethiopia, too, at the start of its history as a great power was ruled over by foreigners. The kingdom of Axum was one of the most important of the nuclei around which feudal Ethiopia eventually emerged, and Axum was founded near the Red Sea coast by a dynasty of Sabean origin from the other side of the Red Sea. But the kings of Axum were never agents of foreign powers, and they became completely Africanized. The founding of Axum goes back to the first century A.D. and its ruling class was Christianized within a few centuries. After that they moved inland and participated in the development of the Christian feudal Ethiopian state.

The Ethiopian, Tigrean, and Amharic ruling class was a proud one, tracing its descent to Solomon. As a state which incorporated several other smaller states and kingdoms, it was an empire in the same sense as feudal Austria or Prussia. The emperor of Ethiopia was addressed as "Conquering Lion of the Tribe of Judah, Elect of God, Emperor of Ethiopia, King of Kings." In practice, however, the "Solomonic" line was not unbroken. Most of the consolidation of the inland Ethiopian plateau was carried out in the twelfth century by an intruding dynasty, the Zagwe, who made claims to descent from Moses. The Zagwe kings distinguished themselves by building several churches cut out of solid rock. The architectural achievements attest to the level of skill reached by Ethiopians as well as the capacity of the state to mobilize labor on a huge scale. Such tasks could not have been achieved by voluntary family labor but only through the labor of an exploited class.

A great deal is known of the superstructure of the Ethiopian empire, especially its Christianity and its literate culture. History was written to glorify the king and the nobility, especially under the restored "Solomonic" dynasty which replaced the Zagwe in 1270 A.D. Fine illuminated books and manuscripts became a prominent element of Amharic culture. Equally fine garments and jewelry were produced for the ruling class and for the church. The top ecclesiastics were part of the nobility, and the institution of the monastery grew to great proportions in Ethiopia. The association of organized religion with the state was implicit in communal societies, where the distinction between politics, economics, religion, medicine, was scarcely drawn. Under feudalism everywhere, church and state were in close alliance. The Buddhists were pre-eminent in feudal Vietnam, Burma, Japan, and to a lesser extent in China. In India, a limited Buddhist influence was overwhelmed by that of the Hindus and Moslems; and of course in feudal Europe it was the Catholic church which played the role paralleled by the Orthodox church in Ethiopia.

The wealth of Ethiopia rested on an agricultural base. The fertile uplands supported cereal growing and there was considerable livestock raising, including the rearing of horses. Craft skills were developed in a number of spheres, and foreign craftsmen were encouraged. For instance, early in the fifteenth century, Turkish artisans settled in the country and made coats of mail and weapons for the Ethiopian army. Coptics from Egypt were also introduced to help run the financial administration. No one denies that the word "feudal" can be applied to Ethiopia in those centuries, because there existed a clear-cut class contradiction between the landlords and the peasants. Those relations grew out of the communalism that had characterized Ethiopia, like other parts of Africa, much earlier.

Feudal Ethiopia included lands that were communally owned by village and ethnic communities as well as lands belonging directly to the crown; but in addition large territories were conferred by the conquering Amharic dynasties on members of the royal family and on soldiers and priests. Those who received huge areas of land became *Ras*, or provincial princes, and they had judges appointed by the emperor attached to them. The peasants in their domain were reduced to tenants who could earn their living only by offering produce to the landlord and taxes to the state (also in produce). The landlords exempted themselves from tax—a typical situation in feudal societies, and one which fed the fires of revolution in Europe when the bourgeois class grew powerful enough to challenge the fact that the feudalists were using political power to tax everyone but themselves. Ethiopia, of course, never reached that stage of transition to capitalism. What is clear is that the transition to feudalism had been made.

Nubia

Nubia was another Christian region in Africa, but one which is not so famous as Ethiopia. In the sixth century A.D., Christianity was introduced into the middle Nile in the districts once ruled by the famous state of Kush, or Meroë. In the period before the birth of Christ, Kush was a rival to Egypt in splendor, and it ruled Egypt for a number of years. Its decline in the fourth century A.D. was completed by attacks from the then expanding Axum. The three small Nubian states which arose some time afterwards were to some extent the heirs of Kush, although after their conversion to Christianity it was this religion which dominated Nubian culture.

The Nubian states (which had consolidated to two by about the eighth century) achieved most from the ninth to the eleventh centuries, in spite of great pressures from Arab and Islamic enemies; and they did not finally succumb until the fourteenth century. Scholarly interest in Nubia has focused on the ruins of large red-brick churches and monasteries which had murals and frescoes of fine quality. Several conclusions can be drawn from the material evidence. In the first place, a great deal of labor was required to build those churches along with the stone fortifications which often surrounded them. As with the pyramids of Egypt or the feudal castles of Europe, the common builders were intensely exploited and probably coerced. Secondly, skilled labor was involved in the making of the bricks and in the architecture. The paintings indicate that the skills surpassed mere manual dexterity, and the same artistic merit is noticeable in fragments of painted pottery recovered from Nubia.

It has already been indicated that the churches and monasteries played a major role in Ethiopia, and this is worth elaborating on with respect to Nubia. The monastery was a major unit of production. Numerous peasant huts were clustered around each monastery, which functioned very much as did the manor of a feudal lord. The wealth that accumulated inside the churches was alienated from the peasants, while the finest aspects of the non-material culture, such as books, were accessible only to a small minority. Not only were the peasants illiterate, but in many cases they were non-Christians or only nominally Christian—judging from the better known Ethiopian example of the same date. When the Christian ruling class of Nubia was eliminated by the Moslems, very little of the achievements of the old state remained in the fabric of the people's daily lives. Such reversals in the historical process are not uncommon throughout human experience. Ultimately, the dialectic of development asserts itself, but some ebbing and flowing is inevitable. The Nubian states were not in existence in the fifteenth century, but they constitute a legitimate example of the potentialities of African development.

One can go further and discern that Kush was still contributing to African development long after the kingdom had declined and given way to Christian Nubia. It is clear that Kush was a center from which many positive cultural elements diffused to the rest of Africa. Brasswork of striking similarity to that of Meroe was reproduced in West Africa, and the technique by which West Africans cast their brass is generally held to have originated in Egypt and to have been passed on by way of Kush. Above all, Kush was one of the earliest and most vigorous centers of iron mining and smelting in Africa, and it was certainly one of the sources from which this crucial aspect of technology passed to the rest of the continent. That is why the middle Nile was a leading force in the social, economic, and political development of Africa as a whole.

The Maghreb

Islam was the great "revealed" religion which played the major role in the period of the feudal development of the Maghreb—the lands at the western extremity of the Islamic empires that stretched across Africa, Asia, and Europe within years of the Prophet Mohammed's death in the seventh century of the Christian era. The Arab empire-building under the banner of Islam is a classic example of the role of religion in that respect. Ibn Khaldun, a great fourteenth-century North African historian, was of the opinion that Islam was the most important force allowing the Arabs to transcend the narrow boundaries of small family communities which were constantly struggling among each other. He wrote:

> Arab pride, touchiness and intense jealousy of power render it impossible for them to agree. Only when their nature has been permeated by a religious impulse are they transformed, so that the tendency to anarchy is replaced by a spirit of mutual defense. Consider the moment when religion dominated their policy and led them to observe a religious law designed to promote the moral and material interests of civilization. Under a series of successors to the Prophet [Mohammed], how vast their empire became and how strongly was it established.

The above remarks by Ibn Khaldun cover only one aspect of Arab imperial expansion, but it was certainly a crucial one, and attested to the essential role of ideology in the developmental process. That has to be considered in relation to and in addition to the material circumstances. Furthermore, in judging the material conditions at any given time which might form the basis for further expansion of production and further growth of the society's power, it is also necessary to consider the historical legacy. Like Islamic Egypt and Christian Nubia, the Maghreb of the Islamic dynasties inherited a rich historical and cultural tradition. It was the seat of the famous society of Carthage which flourished between 1200 B.C. and 200 B.C., and which was a blend of foreign influences from the eastern Mediterranean with the Berber peoples of the Maghreb. The region had subsequently been an important section of the Roman and Byzantine empires; and before becoming Moslem the Maghreb had actually distinguished itself as a center of non-conformist Christianity which went under the name of Donatism.

The striking achievements of Moslem Maghreb were spread over the naval, military, commercial, and cultural spheres. Its navies controlled the western Mediterranean and its armies took over most of Portugal and Spain. When the Moslem advance into Europe was turned back in the year 732 A.D., North African armies were already deep into France. In the eleventh century, the armies of the Almoravid dynasty gathered strength from deep within Senegal and Mauritania and launched themselves across the Strait of Gibraltar to reinforce Islam in Spain, which was being threatened by Christian kings. For over a century, the Almoravid rule in North Africa and Iberia was characterized by commercial wealth and a resplendent literary and architectural record. After being ejected from Spain in the 1230s the Maghreb Moslems, or Moors as they were called, continued to maintain a dynamic society on African soil. As one index to the standard of social life, it has been pointed out that public baths were common in the cities of Maghreb at a time when in Oxford the doctrine was still being propounded that the washing of the body was a dangerous act.

One of the most instructive aspects of the history of the Maghreb is the interaction of social formations to produce the state. A major problem that had to be resolved was that of integrating the isolated Berber groups into larger political communities. There were also contradictions between sedentary groups and nomadic pastoral sectors of the populations.

The Berbers were mainly pastoralists organized in patriarchal clans, and in groups of clans, and in groups of clans connected by a democratic council of all adult males. Grazing land was under communal ownership, and maintaining irrigation was also a collective responsibility for the agriculturalists. Yet, cooperation within kin-groups contrasted with hostility between those who had no immediate blood ties, and it was only in the face of the Arab invaders that the Berbers united—using a non-conformist Kharijite Islam as their ideology. The Kharijite revolt of 739 A.D. is considered in one sense as being nationalistic and in another sense a revolt of the exploited classes against the Arab military, bureaucratic, and theocratic elite, who professed the orthodox Sunni Islam. That revolt of the Berber masses laid the basis for Moroccan nationalism, and three centuries later the Almohad dynasty (1147–1270) brought political unity to the whole of Maghreb as a product of the synthesis of Berber and Arab achievements in the sphere of state-building.

Unfortunately, the Maghreb nation did not last; and instead the region was bequeathed the nuclei of three nation states—Morocco, Algeria, and Tunisia. Within each of the three areas, divisive tendencies were very strong in the fourteenth and fifteenth centuries. For instance, in Tunisia the ruling Hafsid dynasty was constantly involved in crushing local rebellions and defending the integrity of the state. It has been noted already that the political state in Africa and elsewhere was a consequence of development of the productive forces, but the state in turn also conditioned the rate at which the economy advanced, because the two were dialectically interrelated. Therefore, the failure of the Maghreb to build a nation-state and the difficulties of consolidating state power even within the three divisions of Morocco, Algeria, and Tunisia were factors holding back the further development of the region. Moreover, political division weakened the Maghreb vis-à-vis foreign enemies, and Europe was soon to take advantage of those internal weaknesses, by launching attacks from the year 1415 onwards.

The experience of the Maghreb can be drawn upon to illustrate the lengthy nature of transition from the one mode of production to another and the fact that two different ways of organizing society could coexist side by side over centuries. Throughout the period under discussion, a great deal of land in that part of Africa retained its communal ownership and family labor. Meanwhile, considerable socio-economic stratification had taken place and antagonistic classes had emerged. At the very bottom of the ladder were the slaves, or *harratine*, who were most often black Africans from south of the Sahara. Then came the *akhamme*, or landless peasants, who worked the proprietors' land and gave the latter four-fifths of whatever was produced. Special mention should be made of the position of women, who were not a class by themselves but who suffered from deprivations at the hands of their own menfolk and of the male-controlled ruling class. Therefore, the women in the *akhamme* class were in a very depressed condition. At the top of the society were the big landowners, who wielded political power along with other devotees of the Moslem religion.

None of the African societies discussed so far can be said to have thrown up capitalist forms to the point where the accumulation of capital became the principal motive force. However, they all had flourishing commercial sectors, moneylenders, and strong handicraft industries which were the features which ultimately gave birth to modern capitalism through evolution and revolution. The Maghreb merchants were quite wealthy. They gained from the energies of the cultivators, cattlemen, and shepherds; they indirectly or directly mobilized the labor in the mines of copper, lead, antimony, and iron; and they appropriated surplus from the skills of the craftsmen making textiles, carpets, leather, pottery, and articles of brass and iron. The merchants were a class of accumulators, and their dynamism made itself felt not only in the Maghreb but also in the Sahara and across the Sahara in West Africa. In that way, the development of the Maghreb acted as a factor in the development of what was called the Western Sudan.

The Western Sudan

To the Arabs, the whole of Africa south of the Sahara was the *Bilad as Sudan*—the Land of the Blacks. The name survives today only in the Republic of Sudan on the Nile, but references to the Western Sudan in early times concern the zone presently occupied by Senegal, Mali, Upper Volta, and Niger, plus parts of Mauritania, Guinea, and Nigeria. The Western Sudanic empires of Ghana, Mali, and Songhai have become by-words in the struggle to illustrate the achievements of the African past. That is the area to which African nationalists and progressive whites point when they want to prove that Africans too were capable of political, administrative, and military greatness in the epoch before the white men. However, a people's demands at any given time change the kinds of questions to which historians are expected to provide answers. Today the masses of Africa seek "development" and total emancipation. The issues that need resolution with regard to Western Sudanic history are those which illumine the principles underlying the impressive development of certain states in the heart of Africa.

The origins of the empire of Ghana go back to the fifth century A.D., but it reached its peak between the ninth and eleventh centuries. Mali had its prime in the thirteenth and fourteenth centuries, and Songhai in the two subsequent centuries. The three were not in exactly the same location; and the ethnic origin of the three ruling classes was different; but they should be regarded as "successor states," following essentially the same line of evolution and growth. They have been called trading states so often that it is almost forgotten that the principal activity of the population was agriculture. It was a zone in which several species of millet were domesticated, along with a species of rice, several other food plants, and at least one type of cotton. It was a zone which saw the relatively early introduction of iron in the millennium before the birth of Christ, and iron tools exercised their attendant benefits on agriculture. The open savannah country of the Western Sudan also favored livestock. Some groups such as the Fulani were exclusively pastoralist, but livestock was to be found in varying degrees throughout the huge region. Cattle were the most significant domesticated animals, followed by goats. The rearing of horses, mules, and donkeys was also carried on, which was made possible by wide tsetse-free areas. To add further variety, the great Niger River allowed for the rise of specialist fishermen.

Population, the indispensable factor of production, could only have reached the density which it did because of increasing food supplies; while handicraft industry and trade sprang primarily from the products of agriculture. Cotton cultivation led to the making of cotton cloth with such a variety of specialization that there was internal trade in particular cotton cloths, such as the unbleached fabric of Futa Djalon and the blue cloth of Jenne. Pastoralism provided a variety of products for manufacture, notably cattle hides and goatskins which went into the making of sandals, leather jackets for military use, leather pouches for amulets, and so on. Horses served as a means of transport to the ruling class and made a major contribution to warfare and the size of the state. For the purpose of interbreeding, some horses were imported from North Africa where the Arab bloodstock was of the finest quality. For pack transport, the donkey was of course better fitted; and the Mossi kingdom of Upper Volta for a long time specialized in breeding those pack animals which were associated with long distance trade within the vast region. On the edge of the Sahara, the camel took over—another "technological" asset introduced from the north.

Mining was a sphere in which production was important. Some of the royal clans in the Western Sudan, such as that of the Kante, were specialist blacksmiths. In a period of expansion by warfare, the control over iron supplies and over iron-working skills was obviously decisive. Besides, the two most important articles of long distance trade were salt and gold, both obtained principally by mining. Neither the salt supplies nor the gold supplies were originally within the domains of Ghana, but it took steps to integrate them either by trade or by territorial expansion. Ghana struck north into the Sahara, and towards the very end of the tenth century it captured the town of Awdaghast from the Berbers—a town useful for the control of the incoming salt mined in the middle of the desert. Similarly Mali and Songhai sought to secure control of Taghaza, which was the largest single center of salt mining. Songhai took the prize of Taghaza from the desert Berbers and held it for many years in the face of opposition from Morocco. Another crucial but seldom stressed element in the pattern of production was the ownership of copper mines in the Sahara by both Mali and Songhai.

To the south of Ghana lay the important sources of gold on the Upper Senegal and its tributary the Falémé. It is said that Ghana obtained its gold by "silent" or "dumb" barter which was described as follows:

> The merchants beat great drums to summon the local natives, who were naked and lived in holes in the ground. From these holes, which were doubtless the pits from which they dug the gold, they refused to emerge in the presence of the foreign merchants. The latter, therefore, used to

arrange their trade goods in piles on the river bank and retire out of sight. The local natives then came and placed a heap of gold beside each pile and withdrew. If the merchants were satisfied they took the gold and retreated, beating their drums to signify that the market was over.

The writer of the above lines (E. W. Bovill), a supposed European authority on the Western Sudan, then goes on to say that silent trade or dumb barter was a feature of the Western Sudan's gold trade throughout all the centuries until modern times. Actually, the only thing dumb about the trade is what he writes about it. The story of dumb barter for gold in West Africa is repeated in several accounts, starting with ancient Greek scripts. It is clearly a rough approximation of the first attempts at exchange of a people coming into contact with strangers, and it was not a permanent procedure. During the rule of Ghana, the people of the two principal gold-fields of Bambuk and Boure were drawn into regular trade relations with the Western Sudan. Ghana probably, and Mali certainly, exercised political rule over the two regions, where the mining and distribution of gold became a very complicated process. During the centuries of Mali's greatness, extensive mining of gold began in the forest of modern Ghana to supply the trans-Saharan gold trade. The existing social systems expanded and strong states emerged to deal with the sale of gold. The merchants who came from the great cities of the Western Sudan had to buy the gold by weight, using a small accurate measurement known as the *benda*.

When the Portuguese arrived at the river Gambia and got a glimpse at how gold was traded on the upper reaches of the river, they marveled at the dexterity shown by the Mandinga merchants. The latter carried very finely balanced scales, inlaid with silver and suspended from cords of twisted silk. The gold dust and nuggets were weighted with brass weights. The expertise of the Mandinga in measuring gold and in other forms of commerce was largely due to the fact that within that ethnic group there was a core of professional traders, commonly referred to as the Dioulas. They were not very wealthy, but were distinguished by their willingness to travel thousands of miles from one end of the Western Sudan to another. They also reached the coast or very near to the coast of Gambia, Sierra Leone, Liberia, Ivory Coast, and Ghana. The Dioulas handled a long list of African products—salt from the Atlantic coast and the Sahara; kola nuts from the forests of Liberia and Ivory Coast; gold from Akan country in modern Ghana; leather from Hausaland; dried fish from the coast; cotton cloth from many districts and especially from the central area of the Western Sudan; iron from Futa Djalon in modern Guinea; shea butter from the upper Gambia; and a host of other local articles. In addition, the trade of the Western Sudan involved the circulation of goods originating in North Africa, notably fabrics from Egypt and the Maghreb and coral beads from Ceuta on the Mediterranean coast. Therefore, the pattern of Western Sudanic and trans-Saharan commerce was integrating the resources of a wide area stretching from the Mediterranean to the Atlantic Ocean.

Long-distance trade across the Sahara had special characteristics. Some scholars have spoken of the camel as the ship of the Sahara, and the towns which the camel caravans entered on either side of the desert were called "ports." In practice, the trans-Saharan trade was as great an achievement as crossing an ocean. Much more than local trade, it stimulated the famous cities of the region such as Walata, Timbuktu, Gao, and Jenne; and it brought in the literate Islamic culture. Long-distance trade strengthened state power, which meant in effect the power of the lineages who transformed themselves into a permanent aristocracy. However, it is a gross oversimplification of cause and effect to say that it was the trans-Saharan trade which built the Western Sudanic empires. Ghana, Mali, and Songhai grew out of their environment, and out of the efforts of their own populations; and it was only after they had a certain status that their ruling classes could express an interest in long-distance trade and could provide the security to permit that trade to flourish.

It is significant that the Western Sudan never provided any significant capital for the trans-Saharan trade. The capital came from the merchants of Fez, Tlemcen, and other cities of the Maghreb; and they sent their agents to reside in the Western Sudan. To some extent, it was a colonial relationship because the exchange was unequal in North Africa's favor. However, the gold trade was at least capable of stimulating the development of the productive forces within West Africa, while the accompanying trade in slaves had no such benefits. Ghana, Mali, and Songhai all exported small numbers of slaves, and the empire of Kanem-Bornu gave slave exports a much higher priority because it controlled no gold supplies. Kanem-Bornu used its power to raid for captives to the south as far as Adamawa in modern Cameroon. The negative implications of such policies were to be fully brought out in later centuries, when the steady trickle of slaves from a few parts of West Africa across the Sahara was joined by the massive flow of the continent's peoples towards destinations named by Europeans.

Though falling considerably short of the feudal stage, state formation was more advanced in the Western Sudan than in most other parts of Africa in the period 500 A.D. to 1500 A.D. Apart from Ghana, Mali, Songhai, and Kanem-Bornu, there were outstanding kingdoms in Hausaland, in Mossi, in Senegal, in the Futa Djalon mountains of Guinea, and in the basin of the Benue tributary of the river Niger. The Western Sudanic techniques of political organization and administration spread out to many neighboring regions, and influenced the rise of innumerable small states scattered throughout the coastal region from the river Senegal to the Cameroon mountains. Some specific Sudanic features were discernible in many kingdoms, notably the position of the "Queen Mother" in the political structure.

The strengths and weaknesses of the Western Sudanic states attest to the point which they had reached on the long road away from communalism—with respect to social relations and to the level of production. The state held together several clashing social formations and ethnic groups. In the case of Kanem-Bornu, pastoralists and cultivators were even able to integrate the camel nomads of the desert. Elsewhere, the Tuareg nomads were kept at bay, so that cultivators and other sedentary peoples could live their lives in peace. Men, domestic beasts, and goods were free to move for thousands of miles in security. However, the state had not yet broken down the barriers between different social formations. The state existed as an institution which collected tribute from the various communities and restrained them from clashing. In periods of weakness, the superstructure of the state almost disappeared and left free scope for divisive political and social tendencies. Each successive great state was a further experiment to deal with the problem of unity, sometimes on a conscious level and more often as an unconscious by-product of the struggle for survival.

Under feudalism, the ruling class in the state for the first time tore away the social institutions which prevented the first embryo states from exercising direct action on each subject. That is to say, feudalism brought about a series of direct obligatory ties between the landed rulers and the landless subjects. In the Western Sudan, that clear-cut class division had not come into existence. By the time of Mali's pre-eminence in the thirteenth and fourteenth centuries, a small amount of local slavery had come into existence, and by the end of the fifteenth century there were both chattel slaves and "domestic slaves" comparable to feudal serfs. For instance, in Senegal, the Portuguese traders found that there were elements in the population who worked most days for their masters and a few days per month for themselves—a budding feudalist tendency. Nevertheless, most of the population still had ample access to land through their kin, and in political terms that meant that the authority of the ruling class was exercised over heads of families and clans rather than over each subject.

Although communal egalitarianism was on its way out, communal relations still persisted and had by the fifteenth century become a brake on the development of the Western Sudan. Such surplus as was being produced by the society over and above subsistence needs came out of tribute from the collective communities rather than directly from the producer to the exploiting class. That gave an incentive for maintaining the old social structures, although they were incapable of increasing labor mobilization and specialization to a much greater degree. It was unlikely that there would be a violent social revolution. Under those circumstances, major advances of technology were required to spark off further changes. The degree of economic integration had to be enhanced by greater productivity in various areas—allowing for more trade, more specialization in the division of labor, and the possibility of surplus accumulation. But wheeled vehicles and the plow stopped in North Africa, and so too did large-scale irrigation. Indeed, through the critical absence of large-scale irrigation, the productive base in the Western Sudan actually decreased, for the Sahara was advancing. Ghana had stood on fertile agricultural land, but both Mali and Songhai had their centers farther south, because the former northern terrain of Ghana was claimed by the Sahara through desiccation. Techniques necessary for the control of this hostile environment and for the increase of agricultural and manufacturing capacity had either to evolve locally or to be brought in from outside. In the next phase of African history after the coming of the white men, both of those alternatives were virtually ruled out in West Africa.

The Interlacustrine Zone

The high level of social evolution in the Western Sudan has been the cause of lengthy debates as to whether the region had achieved feudalism of the European variety, or whether it should be classed together with the great Asian empires, or whether it created a new and unique category of its own. On the eastern side of the continent, development in the same period was definitely slower. For one thing, the people of East Africa acquired iron tools at a much later date than their brothers in the north and west; and, secondly, the range of their technology and skills was narrower. However, by the fourteenth century, state formation was well under way, and the principles of development revealed in the process are worth considering. An area of special interest is that of the great lakes of Africa and particularly the zone around the group of lakes which the British thought fit to rename in honor of various members of the British ruling family—Victoria, Albert, Edward, George. In that interlacustrine zone, several famous states eventually emerged, one of the earliest and largest being that of Bunyoro-Kitara.

Bunyoro-Kitara comprised in whole or in part the regions which today are called Bunyoro, Ankole, Toro, Karagwe, and Buganda—all of which fall in Uganda, except Karagwe which is in Tanzania. The historical traditions have been orally preserved by these various peoples who at one time fell within the boundaries of Bunyoro-Kitara; and the traditions concentrate on the ruling dynasty, which is known as the Bachwezi. The Bachwezi were supposedly an immigrant pastoralist group. They introduced long-horned humped cattle, which later became the major species in the interlacustrine zone. Possession of these cattle undoubtedly aided them to become a ruling aristocracy in the fourteenth and fifteenth centuries. They became a social stratum above the clans which previously existed, and which had narrow territorial bases. The period of Bachwezi pre-eminence is also associated with ironworking, the manufacture of barkcloth, the technique of sinking well shafts through rocks, and (most striking of all) the construction of extensive earthwork systems, used apparently both for defense and for enclosing large herds of cattle. The largest of the earthworks was at Bigo, with ditches extending over six and a half miles.

The division of labor between pastoralists and cultivators and the nature of their contacts intensified the process of caste formation and class stratification in the interlacustrine area. The pastoralist Bahima had imposed their rule over the cultivators, or *Bairu*. Social classes grew out of a situation of changing labor relations. The earthworks of Bigo and elsewhere were not built by voluntary family labor, and some form of coercion must also have been used to get the cultivators to produce a surplus for their new lords. For instance, the Bachwezi are said to have established a system by which young men were conscripted into the king's service and were maintained by *Bairu* who occupied and cultivated land assigned for the support of the army. They also introduced slave artisans and administrators. When administrative officials were appointed at a local level to rule on behalf of the aristocrats, that was a first step toward setting up feudal fiefs as in Ethiopia; for while the question of land grants had not yet entered the picture, it must be borne in mind that inequality in the distribution of cattle meant in fact unequal access to the means of production.

Much uncertainty surrounds the precise identification of the Bachwezi. It is possible that they were not immigrants. Nevertheless, it is generally held that they were light-complexioned pastoralists coming from the north. Assuming that this was so, it is essential to stress that whatever was achieved in the interlacustrine region in the fourteenth and fifteenth centuries was a product of the evolution of African society as a whole and not a transplant from outside. In order to place those East African events within the context of universal human achievement, a parallel can be drawn with India. Centuries before the birth of Christ, Northern India was also the recipient of light-complexioned pastoral immigrants known as Aryans. There was a time when everything in Indian culture was attributed to the Aryans; but then careful scrutiny revealed that the basis of Indian society and culture had been laid by the earlier population known as the Dravidians. Therefore, it is now considered far more sensible to see the achievements of North India as a product of synthesis or combination of Aryan and Dravidian. Similarly in East Africa, one needs to seek the elements of synthesis between the new and the old and that in effect was the path of development in the interlacustrine zone in the fourteenth and fifteenth centuries.

As has just been noted, the Bachwezi are *associated with* techniques such as ironworking and barkcloth manufacture. It is not at all clearly established that they introduced such techniques for the first time, and it is much more probable that they presided over the *elaboration* of such skills. Certainly, iron-using societies were known in East Africa several centuries before the Bachwezi period. At Engaruka, just south of the present Kenya-Tanzania border, there are to be found the ruins of a small but impressive iron-age society, which flourished sometime before the end of the first millennium A.D. (i.e., before 1000 A.D.). Engaruka was a concentrated agricultural settlement engaging in terracing, irrigation, and the construction of walls by the technique known as dry stone building, whereby no lime was required to hold the stones together. In the interlacustrine area itself, there had emerged a banana-based agriculture, which was capable of supporting a large sedentary population. That was the sort of precondition for moving from communal isolation to statehood.

It is significant that orally preserved traditions imply the existence of kingdoms in Bunyoro and Karagwe before the Bachwezi. State formation was already in an embryo stage when the outsiders arrived, and the likelihood is that they did not remain outsiders for long. Unlike the Aryans in India, the Bachwezi did not even impose their own language, but adopted the Bantu speech of the local inhabitants. That reflects the dominance of local rather than foreign elements in the synthesis. In any event, the cultural product was *African*, and was part of the pattern of development through localized evolution combined with the interplay of social formations on a continent-wide scale.

Among the contributions supposedly made by the Bachwezi to the interlacustrine kingdoms was the introduction of religion based on the phases of the moon. In all of the situations examined so far, religion played a significant role in promoting the building of the state, leading away from the simple organization of the family community. Christianity and Islam have been most frequently associated with large-scale building both inside and outside of Africa. That is to be explained not so much by the actual religious beliefs, but because membership in a powerful universal church gave the ruling class of a young state many advantages. A Christian or Moslem prince had access to a literate culture and a wider world. He dealt with traders and craftsmen professing that religion; he used administrators and churchmen who were literate; and he could travel to parts of the world such as Mecca. Above all, the universal religions replaced "traditional" African ancestral religions in Ethiopia, Sudan, Egypt, the Maghreb, and progressively in the Western Sudan because Christianity and Islam were not rooted in any given family community and therefore could be used to mobilize the many communities that were merging into the state. However, religious beliefs which had been accepted by a single clan or ethnic group could be elevated in the same form or in a slightly altered form to become the religion of the whole state. This was the situation in the interlacustrine zone, and indeed in most other parts of Africa outside the regions already described.

Zimbabwe

In Zimbabwe, one of the great constructions in brick (dated around the fourteenth century) is commonly referred to as a "temple" and is felt to have served religious purposes. Even from the scanty evidence, it is clear that the religious aspect of social development was of the greatest importance in serving to cement ties between individuals in that emergent African society. For instance, the ruling class in the fifteenth century empire of Mutapa in Zimbabwe were pastoralists and their religious ritual included objects that were symbolic of cattle, as was found in the interlacustrine kingdoms such as Bunyoro and Karagwe. One can guess that the rituals also symbolized the dominance of the cattle owners, just as they also paid respect to pre-existing ideas of the cultivators in order to effect a stable synthesis. The details of the picture are not available in the present stage of knowledge, but what is required is that any discussion of African religion must seek to present it in a mobile evolutionary manner and to relate it to changing socio-economic forms and institutions. That task being beyond the confines of the present study, it is proposed to examine Zimbabwe as yet another region where the productive base and the political superstructure can be ascertained to have developed appreciably in the last few centuries before Africa was drawn into contact with Europe.

Within the southernmost section of the continent, the area in which striking achievements were registered by the fifteenth century was that between the rivers Zambezi and Limpopo, covering the territories that were later to be called Mozambique and Rhodesia. Iron-using and state-building peoples were active there from early in the first millennium A.D., and eventually there emerged in the fifteenth century the empire which Europeans called Monomotapa. The term "Zimbabwe" is being used here to designate the Zambesi-Limpopo cultures in the few centuries preceding the European arrival, because it was from the eleventh to the fourteenth century that there flourished the societies, whose most characteristic feature was the building of large stone palaces, known collectively as Zimbabwe.

Much has been written about the buildings which distinguish the Zimbabwe culture. They are a direct response to the environment of granite rocks, being built upon granite hills and of flaked granite. The most famous site of surviving stone ruins is that of Great Zimbabwe, north of the river Sabi. One of the principal structures at Great Zimbabwe was some 300 feet long and 220 feet broad, with the walls being 30 feet high and 20 feet thick. The technique of laying the bricks one on the other without lime to act as a cement was the same style noted in the description of Engaruka in northern Tanzania. It was in fact a peculiar aspect of material culture in Africa, being widely found in Ethiopia and the Sudan. The style of the encircling brick walls at Great Zimbabwe and other sites was also characteristically African in that it was an elaboration of the mud enclosures, or kraals, of many Bantu-speaking people.

One European archaeologist is reported to have said that there was as much labor expended in Zimbabwe as on the pyramids in Egypt. That is surely an overstatement, for the pyramids were raised through an incredible amount of slave labor, which could not possibly have been at the disposal of the rulers in Zimbabwe. However, it is definitely necessary to reflect on the amount of labor which would have been required to construct the buildings within the Zimbabwe region up until the fifteenth century. The workers may well have been from particular ethnic groups who were subjugated by other ethnic groups, but in the process of subjugation they were acquiring the character of a social class whose labor was being exploited. Nor was it sheer manual labor. Skill, creativity, and artistry went into the construction of the walls, especially with regard to the decorations, the inner recesses, and the doors.

When Cecil Rhodes sent in his agents to rob and steal in Zimbabwe, they and other Europeans marveled at the surviving ruins of the Zimbabwe culture, and automatically assumed that it had been built by white people.

Even today there is still a tendency to consider the achievements with a sense of wonder rather than with the calm acceptance that it was a perfectly logical outgrowth of human social development within Africa, as part of the universal process by which man's labor opened up new horizons. The sense of reality can only be restored by making it clear that the architecture rested on a foundation of advanced agriculture and mining, which had come into existence over centuries of evolution.

Zimbabwe was a zone of mixed farming, with cattle being very important, since the area is free from tsetse flies. Irrigation and terracing reached considerable proportions. There was no single dam or aqueduct comparable to those in Asia or ancient Rome, but countless small streams were diverted and made to flow around hills, in a manner that indicated an awareness of the scientific principles governing the motion of water. In effect, the people of Zimbabwe had produced "hydrologists" through their understanding of the material environment. On the mining side, it is equally striking that the African peoples in the zone in question had produced prospectors and "geologists" who had a clear idea of where to look for gold and copper in the subsoil. When the European colonialists arrived in the nineteenth century, they found that virtually all the gold-bearing and copper-bearing strata had been mined previously by Africans—though of course not on the same scale as Europeans were to achieve with drilling equipment. Among the Zimbabwe people, there also arose craftsmen who worked the gold into ornaments with tremendous skill and lightness of touch.

The presence of gold in particular was a stimulus to external trade, and in turn it was external demand which did most to accelerate mining. In the first millennium A.D., there was a gold-using aristocracy at Ingombe Ilede just north of the Zambezi. Presumably, they got their supplies from gold mines farther south. However, gold is required in large quantities only in a society which produces a very large economic surplus and can afford to transform part of that surplus into gold for prestige purposes (as in India) or into coinage and money to promote capitalism (as in Western Europe). The pre-feudal African societies did not have such a surplus, nor the social relations which made it necessary for gold to circulate a great deal *internally*. Hence, it was the presence of Arab traders as far south as Sofala in the Mozambique channel which spurred Zimbabwe to mine more gold for *export* just about the same time in the eleventh century when stone-building was beginning. The implication is that a number of factors coincided: namely, the intensification of class stratification, of state consolidation, of production and building techniques, and of trade.

Several different ethnic groups contributed to Zimbabwe society. The earliest populations of the region were the "Bushmen" and Khoisan type of hunters who today are found only in small numbers in Southern Africa. They were incorporated into the physical stock of newcomers from farther north speaking Bantu languages, and in fact they made their contribution to the Bantu languages of the area. Among the Bantu speakers, there were also several different groups coming into their own at different times. The material evidence which has been revealed by archaeologists shows various pottery styles, contrasting burial positions, and different bone structures among skeletons. Other material artifacts show that over the centuries many societies occupied the region of Zimbabwe. Much of the interpenetration of one group by another was done peacefully, although at the same time, the very existence of the fortified hilltops and stone defenses shows that the largest states were engaged in military struggles for survival and pre-eminence. Furthermore, some ethnic groups must have been permanently relegated to inferior status, so as to provide the labor for agriculture, building, and mining. Other clans specialized in pastoralism, warfare, and the control of religious apparatus such as divination and rainmaking.

It is believed that the inhabitants of Zimbabwe in the eleventh to the fourteenth centuries were Sotho-speaking; but by the time the Portuguese arrived a Shona-speaking dynasty had taken control of most of the region. That was the Rozwi clan, which set up the state of Mutapa, between the Zambezi and the Limpopo. The ruler was known as the Mwene Mutapa, which apparently meant "the great Lord of Mutapa" to his own followers, but was held to mean "the great pillager" by peoples whom he conquered and wielded together into a single empire. The first individual to hold the title Mwene Mutapa ruled from about 1415 to 1450, but the dynasty had already been growing prominent before that date. The capital was at first sited at Great Zimbabwe, and later moved north. What was important was that the Mwene Mutapa appointed governors to rule over various localities outside the capital, in a manner comparable to that of the Western Sudanic empires or the interlacustrine Bachwezi states.

The Rozwi lords of Mutapa did most to encourage production for export trade, notably in gold, ivory, and copper. Arab merchants came to reside in the kingdom and the Zimbabwe region became involved in the network of Indian Ocean commerce, which linked them with India, Indonesia, and China. One of the principal achievements of the Rozwi lords of Mutapa was to organize a single system of production and trade. They exacted tribute from the various communities in their kingdoms, which was both a sign of sovereignty and a form of trade, because the movement of goods was stimulated. There is no doubt that the foreign trade strengthened the

Mutapa state; but above all it strengthened the ruling strata which had a monopoly over that aspect of economic activity. In comparison with other African elites at that time, the Rozwi of Zimbabwe still had a long way to go. They were not in the same category as the Amharic nobility of Ethiopia or the Arab-Berber feudal lords of the Maghreb. They did imbibe a few influences from outside, but they did not travel, as did the rulers of Mali and Songhai, who made the pilgrimage to Mecca. Their dress was still mainly animal skins, and such cloths as they utilized were recent imports from the Arab traders rather than the product of the evolution of their own skills in that field. In that respect, Zimbabwe also trailed behind other early African states such as Oyo in Yorubaland, Benin in the same area, and the fourteenth-century empire of Kongo (which Europeans referred to as the greatest state in West Africa at the time of their arrival).

It has been considered necessary for the purposes of illustration to consider some (though by no means all) of the outstanding areas of development in Africa before the coming of the Europeans. Nor should it be forgotten that there were innumerable village communities emerging to become states that were small in size, but were sometimes sharply stratified internally and displayed an impressive level of material advance. Those described above should be sufficient to establish that Africa in the fifteenth century was not just a jumble of different "tribes." There was a pattern and there was historical movement. Societies such as feudal Ethiopia and Egypt were at the furthest point of the process of evolutionary development. Zimbabwe and the Bachwezi states were also clearly on the ascendant away from communalism, but at a lower level than the feudal states and a few others that were not yet feudal such as those in the Western Sudan.

Conclusion

In introducing the concept of development, attention was drawn to the fact that the slow, imperceptible expansion in social productive capacity ultimately amounted to a qualitative difference, with the arrival at the new stage sometimes being announced by social violence. It can be said that most African societies had not reached a new stage that was markedly different from communalism, and hence the use in this study of the cautious term "transitional." It can also be noted that nowhere had there been any internal social revolutions. The latter have taken place in European and world history only where class consciousness led to the massive intervention of people's wills within the otherwise involuntary socio-economic process. Such observations help to situate African development up to the fifteenth century at a level that was below mature, class-ridden feudalism.

It should also be reiterated that slavery as a mode of production was not present in any African society, although some slaves were to be found where the decomposition of communal equality had gone furthest. This is an outstanding feature illustrating the autonomy of the African path within the broader framework of universal advance. One of the paradoxes in studying this early period of African history is that it cannot be fully comprehended without first deepening our knowledge of the world at large, and yet the true picture of the complexities of the development of man and society can only be drawn after intensive study of the long-neglected African continent. There is no escaping the use of comparisons as an aid to clarity; and indeed the parallels have been narrowly restricted to Europe even though they could also be provided by examples from Asian history. Therein lies the cultural imperialism which makes it easier for the European-educated African to recall names like the (French) Capetians and the (Prussian) Hohenzollerns rather than the Vietnamese dynasties of Id and Tran, for the latter are either unknown to him, or would be considered unimportant if known, or might even be judged too difficult to pronounce!

Several historians of Africa have pointed out that after surveying the developed areas of the continent in the fifteenth century and those within Europe at the same date, the difference between the two was in no way to Africa's discredit. Indeed, the first Europeans to reach West and East Africa by sea were the ones who indicated that in most respects African development was comparable to that which they knew. To take but one example, when the Dutch visited the city of Benin they described it thus:

> The town seems to be very great. When you enter into it, you go into a great broad street, not paved, which seems to be seven or eight times broader than the Warmoes street in Amsterdam. . . .

> The king's palace is a collection of buildings which occupy as much space as the town of Harlem, and which is enclosed with walls. There are numerous apartments for the Prince's ministers and fine galleries, most of which are as big as those on the Exchange at Amsterdam. They are supported by wooden pillars encased with copper, where their victories are depicted, and which are carefully kept very clean.

> The town is composed of thirty main streets, very straight and 120 feet wide, apart from an infinity of small intersecting streets. The houses are close to one another, arranged in good order. These people are in no way inferior to the Dutch as regards cleanliness; they wash and scrub their houses so well that they are polished and shining like a looking-glass.

Yet, it would be self-delusion to imagine that all things were exactly equal in Benin and in Holland. European society was already more aggressive, more expansionist, and more dynamic in producing new forms. The dynamism within Europe was contained within the merchant and manufacturing class. In the galleries of the exchange at Amsterdam sat Dutch burghers—the ancestors of the modern bourgeoisie of industry and finance. This class in fifteenth-century Europe was able to push the feudal landowners forward or aside. They began to discard conservatism and to create the intellectual climate in which change was seen as desirable. A spirit of innovation arose in technology, and transformation of the mode of production was quickened. When Europe and Africa established close relations through trade, there was therefore already a slight edge in Europe's favor—an edge representing the difference between a fledgling capitalist society and one that was still emerging from communalism.

Brief Guide to Reading

Studies on early African history are lacking for many reasons, the most obvious being that African history was for a long time considered by the colonialists as having so little value that it was not worth reconstructing. Another decisive factor is that studies of Africa were mainly carried out by European bourgeois anthropologists, whose philosophical outlook on "primitive societies" caused them to separate African society from its historical context. There was a concentration on micro-units and no reference to overall patterns. The new African scholarship has been under way for too short a time to have provided any significant breakthrough. The few books cited below are part of the new approach.

BASIL DAVIDSON, *Africa in History*. New York: Macmillan, 1969.

HENRI LABOURET, *Africa before the White Man*. New York: Walker and Co., 1962.

MARGARET SHINNIE, *Ancient African Kingdoms*. New York: St. Martin's Press, 1965.

K. M. PANIKKAR, *The Serpent and the Crescent*. New York: Asia Publishing House, 1963.

   The above group of books are assessments by non-Africans from a sympathetic perspective and with sufficient value for them to be respected and widely used inside Africa. K. M. Panikkar is an unusual example of an Asian scholar with a professional interest in the African continent.

J. AJAYI and I. ESPIE (editors), *A Thousand Years of West African History*. New York: Humanities Press, 1969.

B. A. OGOT and J. A. KIERAN (editors), *Zamani, a Survey of East African History*. New York: Humanities Press, 1968.

African historians have begun to provide syntheses of the continent's history by putting together relevant collections—usually on some section of the continent, as in the two examples above. Unfortunately, the quality varies from one selection to another, and African writers have not as yet provided any coherent overview of the regions with which they are supposedly dealing.

G. J. AFOLABI OJO, *Yoruba Culture, a Geographical Analysis.* London: University of London Press, 1967.

B. M. FAGAN, *Southern Africa during the Iron Age.* New York: Praeger, 1965.

What these two dissimilar books have in common is an awareness of the material environment. Afolabi Ojo is a Nigerian geographer and B. M. Fagan is an English archaeologist.

CHAPTER

III

Africa's Contribution to European Capitalist Development—The Pre-Colonial Period

· How Europe Became the Dominant Section of a World-Wide Trade System · Africa's Contribution to the Economy and Beliefs of Early Capitalist Europe

BRITISH TRADE IS A MAGNIFICENT SUPERSTRUCTURE OF AMERICAN COM-
merce and naval power on an African foundation.

—MALACHI POSTLETHWAYT, *The African Trade, the Great Pillar and
Support of the British Plantation Trade in North America, 1745.*

If you were to lose each year more than 200 million livres that you now
get from your colonies: if you had not the exclusive trade with your
colonies to feed your manufactures, to maintain your navy, to keep your
agriculture going, to repay for your imports, to provide for your luxury
needs, to advantageously balance your trade with Europe and Asia, then I
say it clearly, the kingdom would be irretrievably lost.

—BISHOP MAURY (of France): *Argument against France's ending
the slave trade and giving freedom to its slave colonies.* Presented
in the French National Assembly, 1791.

How Europe Became the Dominant Section of a World-Wide Trade System

Because of the superficiality of many of the approaches to "underdevelopment," and because of resulting misconceptions, it is necessary to re-
emphasize that development and underdevelopment are not only comparative terms, but that they also have a dialectical relationship one to the
other: that is to say, the two help produce each other by interaction.
Western Europe and Africa had a relationship which insured the transfer
of wealth from Africa to Europe. The transfer was possible only after
trade became truly international; and that takes one back to the late
fifteenth century when Africa and Europe were drawn into common relations for the first time—along with Asia and the Americas. The developed
and underdeveloped parts of the present capitalist section of the world
have been in continuous contact for four and a half centuries. The contention here is that over that period Africa helped to develop Western
Europe in the same proportion as Western Europe helped to underdevelop
Africa.

The first significant thing about the internationalization of trade in the
fifteenth century was that Europeans took the initiative and went to other
parts of the world. No Chinese boats reached Europe, and if any African
canoes reached the Americas (as is sometimes maintained) they did not
establish two-way links. What was called international trade was nothing

75

but the extension overseas of European interests. The strategy behind international trade and the production that supported it was firmly in European hands, and specifically in the hands of the sea-going nations from the North Sea to the Mediterranean. They owned and directed the great majority of the world's sea-going vessels, and they controlled the financing of the trade between four continents. Africans had little clue as to the tri-continental links between Africa, Europe, and the Americas. Europe had a monopoly of knowledge about the international exchange system seen as a whole, for Western Europe was the only sector capable of viewing the system as a whole.

Europeans used the superiority of their ships and cannon to gain control of all the world's waterways, starting with the western Mediterranean and the Atlantic coast of North Africa. From 1415, when the Portuguese captured Ceuta, near Gibraltar, they maintained the offensive against the Maghreb. Within the next sixty years, they seized ports such as Arzila, El-Ksar-es-Seghir, and Tangier, and fortified them. By the second half of the fifteenth century, the Portuguese controlled the Atlantic coast of Morocco and used its economic and strategic advantages to prepare for further navigations which eventually carried their ships round the Cape of Good Hope in 1495. After reaching the Indian Ocean, the Portuguese sought with some success to replace Arabs as the merchants who tied East Africa to India and the rest of Asia. In the seventeenth and eighteenth centuries, the Portuguese carried most of the East African ivory which was marketed in India; while Indian cloth and beads were sold in East and West Africa by the Portuguese, Dutch, English, and French. The same applied to cowry shells from the East Indies. Therefore, by control of the seas, Europe took the first steps towards transforming the several parts of Africa and Asia into economic satellites.

When the Portuguese and the Spanish were still in command of a major sector of world trade in the first half of the seventeenth century, they engaged in buying cotton cloth in India to exchange for slaves in Africa to mine gold in Central and South America. Part of the gold in the Americas would then be used to purchase spices and silks from the Far East. The concept of metropole and dependency automatically came into existence when parts of Africa were caught up in the web of international commerce. On the one hand, there were the European countries who decided on the role to be played by the African economy; and on the other hand, Africa formed an extension to the European capitalist market. As far as foreign trade was concerned, Africa was dependent on what Europeans were prepared to buy and sell.

Europe exported to Africa goods which were already being produced and used in Europe itself—Dutch linen, Spanish iron, English pewter, Portuguese wines, French brandy, Venetian glass beads, German muskets. Europeans were also able to unload on the African continent goods which had become unsalable in Europe. Thus, items like old sheets, cast-off uniforms, technologically outdated firearms, and lots of odds and ends found guaranteed markets in Africa. Africans slowly became aware of the possibility of demanding and obtaining better imported goods, and pressure was exerted on the captains of European ships; but the overall range of trade goods which left the European ports of Hamburg, Copenhagen, and Liverpool was determined almost exclusively by the pattern of production and consumption within Europe.

From the beginning, Europe assumed the power to make decisions within the international trading system. An excellent illustration of that is the fact that the so-called international law which governed the conduct of nations on the high seas was nothing else but European law. Africans did not participate in its making, and in many instances, African people were simply the victims, for the law recognized them only as transportable merchandise. If the African slave was thrown overboard at sea, the only legal problem that arose was whether or not the slave ship could claim compensation from the insurers! Above all, European decision-making power was exercised in selecting what Africa should export—in accordance with European needs.

The ships of the Portuguese gave the search for gold the highest priority, partly on the basis of well-known information that West African gold reached Europe across the Sahara and partly on the basis of guesswork. The Portuguese were successful in obtaining gold in parts of West Africa and in eastern Central Africa; and it was the Gold Coast which attracted the greatest attention from Europeans in the sixteenth and seventeenth centuries. The number of forts built there was proof to that effect, and the nations involved included the Scandinavians and the Prussians (Germans) apart from other colonial stalwarts like the British, Dutch, and Portuguese.

Europeans were anxious to acquire gold in Africa because there was a pressing need for gold coin within the growing capitalist money economy. Since gold was limited to very small areas of Africa, as far as Europeans were then aware, the principal export was human beings. Only in a very few places at given times was the export of another commodity of equal or greater importance. For instance, in the Senegal there was gum, in Sierra Leone camwood, and in Mozambique ivory. However, even after taking those things into account, one can say that Europe allocated to Africa the role of supplier of human captives to be used as slaves in various parts of the world.

When Europeans reached the Americas, they recognized its enormous potential in gold and silver and tropical produce. But that potential could not be made a reality without adequate labor supplies. The indigenous Indian population could not withstand new European diseases such as smallpox, nor could they bear the organized toil of slave plantations and slave mines, having barely emerged from the hunting stage. That is why in islands like Cuba and Hispaniola, the local Indian population was virtually wiped out by the white invaders. At the same time, Europe itself had a very small population and could not afford to release the labor required to tap the wealth of the Americas. Therefore, they turned to the nearest continent, Africa, which incidentally had a population accustomed to settled agriculture and disciplined labor in many spheres. Those were the objective conditions lying behind the start of the European slave trade, and those are the reasons why the capitalist class in Europe used their control of international trade to insure that Africa specialized in exporting captives.

Obviously, if Europe could tell Africans what to export, that was an expression of European power. However, it would be a mistake to believe that it was an overwhelming military power. Europeans found it impossible to conquer Africans during the early centuries of trade, except in isolated spots on the coast. European power resided in their system of production which was at a somewhat higher level than Africa's at that time. European society was leaving feudalism and was moving towards capitalism; African society was then entering a phase comparable to feudalism.

The fact that Europe was the first part of the world to move from feudalism towards capitalism gave Europeans a headstart over humanity elsewhere in the scientific understanding of the universe, the making of tools, and the efficient organization of labor. *European technical superiority did not apply to all aspects of production, but the advantage which they possessed in a few key areas proved decisive.* For example, African canoes on the river Nile and the Senegal coast were of a high standard, but the relevant sphere of operations was the ocean, where European ships could take command. West Africans had developed metal casting to a fine artistic perfection in many parts of Nigeria, but when it came to the meeting with Europe, beautiful bronzes were far less relevant than the crudest cannon. African wooden utensils were sometimes works of great beauty, but Europe produced pots and pans that had many practical advantages. Literacy, organizational experience, and the capacity to produce on an ever expanding scale also counted in the European favor.

European manufactures in the early years of trade with Africa were often of poor quality, but they were of new varieties and were found attractive. Estaban Montejo, an African who ran away from a Cuban slave plantation in the nineteenth century, recalled that his people were enticed into slavery by the color red. He said:

> It was the scarlet which did for the Africans; both the kings and the rest surrendered without a struggle. When the kings saw that the whites were taking out these scarlet handkerchiefs as if they were waving, they told the blacks, "Go on then, go and get a scarlet handkerchief" and the blacks were so excited by the scarlet they ran down to the ships like sheep and there they were captured.

That version by one of the victims of slavery is very poetic. What it means is that some African rulers found European goods sufficiently desirable to hand over captives which they had taken in warfare. Soon, war began to be fought between one community and another for the sole purpose of getting prisoners for sale to Europeans, and even inside a given community a ruler might be tempted to exploit his own subjects and capture them for sale. A chain reaction was started by European demand for slaves (and only slaves) and by their offer of consumer goods—this process being connected with divisions within African society.

It is often said for the colonial period that vertical political divisions in Africa made conquest easy. This is even truer of the way that Africa succumbed to the slave trade. National unification was a product of mature feudalism and of capitalism. Inside Europe, there were far fewer political divisions than in Africa where communalism meant political fragmentation with the family as the nucleus, and there were only a few states that had real territorial solidity. Furthermore, when one European nation challenged another to obtain captives from an African ruler, Europe benefited from whichever of the two nations won the conflict. Any European trader could arrive on the coast of West Africa and exploit the political differences which he found there. For example, in the small territory that the Portuguese later claimed as Guinea-Bissau, there were more than a dozen ethnic groups. It was so easy to set one off against another that Europeans called it a "slave trader's paradise."

Although class divisions were not pronounced in African society, they too contributed to the ease with which Europe imposed itself commercially on large parts of the African continent. The rulers had a certain status and authority, and when bamboozled by European goods they began to use that position to raid outside their societies as well as to exploit internally by victimizing some of their own subjects. In the simplest of societies where there were no kings, it proved impossible for Europeans to strike up the alliance which was necessary to carry on a trade in captives on the coast. In those societies with ruling groups, the association with

Europeans was easily established; and afterwards Europe hardened the existing internal class divisions and created new ones.

In effect, particular aspects of African society became weaknesses when Europeans arrived as representatives of a different phase of development. And yet the subjugation of the African economy through slave trade was a slow process at the outset, and in some instances African opposition or disinterest had to be overcome. In the Congo, the slave trade did not get under way without grave doubts and opposition from the king of the state of Kongo at the beginning of the sixteenth century. He asked for masons, priests, clerks, physicians; but instead he was overwhelmed by slave ships sent from Portugal, and a vicious trade was opened up by playing off one part of the Kongo kingdom against another. The king of the Kongo had conceived of possibilities of mutually beneficial interchange between his people and the European state, but the latter forced him to specialize in the export of human cargo. It is also interesting to note that while the *Oba* (king) of Benin was willing to sell a few female captives, it took a great deal of persuasion and pressure from Europeans to get him to sell male African prisoners of war, who would otherwise have been brought into the ranks of Benin society.

Once trade in slaves had been started in any given part of Africa, it soon became clear that it was beyond the capacity of any single African state to change the situation. In Angola, the Portuguese employed an unusual number of their own troops and tried to seize political power from Africans. The Angolan state of Matamba on the river Kwango was founded around 1630 as a direct reaction against the Portuguese. With Queen Nzinga at its head, Matamba tried to coordinate resistance against the Portuguese in Angola. However, Portugal gained the upper hand in 1648, and this left Matamba isolated. Matamba could not forever stand aside. So long as it opposed trade with the Portuguese, it was an object of hostility from neighboring African states which had compromised with Europeans and slave trading. So in 1656, Queen Nzinga resumed business with the Portuguese—a major concession to the decision-making role of Europeans within the Angolan economy.

Another example of African resistance during the course of the slave trade comes from the Baga people in what is now the Republic of Guinea. The Baga lived in small states, and in about 1720 one of their leaders (Tomba by name) aimed at securing an alliance to stop the slave traffic. He was defeated by local European resident-traders, mulattos, and other slave trading Africans. It is not difficult to understand why Europeans should have taken immediate steps to see that Tomba and his Baga followers did not opt out of the role allocated to them by Europe. A parallel which presents itself is the manner in which Europeans got together to wage the "Opium War" against China in the nineteenth century to insure that Western capitalists would make profit while the Chinese were turned into dope addicts.

Of course, it is only as a last resort that the capitalist metropoles need to use armed force to insure the pursuit of favorable policies in the dependent areas. Normally, economic weapons are sufficient. In the 1720s, Dahomey opposed European slave traders, and was deprived of European imports—some of which had become necessary by that time. Agaja Trudo, Dahomey's greatest king, appreciated that European demand for slaves and the pursuit of slaving in and around Dahomey was in conflict with Dahomey's development. Between 1724 and 1726, he looted and burned European forts and slave camps; and he reduced the trade from the "Slave Coast" to a mere trickle, by blocking the paths leading to sources of supply in the interior. European slave dealers were very bitter, and they tried to sponsor some African collaborators against Agaja Trudo. They failed to unseat him or to crush the Dahomean state, but in turn Agaja failed to persuade them to develop new lines of economic activity, such as local plantation agriculture; and, being anxious to acquire firearms and cowries through the Europeans, he had to agree to the resumption of slave trading in 1730.

After 1730, Dahomean slaving was placed under royal control and was much more restricted than previously. Yet, the failure of this determined effort demonstrated that a single African state at that time could not emancipate itself from European control. The small size of African states and the numerous political divisions made it so much easier for Europe to make the decisions as to Africa's role in world production and trade.

Many guilty consciences have been created by the slave trade. Europeans know that they carried on the slave trade, and Africans are aware that the trade would have been impossible if certain Africans did not cooperate with the slave ships. To ease their guilty consciences, Europeans try to throw the major responsibility for the slave trade on to the Africans. One European author of a book on the slave trade (appropriately entitled *Sins of Our Fathers*) explained how many other white people urged him to state that the trade was the responsibility of African chiefs, and that Europeans merely turned up to buy the captives—as though without European demand there would have been captives sitting on the beach by the millions! Issues such as those are not the principal concern of this study, but they can be correctly approached only after understanding

that Europe became the center of a world-wide system and that it was
European capitalism which set slavery and the Atlantic slave trade in
motion.

The trade in human beings from Africa was a response to *externa*
factors. At first, the labor was needed in Portugal, Spain, and in Atlantic
islands such as São Tomé, Cape Verde, and the Canaries; then came the
period when the Greater Antilles and the Spanish-American mainland
needed replacements for the Indians who were victims of genocide; and
then the demands of Caribbean and mainland plantation societies had to
be met. The records show direct connections between levels of exports
from Africa and European demand for slave labor in some part of the
American plantation economy. When the Dutch took Pernambuco in
Brazil in 1634, the director of the Dutch West Indian Company immediately informed their agents on the Gold Coast that they were to
take the necessary steps to pursue the trade in slaves on the adjacent coast
east of the Volta—thus creating for that area the infamous name of the
"Slave Coast." When the British West Indian islands took to growing
sugar cane, Gambia was one of the first places to respond. Examples
of this kind of external control can be cited right up to the end of the
trade, and this embraces Eastern Africa also, since European markets in
the Indian Ocean islands became important in the eighteenth and nineteenth centuries, and since demand in places like Brazil caused Mozambicans to be shipped around the Cape of Good Hope.

Africa's Contribution to the Economy and Beliefs of Early Capitalist Europe

The kinds of benefits which Europe derived from its control of world
commerce are fairly well known, although it is curious that the recognition of Africa's major contribution to European development is usually
made in works devoted specifically to that subject; while European
scholars of Europe often treat the European economy as if it were entirely independent. European economists of the nineteenth century certainly
had no illusions about the interconnections between their national economies and the world at large. J. S. Mill, as spokesman for British capitalism, said that as far as England was concerned, "the trade of the West
Indies is hardly to be considered as external trade, but more resembles the
traffic between town and country." By the phrase "trade of the West Indies"
Mill meant the commerce between Africa, England, and the West Indies,
because without African labor the West Indies were valueless. Karl Marx
also commented on the way that European capitalists tied Africa, the

West Indies, and Latin America into the capitalist system; and (being the most bitter critic of capitalism) Marx went on to point out that what was good for Europeans was obtained at the expense of untold suffering by Africans and American Indians. Marx noted that "the discovery of gold and silver in America, the extirpation, enslavement and entombment in mines of the aboriginal population, the turning of Africa into a commercial warren for the hunting of black skins signalized the rosy dawn of the era of capitalist production."

Some attempts have been made to quantify the actual monetary profits made by Europeans from engaging in the slave trade. The actual dimensions are not easy to fix, but the profits were fabulous. John Hawkins made three trips to West Africa in the 1560s, and stole Africans whom he sold to the Spanish in America. On returning to England after the first trip, his profit was so handsome that Queen Elizabeth I became interested in directly participating in his next venture; and she provided for that purpose a ship named the *Jesus*. Hawkins left with the *Jesus* to steal some more Africans, and he returned to England with such dividends that Queen Elizabeth made him a knight. Hawkins chose as his coat of arms the representation of an African in chains.

Of course, there were inevitably voyages that failed, slave ships that were lost at sea. Sometimes trade in Africa did well, while at other times it was the profit in the Americas that was really substantial. When all the ups and downs are ironed out, the level of profit had to be enough to justify continued participation in that particular form of trade for centuries. A few bourgeois scholars have tried to suggest that the trade in slaves did not have worthwhile monetary returns. They would have us believe that the same entrepreneurs whom they praise in other contexts as the heroes of capitalist development were so dumb with regard to slavery and slave trade that for centuries they absorbed themselves in a non-profit venture! This kind of argument is worth noting more as an example of the distortions of which white bourgeois scholarship is capable than as something requiring serious consideration. Besides, quite apart from capital accumulation, Europe's trade with Africa gave numerous stimuli to Europe's growth.

Central and South American gold and silver—mined by Africans— played a crucial role in meeting the need for coin in the expanding capitalist money economy of Western Europe, while African gold helped the Portuguese to finance further navigations around the Cape of Good Hope and into Asia from the fifteenth century on. African gold was also the main source for the mintage of Dutch gold coin in the seventeenth century, helping Amsterdam to become the financial capital of Europe in that period; and further it was no coincidence that when the English struck a new gold coin in 1663, they called it the "guinea." The Encyclopaedia Britannica explains that the guinea was "a gold coin at one time current in the United Kingdom. It was first coined in 1663, in the reign of Charles II, from gold imported from the Guinea Coast of West Africa by a company of merchants trading under charter from the British crown—hence the name."

Throughout the seventeenth and eighteenth centuries, and for most of the nineteenth century, the exploitation of Africa and African labor continued to be a source for the accumulation of capital to be reinvested in Western Europe. The African contribution to European capitalist growth extended over such vital sectors as shipping, insurance, the formation of companies, capitalist agriculture, technology, and the manufacture of machinery. The effects were so wide-ranging that many are seldom brought to the notice of the reading public. For instance, the French Saint-Malo fishing industry was revived by the opening up of markets in the French slave plantations; while the Portuguese in Europe depended heavily on dyes like indigo, camwood, Brazil wood, and cochineal brought from Africa and the Americas. Gum from Africa also played a part in the textile industry, which is acknowledged as having been one of the most powerful engines of growth within the European economy. Then there was the export of ivory from Africa, enriching many merchants in London's Mincing Lane, and providing the raw material for industries in England, France, Germany, Switzerland, and North America—producing items ranging from knife handles to piano keys.

Africa's being drawn into the orbit of Western Europe speeded up the latter's technological development. For example, the evolution of European shipbuilding from the sixteenth century to the nineteenth century was a logical consequence of their monopoly of sea commerce in that period. During that time, the North Africans were bottled up in the Mediterranean, and although it was from them that Europeans initially borrowed a great deal of nautical instrumentation, the North Africans made no further worthwhile advances. Where the original European advantage was not sufficient to assure supremacy, they deliberately undermined other people's efforts. The Indian navy, for instance, suffered from the rigid enforcement of the English Navigation Laws. Yet, the expenses involved in building new and better European ships were met from the profits of overseas trade with India and Africa. The Dutch were pioneers in improving upon the caravels which took the Spanish and Portuguese out across the Atlantic, and the successive Dutch trading companies operating in Asia, Africa, and America were the ones responsible for experimentation. By the eighteenth century, the British were using Dutch know-how as a basis for surpassing the Dutch themselves, and the Atlantic was their laboratory. It used to be said that the slave trade was a training ground for British seamen. It is probably more significant to note that the Atlantic trade was the stimulator of consistent advances in naval technology.

The most spectacular feature in Europe which was connected with African trade was the rise of seaport towns—notably, Bristol, Liverpool, Nantes, Bordeaux, and Seville. Directly or indirectly connected to those ports, there often emerged the manufacturing centers which gave rise to the Industrial Revolution. In England, it was the county of Lancashire which was the first center of the Industrial Revolution, and the economic advance in Lancashire depended first of all on the growth of the port of Liverpool through slave trading.

The connections between slavery and capitalism in the growth of England is adequately documented by Eric Williams in his well-known book *Capitalism and Slavery*. Williams gives a clear picture of the numerous benefits which England derived from trading and exploiting slaves, and he identified by name several of the personalities and capitalist firms who were the beneficiaries. Outstanding examples are provided in the persons of David and Alexander Barclay, who were engaging in slave trade in 1756 and who later used the loot to set up Barclays Bank. There was a similar progression in the case of Lloyds—from being a small London coffee house to being one of the world's largest banking and insurance houses, after dipping into profits from slave trade and slavery. Then there was James Watt, expressing eternal gratitude to the West Indian slave owners who directly financed his famous steam engine, and took it from the drawing board to the factory.

A similar picture would emerge from any detailed study of French capitalism and slavery, given the fact that during the eighteenth century the West Indies accounted for 20 per cent of France's external trade— much more than the whole of Africa in the present century. Of course, benefits were not always directly proportionate to the amount of involvement of a given European state in the Atlantic trade. The enormous profits of Portuguese overseas enterprise passed rapidly out of the Portuguese economy into the hands of the more developed Western European capitalist nations who supplied Portugal with capital, ships, and trade goods. Germany was included in this category, along with England, Holland, and France.

Commerce deriving from Africa helped a great deal to strengthen transnational links within the Western European economy, bearing in mind that American produce was the consequence of African labor. Brazilian dyewoods, for example, were re-exported from Portugal into the Mediterranean, the North Sea, and the Baltic, and passed into the continental cloth industry of the seventeenth century. Sugar from the Caribbean was re-exported from England and France to other parts of Europe to such an extent that Hamburg in Germany was the biggest sugar-refining center in Europe in the first half of the eighteenth century. Germany supplied manufactures to Scandinavia, Holland, England, France, and Portugal for resale in Africa. England, France, and Holland found it necessary to exchange various classes of goods the better to deal with Africans for gold, slaves, and ivory. The financiers and merchants of Genoa were the powers behind the markets of Lisbon and Seville; while Dutch bankers played a similar role with respect to Scandinavia and England.

Western Europe was that part of Europe in which by the fifteenth century the trend was most visible that feudalism was giving way to capitalism. (In Eastern Europe, feudalism was still strong in the nineteenth century.) The peasants were being driven off the land in England, and agriculture was becoming technologically more advanced—producing food and fibers to support a larger population and to provide a more effective basis for the woolen and linen industries in particular. The technological base of industry, as well as its social and economic organization, was being transformed. African trade speeded up several aspects, including the integration of Western Europe, as noted above. That is why the African connection contributed not merely to economic growth (which relates to quantitative dimensions) but also to real development in the sense of increased capacity for further growth and independence.

In speaking of the European slave trade, mention must be made of the U.S.A., not only because its dominant population was European but also because Europe transferred its capitalist institutions more completely to North America than to any other part of the globe, and established a powerful form of capitalism—after eliminating the indigenous inhabitants and exploiting the labor of millions of Africans. Like other parts of the New World, the American colonies of the British crown were used as means of accumulating primary capital for re-export to Europe. But the Northern colonies also had direct access to benefits from slavery in the American South and in the British and French West Indies. As in Europe, the profits made from slavery and slave trade went firstly to commercial ports and industrial areas, which meant mainly the northeastern seaboard district known as New England and the state of New York. The Pan-Africanist, W. E. B. Du Bois, in a study of the American slave trade, quoted a report of 1862 as follows:

The number of persons engaged in the slave trade and the amount of capital embarked in it exceed our powers of calculation. The city of New York has been until of late (1862) the principal port of the world for this infamous commerce; although the cities of Portland and Boston are only second to her in that distribution.

American economic development up to mid-nineteenth century rested squarely on foreign commerce, of which slavery was a pivot. In the 1830s, slave-grown cotton accounted for about half the value of all exports from the United States of America. Furthermore, in the case of the American colonies of the eighteenth century, it can again be observed that Africa contributed in a variety of ways—one thing leading to another. For instance, in New England, trade with Africa, Europe, and the West Indies in slaves and slave-grown products supplied cargo for their merchant marine, stimulated the growth of their shipbuilding industry, built up their towns and their cities, and enabled them to utilize their forests, fisheries, and soil more effectively. Finally, it was the carrying trade between the West Indian slave colonies and Europe which lay behind the emancipation of the American colonies from British rule, and it was no accident that the struggle for American independence started in the leading New England town of Boston. In the nineteenth century, the connection with Africa continued to play an indirect role in American political growth. In the first place, profits from the slave activities went into the coffers of political parties, and even more important the African stimulation and black labor played a vital role in extending European control over the present territory of the United States—notably in the South, but including also the "Wild West," where black cowboys were active.

Slavery is useful for early accumulation of capital, but it is too rigid for industrial development. Slaves had to be given crude non-breakable tools which held back the capitalist development of agriculture and industry. That explains the fact that the northern portions of the U.S.A. gained far more industrial benefits from slavery than the South, which actually had slave institutions on its soil; and ultimately the stage was reached during the American Civil War when the Northern capitalists fought to end slavery within the boundaries of the U.S.A. so that the country as a whole could advance to a higher level of capitalism.

In effect, one can say that within the U.S.A. the slave relations in the South had by the second half of the nineteenth century come into conflict with the further expansion of the productive base inside the U.S.A. as a whole, and a violent clash ensued before the capitalist relations of legally free labor became generalized. Europe maintained slavery in places that were physically remote from European society; and therefore inside Europe itself, capitalist relations were elaborated without being adversely affected by slavery in the Americas. However, even in Europe there came a moment when the leading capitalist states found that the trade in slaves and the use of slave labor in the Americas was no longer in the interest of their further development. Britain made this decision early in the nineteenth century, to be followed later by France.

Since capitalism, like any other mode of production, is a total system which involves an ideological aspect, it is also necessary to focus on the effects of the ties with Africa on the development of ideas within the superstructure of European capitalist society. In that sphere, the most striking feature is undoubtedly the rise of racism as a widespread and deeply rooted element in European thought. The role of slavery in promoting racist prejudice and ideology has been carefully studied in certain situations, especially in the U.S.A. The simple fact is that no people can enslave another for centuries without coming out with a notion of superiority, and when the color and other physical traits of those peoples were quite different it was inevitable that the prejudice should take a racist form. Within Africa itself, the same can be said for the situation in the Cape Province of South Africa where white men have been establishing military and social superiority over non-whites since 1650.

It would be much too sweeping a statement to say that all racial and color prejudice in Europe derived from the enslavement of Africans and the exploitation of non-white peoples in the early centuries of international trade. There was also anti-Semitism at an even earlier date inside Europe and there is always an element of suspicion and incomprehension when peoples of different cultures come together. However, it can be affirmed without reservations that the white racism which came to pervade the world was an integral part of the capitalist mode of production. Nor was it merely a question of how the individual white person treated a black person. The racism of Europe was a set of generalizations and assumptions, which had no scientific basis, but were rationalized in every sphere from theology to biology.

Occasionally, it is mistakenly held that Europeans enslaved Africans for racist reasons. European planters and miners enslaved Africans for *economic* reasons, so that their labor power could be exploited. Indeed, it would have been impossible to open up the New World and to use it as a constant generator of wealth, had it not been for African labor. There were no other alternatives: the American (Indian) population was virtually wiped out and Europe's population was too small for settlement overseas at that time. Then, having become utterly dependent on African labor, Europeans at home and abroad found it necessary to rationalize that exploitation in racist terms as well. Oppression follows logically from exploitation, so as to guarantee the latter. Oppression of African people on purely racial grounds accompanied, strengthened, and became indistinguishable from oppression for economic reasons.

C. L. R. James, noted Pan-Africanist *and* Marxist, once remarked that:

> The race question is subsidiary to the class question in politics, and to think of imperialism in terms of race is disastrous. But to neglect the racial factor as merely incidental is an error only less grave than to make it fundamental.

It can further be argued that by the nineteenth century white racism had become so institutionalized in the capitalist world (and notably in the U.S.A.) that it sometimes ranked above the maximization of profit as a motive for oppressing black people.

In the short run, European racism seemed to have done Europeans no harm, and they used those erroneous ideas to justify their further domination of non-European peoples in the colonial epoch. But the international proliferation of bigoted and unscientific racist ideas was bound to have its negative consequences in the long run. When Europeans put millions of their brothers (Jews) into ovens under the Nazis, the chickens were coming home to roost. Such behavior inside of "democratic" Europe was not as strange as it is sometimes made out to be. There was always a contradiction between the elaboration of democratic ideas inside Europe and the elaboration of authoritarian and thuggish practices by Europeans with respect to Africans. When the French Revolution was made in the name of "Liberty, Equality, Fraternity," it did not extend to black Africans who were enslaved by France in the West Indies and the Indian Ocean. Indeed, France fought against the efforts of those people to emancipate themselves, and the leaders of their bourgeois revolution said plainly that they did not make it on behalf of black humanity.

It is not even true to say that capitalism developed democracy at home in Europe and not abroad. At home, it was responsible for a talk or certain rhetoric of freedom, but it was never extended from the bourgeoisie to the oppressed workers; and the treatment of Africans must surely have made such hypocrisy a habit of European life, especially within the ruling class. How else can one explain the fact that the Christian church participated fully in the maintenance of slavery and still talked about saving souls! The hypocrisy reached its highest levels inside the U.S.A. The first martyr in the American national war of liberation against the British colonialists in the eighteenth century was an African descendant, Crispus Attucks; and both slave and free Africans played a key role in Washington's armies. And yet, the American Constitution sanctioned the continued enslavement of Africans. In recent times, it has become an object of concern to some liberals that the U.S.A. is capable of war crimes of the order of My Lai in Vietnam. But the fact of the matter is that the My Lais began with the enslavement of Africans and American Indians. Racism, violence, and brutality were the concomitants of the capitalist system when it extended itself abroad in the early centuries of international trade.

Brief Guide to Reading

The subject of Africa's contribution to European development reveals several of the factors which limit a writer's representation of reality. Language and nationality, for instance, are effective barriers to communication. Works in English seldom take account of the effect brought about in France, Holland, or Portugal by participation in slaving and other forms of commerce which exploited Africa in the pre-colonial period. The ideological gulf is responsible for the fact that most bourgeois scholars write about phenomena such as the Industrial Revolution in England without once mentioning the European slave trade as a factor in primary accumulation of capital. Marx himself had laid great emphasis on sources of overseas capital accumulation. But even Marxists (as prominent as Maurice Dobb and E. J. Hobsbawm) for many years concentrated on examining the evolution of capitalism out of feudalism inside Europe, with only marginal reference to the massive exploitation of Africans, Asians, and American Indians.

ERIC WILLIAMS, *Capitalism and Slavery*. Chapel Hill: University of North Carolina Press, 1944.
OLIVER COX, *Capitalism as a System*. New York: Monthly Review Press, 1964.
    Cox, an African American, makes the basic point that capitalism has from very early times been an international system. Eric Williams, a West Indian, is very precise and very detailed in illustrating the connection between British capitalism and the enslavement of Africans.

W. E. B. DU BOIS, *The Suppression of the Atlantic Slave-Trade to the United States of America—1638–1870*. New York: Social Science Press, 1954.
RICHARD PARES, *Yankees and Creoles: the Trade between North America and the West Indies before the American Revolution*. London: Longmans Green, 1956.
    Both of these provide data on the contribution of African labor to the development of capitalism in the U.S.A. in the epoch of slavery.

LEO HUBERMAN, *Man's Worldly Goods: The Story of the Wealth of Nations*. New York and London: Harper Bros., 1936.

F. CLAIREMONTE, *Economic Liberalism and Underdevelopment.*
Huberman's book is an excellent overall treatment of the development of capitalism out of feudalism in Europe. It includes a section in which the role of slavery is highlighted. Clairemonte's study accords recognition to the role played by the subcontinent of India in building Europe.

PHILIP D. CURTIN, *The Image of Africa.* Madison: University of Wisconsin Press, 1964.
WINTHROP JORDAN, *White Over Black: American Attitudes towards the Negro.* Chapel Hill: Published for the Institute of Early American History and Culture at Williamsburg, 1968.
These two texts are relevant to the question of the rise of white racism, although neither of the two makes sufficiently explicit the connection between racism and capitalism.

CHAPTER
IV

Europe and the Roots of African Underdevelopment—To 1885

· The European Slave Trade as a Basic Factor in African Underdevelopment · Technical Stagnation and Distortion of the African Economy in the Pre-Colonial Epoch · Continuing Politico-Military Developments in Africa—1500 to 1885 · The Coming of Imperialism and Colonialism

THE RELATION BETWEEN THE DEGREE OF DESTITUTION OF PEOPLES OF
Africa and the length and nature of the exploitation they had to endure
is evident. Africa remains marked by the crimes of the slave-traders: up
to now, her potentialities are restricted by under-population.

—AHMED SEKOU TOURE,
Republic of Guinea, 1962

The European Slave Trade as a Basic Factor in African Underdevelopment

To discuss trade between Africans and Europeans in the four centuries before colonial rule is virtually to discuss slave trade. Strictly speaking, the
African only became a slave when he reached a society where he worked
as a slave. Before that, he was first a free man and then a captive. Nevertheless, it is acceptable to speak of the trade in slaves when referring to the
shipment of captives from Africa to various other parts of the world where
they were to live and work as the property of Europeans. The title of this
section is deliberately chosen to call attention to the fact that the shipments
were all by Europeans to markets controlled by Europeans, and this was
in the interest of European capitalism and nothing else. In East Africa and
the Sudan, many Africans were taken by Arabs and were sold to Arab
buyers. This is known (in European books) as the "Arab Slave Trade."
Therefore, let it be clear that when Europeans shipped Africans to European buyers it was the "European Slave Trade" from Africa.

Undoubtedly, with few exceptions such as Hawkins, European buyers
purchased African captives on the coasts of Africa and the transaction between themselves and Africans was a form of trade. It is also true that very
often a captive was sold and resold as he made his way from the interior
to the port of embarkation—and that too was a form of trade. However,
on the whole, the process by which captives were obtained on African soil
was not trade at all. It was through warfare, trickery, banditry, and kidnaping. When one tries to measure the effect of European slave trading
on the African continent, it is essential to realize that one is measuring the
effect of social violence rather than trade in any normal sense of the word.

Many things remain uncertain about the slave trade and its consequences
for Africa, but the general picture of destructiveness is clear, and that
destructiveness can be shown to be the logical consequence of the manner

95

of recruitment of captives in Africa. One of the uncertainties concerns the basic question of how many Africans were imported. This has long been an object of speculation, with estimates ranging from a few millions to over one hundred million. A recent study has suggested a figure of about ten million Africans landed alive in the Americas, the Atlantic islands, and Europe. Because it is a low figure, it is already being used by European scholars who are apologists for the capitalist system and its long record of brutality in Europe and abroad. In order to whitewash the European slave trade, they find it convenient to start by minimizing the numbers concerned. The truth is that any figure of Africans imported into the Americas which is narrowly based on the surviving records is bound to be low, because there were so many people at the time who had a vested interest in smuggling slaves (and withholding data). Nevertheless, if the low figure of ten million was accepted as a basis for evaluating the impact of slaving on Africa as a whole, the conclusions that could legitimately be drawn would confound those who attempt to make light of the experience of the rape of Africans from 1445 to 1870.

On any basic figure of Africans landed alive in the Americas, one would have to make several extensions—starting with a calculation to cover mortality in transshipment. The Atlantic crossing, or "Middle Passage," as it was called by European slavers, was notorious for the number of deaths incurred, averaging in the vicinity of 15 to 20 per cent. There were also numerous deaths in Africa between time of capture and time of embarkation, especially in cases where captives had to travel hundreds of miles to the coast. Most important of all (given that warfare was the principal means of obtaining captives) it is necessary to make some estimate as to the number of people killed and injured so as to extract the millions who were taken alive and sound. The resultant figure would be many times the millions landed alive outside of Africa, and it is that figure which represents the number of Africans directly removed from the population and labor force of Africa because of the establishment of slave production by Europeans.

The massive loss to the African labor force was made more critical because it was composed of able-bodied young men and young women. Slave buyers preferred their victims between the ages of fifteen and thirty-five, and preferably in the early twenties; the sex ratio being about two men to one woman. Europeans often accepted younger African children, but rarely any older person. They shipped the most healthy wherever possible, taking the trouble to get those who had already survived an attack of smallpox, and who were therefore immune from further attacks of that disease, which was then one of the world's great killer diseases.

Absence of data about the size of Africa's population in the fifteenth century makes it difficult to carry out any scientific assessment of the results of the population outflow. But, nothing suggests that there was any increase in the continent's population over the centuries of slaving, although that was the trend in other parts of the world. Obviously, fewer babies were born than would otherwise have been the case if millions of child-bearing ages were not eliminated. Besides, it is essential to recognize that the slave trade across the Atlantic Ocean was not the only connection which Europeans had with slaving in Africa. The slave trade on the Indian Ocean has been called the "East African Slave Trade" and the "Arab Slave Trade" for so long that it hides the extent to which it was also a European slave trade. When the slave trade from East Africa was at its height in the eighteenth century and in the early nineteenth century, the destination of most captives was the European-owned plantation economies of Mauritius, Réunion, and Seychelles—as well as the Americas, via the Cape of Good Hope. Besides, Africans laboring as slaves in certain Arab countries in the eighteenth and nineteenth centuries were all ultimately serving the European capitalist system which set up a demand for slave-grown products, such as the cloves grown in Zanzibar under the supervision of Arab masters.

No one has been able to come up with a figure representing total losses to the African population sustained through the extraction of slave labor from all areas to all destinations over the many centuries that slave trade existed. However, on every other continent from the fifteenth century onwards, the population showed constant and sometimes spectacular natural increase; while it is striking that the same did not apply to Africa. One European scholar gave the following estimates of world population (in millions) according to continents:

	1650	1750	1850	1900
Africa	100	100	100	120
Europe	103	144	274	423
Asia	257	437	656	857

None of the above figures is really precise, but they do indicate a consensus among researchers on population that the huge African continent has an abnormal record of stagnation in this respect, and there is no causative factor other than the trade in slaves to which attention can be drawn.

An emphasis on population loss as such is highly relevant to the question of socio-economic development. Population growth played a major role in European development in providing labor, markets, and the pressures which led to further advance. Japanese population growth had similar positive effects; and in other parts of Asia which remained pre-capitalist, the size of the population led to a much more intensive exploitation of the land than has ever been the case in what is still a sparsely peopled African continent.

So long as the population density was low, then human beings viewed as units of labor were far more important than other factors of production such as land. From one end of the continent to the other, it is easy to find examples showing that African people were conscious that population was in their circumstances the most important factor of production. Among the Bemba, for instance, numbers of subjects were held to be more important than land. Among the Shambala of Tanzania, the same feeling was expressed in the saying "A king is people." Among the Balanta of Guinea-Bissau, the family's strength is represented by the number of hands there are to cultivate the land. Certainly, many African rulers acquiesced in the European slave trade for what they considered to be reasons of self-interest, but on no scale of rationality could the outflow of population be measured as being anything but disastrous for African societies.

African economic activity was affected both directly and indirectly by population loss. For instance, when the inhabitants of a given area were reduced below a certain number in an environment where the tsetse fly was present, the remaining few had to abandon the area. In effect, enslavement was causing these people to lose their battle to tame and harness nature—a battle which is at the basis of development. Violence almost meant insecurity. The opportunity presented by European slave dealers became the major (though not the only) stimulus for a great deal of social violence between different African communities and within any given community. It took the form more of raiding and kidnaping than of regular warfare, and that fact increased the element of fear and uncertainty.

Both openly and by implication, all the European powers in the nineteenth century indicated their awareness of the fact that the activities connected with producing captives were inconsistent with other economic pursuits. That was the time when Britain in particular wanted Africans to collect palm produce and rubber and to grow agricultural crops for export in place of slaves; and it was clear that slave raiding was violently conflicting with that objective in Western, Eastern, and Central Africa. Long before that date, Europeans accepted that fact when their self-interest was involved. For example, in the seventeenth century, the Portuguese and Dutch actually discouraged slave trade on the Gold Coast, for they recognized that it would be incompatible with gold trade. However, by the end of that century, gold had been discovered in Brazil, and the importance of gold supplies from Africa was lessened. Within the total Atlantic pattern, African slaves became more important than gold, and Brazilian gold was offered for African captives at Whydah (Dahomey) and Accra. At that point, slaving began undermining the Gold Coast economy and destroying the gold trade. Slave raiding and kidnaping made it unsafe to mine and to travel with gold; and raiding for captives proved more profitable than gold mining. One European on the scene noted that "as one fortunate marauding makes a native rich in a day, they therefore exert themselves rather in war, robbery and plunder than in their old business of digging and collecting gold."

The above changeover from gold mining to slave raiding took place within a period of a few years between 1700 and 1710, when the Gold Coast came to supply about five thousand to six thousand captives per year. By the end of the eighteenth century, a much smaller number of captives were exported from the Gold Coast, but the damage had already been done. It is worth noting that Europeans sought out different parts of West and Central Africa at different times to play the role of major suppliers of slaves to the Americas. This meant that virtually every section of the long western coastline between the Senegal and Cunene rivers had at least a few years' experience of intensive trade in slaves—with all its consequences. Besides, in the history of eastern Nigeria, the Congo, northern Angola, and Dahomey, there were periods extending over decades when exports remained at an average of many thousands per year. Most of those areas were also relatively highly developed within the African context. They were leading forces inside Africa, whose energies would otherwise have gone towards their own self-improvement and the betterment of the continent as a whole.

The changeover to warlike activities and kidnaping must have affected all branches of economic activity, and agriculture in particular. Occasionally, in certain localities food production was increased to provide supplies for slave ships, but the overall consequences of slaving on agricultural activities in Western, Eastern, and Central Africa were negative. Labor was drawn off from agriculture and conditions became unsettled. Dahomey, which in the sixteenth century was known for exporting food to parts of what is now Togo, was suffering from famines in the nineteenth century. The present generation of Africans will readily recall that in the colonial period when able-bodied men left their homes as migrant laborers, that upset the farming routine in the home districts and often caused famines. Slave trading after all meant migration of labor in a manner one hundred times more brutal and disruptive.

To achieve economic development, one essential condition is to make the maximum use of the country's labor and natural resources. Usually, that demands peaceful conditions, but there have been times in history when social groups have grown stronger by raiding their neighbors for women, cattle, and goods, because they then used the "booty" from the raids for the benefit of their own community. Slaving in Africa did not even have that redeeming value. Captives were shipped outside instead of being utilized within any given African community for creating wealth from nature. It was only as an accidental by-product that in some areas Africans who recruited captives for Europeans realized that they were better off keeping some captives for themselves. In any case, slaving prevented the remaining population from effectively engaging in agriculture and industry, and it employed professional slave-hunters and warriors to destroy rather than build. Quite apart from the moral aspect and the immense suffering that it caused, the European slave trade was economically totally irrational from the viewpoint of African development.

For certain purposes, it is necessary to be more specific and to speak of the trade in slaves not in general continent-wide terms but rather with reference to the varying impact on several regions. The relative intensity of slave-raiding in different areas is fairly well known. Some South African peoples were enslaved by the Boers and some North African Moslems by Christian Europeans, but those were minor episodes. The zones most notorious for human exports were, firstly, West Africa from Senegal to Angola along a belt extending about two hundred miles inland and, secondly, that part of East-Central Africa which today covers Tanzania, Mozambique, Malawi, northern Zambia, and eastern Congo. Furthermore, within each of those broad areas, finer distinctions can be drawn.

It might therefore appear that slave trade did not adversely affect the development of some parts of Africa, simply because exports were nonexistent or at a low level. However, the contention that European slave trade was an underdeveloping factor for the continent as a whole must be upheld, because it does not follow that an African district which did not trade with Europe was entirely free from whatever influences were exerted by Europe. European trade goods percolated into the deepest interior, and (more significantly) the orientation of large areas of the continent towards human exports meant that other positive interactions were thereby ruled out.

The above proposition may be more fully grasped by making some comparisons. In any given economy, the various components reflect the well-being of others. Therefore, when there is depression in one sector, that depression invariably transfers itself to others to some extent. Similarly, when there is buoyancy in one sector, then others benefit. Turning to bio-logical sciences, it will be found that students of ecology recognize that a single change, such as the disappearance of a snail species, could trigger off negative or positive reactions in spheres that superficially appear un-connected. Parts of Africa left "free" by export trends in captives must have been affected by the tremendous dislocation—in ways that are not easy to comprehend, because it is so much a question of what *might* have happended.

Hypothetical questions such as "What might have happened if . . . ?" sometimes lead to absurd speculations. But it is entirely legitimate and very necessary to ask "What might have happened in Barotseland (south-ern Zambia) if there were not generalized slave trading across the whole belt of central Africa which lay immediately north of Barotseland?" "What would have happened in Buganda if the Katangese were concentrating on selling copper to the Baganda instead of captives to Europeans?"

During the colonial epoch, the British forced Africans to sing,

> *Rule Britannia, Britannia rule the waves*
> *Britons never never never shall be slaves.*

The British themselves started singing the tune in the early eighteenth century, at the height of using Africans as slaves. "What would have been Britain's level of development had millions of them been put to work as slaves outside of their homelands over a period of four centuries?" Further-more, assuming that those wonderful fellows could never never never have been slaves, one could speculate further on the probable effects on their development had continental Europe been enslaved. Had that been the case, its nearest neighbors would have been removed from the ambit of fruitful trade with Britain. After all, trade between the British Isles and places like the Baltic and the Mediterranean is unanimously considered by scholars to have been the earliest stimulus to the English economy in the late feudal and early capitalist period, even before the era of overseas ex-pansion.

One tactic that is now being employed by certain European (including American) scholars is to say that the European slave trade was un-doubtedly *a moral evil,* but it was *economically good* for Africa. Here at-tention will be drawn only very briefly to a few of those arguments to indicate how ridiculous they can be. One that receives much emphasis is that African rulers and other persons obtained European commodities in exchange for their captives, and this was how Africans gained "wealth." This suggestion fails to take into account the fact that several European imports were competing with and strangling African products; it fails to take into account the fact that none of the long list of European articles were of the type which entered into the productive process, but were rather items to be rapidly consumed or stowed away uselessly; and it incredibly overlooks the fact that the majority of the imports were of the worst quality even as consumer goods—cheap gin, cheap gunpowder, pots and kettles full of holes, beads, and other assorted rubbish.

Following from the above, it is suggested that certain African kingdoms grew strong economically and politically as a consequence of the trade with Europeans. The greatest of the West African kingdoms, such as Oyo, Benin, Dahomey, and Asante are cited as examples. Oyo and Benin were great long before making contact with Europeans, and while both Dahomey and Asante grew stronger during the period of the European slave trade, the roots of their achievements went back to much earlier years. Furthermore—and this is a major fallacy in the argument of the slave-trade apologists—the fact that a given African state grew politically more powerful at the same time as it engaged in selling captives to Europeans is not automatically to be attributed to the credit of the trade in slaves. A cholera epidemic may kill thousands in a country and yet the population increases. The increase obviously came about *in spite of* and not because of the cholera. This simple logic escapes those who speak about the European slave trade benefiting Africa. The destructive tendency of slave trading can be clearly established; and, wherever a state seemingly progressed in the epoch of slave trading, the conclusion is simply that it did so in spite of the adverse effects of a process that was more damaging than cholera. This is the picture that emerges from a detailed study of Dahomey, for instance, and in the final analysis although Dahomey did its best to expand politically and militarily while still tied to slave trade, that form of economic activity seriously undermined its economic base and left it much worse off.

A few of the arguments about the economic benefits of the European slave trade for Africa amount to nothing more than saying that exporting millions of captives was a way of avoiding starvation in Africa! To attempt to reply to that would be painful and time-wasting. But, perhaps a slightly more subtle version of the same argument requires a reply: namely, the argument that Africa gained because in the process of slave trading new food crops were acquired from the American continent and these became staples in Africa. The crops in question are maize and cassava, which became staples in Africa late in the nineteenth century and in the present century. But the spread of food crops is one of the most common phenomena in human history. Most crops originated in only one of the continents, and then social contact caused their transfer to other parts of the world. Trading in slaves has no special bearing on whether crops spread—

the simplest forms of trade would have achieved the same result. Today, the Italians have (hard) wheat foods like spaghetti and macaroni as their staple, while most Europeans use the potato. The Italians took the idea of the spaghetti-type foods from the Chinese noodle after Marco Polo returned from travels there, while Europe adopted the potato from American Indians. In neither case were Europeans enslaved before they could receive a benefit that was the logical heritage of all mankind, but Africans are to be told that the European slave trade developed us by bringing us maize and cassava.

All of the above points are taken from books and articles published recently, as the fruit of research in major British and American universities. They are probably not the commonest views even among European bourgeois scholars, but they are representative of a growing trend that seems likely to become the new accepted orthodoxy in metropolitan capitalist countries; and this significantly coincides with Europe's struggle against the further decolonization of Africa economically and mentally. In one sense, it is preferable to ignore such rubbish and isolate our youth from its insults; but unfortunately one of the aspects of current African underdevelopment is that the capitalist publishers and bourgeois scholars dominate the scene and help mold opinions the world over. It is for that reason that writing of the type which justifies the trade in slaves has to be exposed as racist bourgeois propaganda, having no connection with reality or logic. It is a question not merely of history but of present-day liberation struggle in Africa.

Technical Stagnation and Distortion of the African Economy in the Pre-Colonial Epoch

It has already been indicated that in the fifteenth century European technology was not totally superior to that of other parts of the world. There were certain specific features which were highly advantageous to Europe —such as shipping and (to a lesser extent) guns. Europeans trading to Africa had to make use of Asian and African consumer goods, showing that their system of production was not absolutely superior. It is particularly striking that in the early centuries of trade, Europeans relied heavily on Indian cloths for resale in Africa, and they also purchased cloths on several parts of the West African coast for resale elsewhere. Morocco, Mauritania, Senegambia, Ivory Coast, Benin, Yorubaland, and Loango were all exporters to other parts of Africa—through European middlemen. Yet, by the time that Africa entered the colonial era, it was concentrating almost entirely on the export of raw cotton and the import of manufactured cotton cloth. This remarkable reversal is tied to technological advance in Europe and to stagnation of technology in Africa owing to the very trade with Europe.

Cloth manufacture in the world went through a stage of handlooms and small-scale craft production. Up to the sixteenth century, that was the general pattern in Africa, Asia, and Europe: with Asian cloth-makers being the most skilled in the world. India is the classic example where the British used every means at their disposal to kill the cloth industry, so that British cloth could be marketed everywhere, including inside India itself. In Africa, the situation was not so clear-cut, nor did it require so much conscious effort by Europeans to destroy African cloth manufacture, but the trend was the same. Europe benefited technologically from its external trade contacts, while Africa either failed to benefit or actually lost. Vital inventions and innovations appeared in England in the late eighteenth century, after profits from external trade had been reinvested. Indeed, the new machinery represented the investment of primary capital accumulated from trading and from slavery. African and Indian trade strengthened British industry, which in turn crushed whatever industry existed in what is now called the "underdeveloped" countries.

African demand for cloth was increasing rapidly in the fifteenth, sixteenth, and seventeenth centuries, so that there was a market for all cloth produced locally as well as room for imports from Europe and Asia. But, directed by an acquisitive capitalist class, European industry increased its capacity to produce on a large scale by harnessing the energy of wind, water, and coal. European cloth industry was able to copy fashionable Indian and African patterns, and eventually to replace them. Partly by establishing a stranglehold on the distribution of cloth around the shores of Africa, and partly by swamping African products by importing cloth in bulk, European traders eventually succeeded in putting an end to the expansion of African cloth manufacture.

There are many varied social factors which combine to determine when a society makes a breakthrough from small-scale craft technology to equipment designed to harness nature so that labor becomes more effective. One of the major factors is the existence of a demand for more products than can be made by hand, so that technology is asked to respond to a definite social need—such as that for clothes. When European cloth became dominant on the African market, it meant that African producers were cut off from the increasing demand. The craft producers either abandoned their tasks in the face of cheap available European cloth, or they continued on the same small hand-worked instruments to create styles and pieces for localized markets. Therefore, there was what can be called "technological arrest" or stagnation, and in some instances actual regression, since people forgot even the simple techniques of their forefathers. The abandonment of traditional iron smelting in most parts of Africa is probably the most important instance of technological regression.

Development means a capacity for self-sustaining growth. It means that an economy must register advances which in turn will promote further progress. The loss of industry and skill in Africa was extremely small, if we measure it from the viewpoint of modern scientific achievements or even by standards of England in the late eighteenth century. However, it must be borne in mind that to be held back at one stage means that it is impossible to go on to a further stage. When a person was forced to leave school after only two years of primary school education, it is no reflection on him that he is academically and intellectually less developed than someone who had the opportunity to be schooled right through to university level. What Africa experienced in the early centuries of trade was precisely a loss of development *opportunity,* and this is of the greatest importance.

One of the features associated with technological advance is a spirit of scientific inquiry closely related to the process of production. This leads to inventiveness and innovation. During the period of capitalist development in Europe, this was very much the case, and historians lay great emphasis on the spirit of inventiveness of the English in the eighteenth century. Socialist societies do not leave inventions merely to chance or good luck— they actively cultivate tendencies for innovation. For instance, in the German Democratic Republic, the youth established a "Young Innovators' Fair" in 1958, calling upon the intellectual creativity of socialist youth, so that within ten years over two thousand new inventions were presented at that fair. The connection between Africa and Europe from the fifteenth century onwards served to block this spirit of technological innovation both directly and indirectly.

The European slave trade was a direct block, in removing millions of youth and young adults who are the human agents from whom inventiveness springs. Those who remained in areas badly hit by slave capturing were preoccupied about their freedom rather than with improvements in production. Besides, even the busiest African in West, Central, or East Africa was concerned more with trade than with production, because of the nature of the contacts with Europe; and that situation was not conducive to the introduction of technological advances. The most dynamic groups over a great area of Africa became associated with foreign trade—notably, the Afro-Portuguese middlemen of Upper Guinea, the Akan market women, the Aro traders of Mozambique, and the Swahili and Wanyamwezi of East Africa. The trade which they carried on was in export items like captives and ivory which did not require the invention of machinery. Apart from that, they were agents for distributing European imports.

When Britain was the world's leading economic power, it used to be referred to as a nation of shopkeepers: but most of the goods in their shops were produced by themselves, and it was while grappling with the problems posed by production that their engineers came up with so many inventions. In Africa, the trading groups could make no contribution to technological improvement because their role and preoccupation took their minds and energies away from production.

Apart from inventiveness, we must also consider the borrowing of technology. When a society for whatever reason finds itself technologically trailing behind others, it catches up not so much by independent inventions but by borrowing. Indeed, very few of man's major scientific discoveries have been separately discovered in different places by different people. Once a principle or a tool is known, it spreads or diffuses to other peoples. Why then did European technology fail to make its way into Africa during the many centuries of contact between the two continents? The basic reason is that the very nature of Afro-European trade was highly unfavorable to the movement of positive ideas and techniques from the European capitalist system to the African pre-capitalist (communal, feudal, and pre-feudal) system of production.

The only non-European society that borrowed effectively from Europe and became capitalist is that of Japan. Japan was already a highly developed feudal society progressing towards its own capitalist forms in the nineteenth century. Its people were neither enslaved nor colonized by Europe, and its foreign trade relations were quite advantageous. For instance, Japanese textile manufacturers had the stimulus of their own growing internal market and some abroad in Asia and Europe. Under those circumstances, the young Japanese capitalist class (including many former feudalist landowners) borrowed technology from Europe and successfully domesticated it before the end of the nineteenth century. The use of this example from outside Africa is meant to emphasize that for Africa to have received European technology the demand would have had to come from inside Africa—and most probably from a class or group who saw profit in the new technology. There had to be both willingness on the part of Europeans to transfer technology and African socio-economic structures capable of making use of that technology and internalizing it.

Hunting for elephants or captives did not usually induce in Africa a demand for any technology other than firearms. The lines of economic activity attached to foreign trade were either destructive, as slavery was, or at best purely extractive, like ivory hunting and cutting camwood trees.

Therefore, there was no reason for wanting to call upon European skills. The African economies would have had little room for such skills unless negative types of exports were completely stopped. A remarkable fact that is seldom brought to light is that several African rulers in different parts of the continent saw the situation clearly, and sought European technology for internal development, which was meant to replace the trade in slaves.

Europeans deliberately ignored those African requests that Europe should place certain skills and techniques at their disposal. This was an element in the Kongo situation of the early sixteenth century, which has already been mentioned. It happened in Ethiopia also, though in Ethiopia no trade in captives was established with Europeans. A Portuguese embassy reached the Ethiopian court in 1520. Having examined Portuguese swords, muskets, clothes, books, and other objects, the emperor Lebna Dengel felt the need to introduce European technical knowledge into Ethiopia. Correspondence exists between the emperor and European rulers, such as kings Manuel I and John III of Portugal, and Pope Leo X, in which requests were made for European assistance to Ethiopian industry. Until late in the nineteenth century, Ethiopian petitions to that effect were being repeated with little or no success.

In the first half of the eighteenth century, there were two further examples of African rulers appreciating European technology, and stating their preference for skills and not slave ships. When Agaja Trudo of Dahomey sought to stop the trade in captives, he made an appeal to European craftsmen, and he sent an ambassador to London for that purpose. One European who stayed at the court of Dahomey in the late 1720s told his countrymen that "if any tailor, carpenter, smith or any other sort of white man that is free be willing to come here, he will find very good encouragement." The Asantehene Opoku Ware (1720–50) also asked Europeans to set up factories and distilleries in Asante, but he got no response.

Bearing in mind the history of Japan, it should be noted that the first requests for technical assistance came from the Ethiopian and Kongo empires, which in the sixteenth century were at a level undoubtedly comparable to that of most European feudal states, with the important exception that they had not produced the seeds of capitalism. During the eighteenth century the great African states of Dahomey and Asante became prominent. They had passed out of the communal stage and had a somewhat feudal class stratification along with specialization in many activities such as the working of gold, iron, and cloth. Asante society under Opoku Ware had already shown a capacity for seeking out innovations, by going to the trouble of taking imported silk and unraveling it so as to combine the silk threads with cotton to make the famous *kente* cloth. In other words, there would have been no difficulty in such African societies mastering European technical skills and bridging the rather narrow gap which existed between them and Europe at that time.

Well into the nineteenth century, Europe displayed the same indifference to requests for practical assistance from Africa, although by that period both African rulers and European capitalists were talking about replacing slave trade. In the early nineteenth century, one king of Calabar (in eastern Nigeria) wrote the British asking for a sugar refinery; while around 1804 King Adandozan of Dahomey was bold enough to ask for a firearms factory! By that date, many parts of West Africa were going to war with European firearms and gunpowder. There grew up a saying in Dahomey that "He who makes the powder wins the war," which was a far-sighted recognition that Africans were bound to fall before the superiority of Europeans in the field of arms technology. Of course, Europeans were also fully aware that their arms technology was decisive, and there was not the slightest chance that they would have agreed to teach Africans to make firearms and ammunition.

The circumstances of African trade with Europe were unfavorable to creating a consistent African demand for technology relevant to development; and when that demand was raised it was ignored or rejected by the capitalists. After all, it would not have been in the interests of capitalism to develop Africa. In more recent times, Western capitalists had refused to build the Volta River Dam for Ghana under Kwame Nkrumah, until they realized that the Czechoslovakians would do the job; they refused to build the Aswan Dam for Egypt, and the Soviet Union had to come to the rescue; and in a similar situation they placed obstacles in the way of the building of a railway from Tanzania to Zambia, and it was the socialist state of China that stepped in to express solidarity with African peasants and workers in a practical way. Placing the whole question in historical perspective allows us to see that capitalism has always discouraged technological evolution in Africa, and blocks Africa's access to its own technology. As will be seen in a subsequent section, capitalism introduced into Africa only such limited aspects of its material culture as were essential to more efficient exploitation, but the general tendency has been for capitalism to underdevelop Africa in technology.

The European slave trade and overseas trade in general had what are known as "multiplier effects" on Europe's development in a very positive sense. This means that the benefits of foreign contacts extended to many areas of European life not directly connected with foreign trade, and the whole society was better equipped for its own internal development. The opposite was true of Africa not only in the crucial sphere of technology but also with regard to the size and purpose of each economy in Africa. Under the normal processes of evolution, an economy grows steadily larger so that after a while two neighboring economies merge into one. That was precisely how national economies were created in the states of Western Europe through the gradual combination of what were once separate provincial economies. Trade with Africa actually helped Europe to weld together more closely the different national economies, but in Africa there was disruption and disintegration at the local level. At the same time, each local economy ceased to be directed exclusively or even primarily towards the satisfaction of the wants of its inhabitants; and (whether or not the particular Africans recognized it) their economic effort served external interests and made them dependent on those external forces based in Western Europe. In this way, the African economy taken as a whole was diverted away from its previous line of development and became distorted.

It has now become common knowledge that one of the principal reasons why genuine industrialization cannot easily be realized in Africa today is that the market for manufactured goods in any single African country is too small, and there is no integration of the markets across large areas of Africa. The kind of relationship which Africa has had with Europe from the very beginning has worked in a direction opposite to integration of local economies. Certain interterritorial links established on the continent were broken down after the fifteenth century because of European trade. Several examples arose on the West African coast down to Angola, because in those parts European trade was most voluminous, and the surviving written record is also more extensive.

When the Portuguese arrived in the region of modern Ghana in the 1470s, they had few commodities to offer the inhabitants in exchange for the gold coveted by Europe. However, they were able to transship from Benin in Nigeria supplies of cotton cloths, beads, and female slaves, which were salable on the Gold Coast. The Portuguese were responding to a given demand on the Gold Coast so that a previous trade must have been in existence between the people of Benin and those of the Gold Coast, particularly the Akan. The Akan were gold producers, and the people of Benin were specialist craftsmen who had a surplus of cloth and beads which they manufactured themselves. As an expansionist state with a large army, Benin also had access to prisoners of war; while the Akan seemed concerned with building their own population and labor force, so the latter acquired female captives from Benin and rapidly integrated them as wives. When the Portuguese intervened in this exchange, it was subordinated to the interests of European trade. As soon as Portugal and other European nations had sufficient goods so as not to be dependent on the re-export of certain commodities from Benin, then all that remained were the links between the Gold Coast and Europe on the one hand and between Benin and Europe on the other.

Probably, Benin products had reached the Gold Coast by way of the creeks behind the coast of what is now Dahomey and Togo. Therefore, it would have been more convenient when Europeans established a direct link across the open sea. As pointed out earlier, the superiority of Europeans at sea was of the greatest strategic value, along with their organizational ability. This was illustrated in several places, beginning with the Maghreb and Mauritania. After the Portuguese took control of the Atlantic coast of Northwest Africa, they were able to secure horses, woolen goods, and beads, which they shipped farther south to West Africa for gold and slaves; up to the early sixteenth century, the most important article brought by the Portuguese for trade in Senegambia was the horse. In exchange for one horse they received as many as fifteen captives. North African woolens and beads were also utilized by the Portuguese in buying gold on the river Gambia and as far south as Sierra Leone.

It needs to be recalled that the Western Sudan had links with the West African coast and with North Africa. Long before the European arrival, horses were moving from North Africa to be interbred with local West African stock. Long before the European arrival, the Arabs and Mauritanians traveled to the river Senegal and farther south to meet the Mandinga Djola traders and hand over to them products such as beads made in Ceuta and cloth spun from the wool of North African sheep. With the advantage of rapidity of transport by sea as opposed to overland across the desert, the Portuguese were in effect breaking up the economic integration of the region. As with the Benin-Akan example, the point to note is that after the Portuguese became middlemen they had the opportunity of developing a new trade pattern by which both Northwest Africa and West Africa looked to Europe and forgot about each other.

A similar situation came into existence on the Upper Guinea coast, and this time the European exploitation was aided by the presence of white settlers in the Cape Verde Islands. The Portuguese and the Cape Verde settlers broke into the pattern of local Upper Guinea trade as early as the 1470s. They intervened in transfers of raw cotton and indigo dye from one African community to another, and the Cape Verdean settlers established a flourishing cotton-growing and cotton-manufacturing industry. They used labor and techniques from the mainland, and exported the finished products along the length of the coast down to Accra.

The Portuguese also took over the trade in cowries in the Kongo and its offshore islands, the trade in salt along the Angolan coast, and the trade in high-quality palm cloth between northern and southern Angola. In some instances, they achieved dominance not just because of their ships and commercial skills but also by the use of force—provided they were operating on the coast and could bring their cannon into use. In East Africa, for instance, the Portuguese used violence to capture trade from the Arabs and Swahili. The disruption of African commerce between the Ivory Coast and the Gold Coast followed that pattern. A strong coastal canoe trade existed between these two regions, with the people of Cape Lahou (modern Ivory Coast) sailing past Cape Three Points to sell their cloth as far east as Accra. The Portuguese set up a fort at Axim near Cape Three Points to service gold trade with the hinterland; and one of its functions was to chop the east-west coastal African trade. They banned Axim residents from going to Cape Lahou, and they stopped canoes from Ivory Coast from traveling east beyond Axim. The purpose was obviously to make both areas separate economic entities exclusively tied to Europe.

The above-mentioned African commerce proved to have deep roots. The Dutch found it still going on when they took over Axim in 1637. The servants of the Dutch West India Company which was operating on the Gold Coast wanted to put a complete stop to the African trade; and when that was not achieved they tried to force the people of the Ivory Coast to buy a certain amount of Dutch goods. The Dutch ruled that each Axim canoe-man going to Cape Lahou should carry Dutch goods worth at least four ounces of gold. The purpose was to convert a purely inter-African exchange into a European-African trade.

What was doubly detrimental to African attempts to integrate their own economies was the fact that when Europeans became middlemen in local trade networks, they did so mainly to facilitate the extraction of captives, and thereby subordinated the whole economy to the European slave trade. In Upper Guinea and the Cape Verde Islands, the Portuguese and their mulatto descendants engaged in a large variety of exchanges involving cotton, dyes, kola nuts, and European products. The purpose of it all was to fill the holds of slave ships. In Congo and Angola, the same picture emerges. The salt, cowry shells, and palm cloth that came in Portuguese hands made up for their shortage of trade goods and served to purchase captives on different parts of the coast and deep in the interior.

The element of subordination and dependence is crucial to an understanding of African underdevelopment today, and its roots lie far back in the era of international trade. It is also worth noting that there is a type of false or pseudo integration which is a camouflage for dependence. In contemporary times, it takes the form of free-trade areas in the formerly colonized sections of the world. Those free-trade areas are made to order for the penetration of multinational corporations. From the fifteenth century onwards, pseudo integration appeared in the form of the interlocking of African economies over long distances from the coast, so as to allow the passage of human captives and ivory from a given point inland to a given port on the Atlantic or Indian Ocean. For example, captives were moved from Congo through what is now Zambia and Malawi to Mozambique, where Portuguese, Arab, or French buyers took them over. That was not genuine integration of the economies of the African territories concerned. Such trade merely represented the extent of foreign penetration, thereby stifling local trades.

The West African gold trade was not destroyed, but it became directly dependent on European buyers by being diverted from the northward routes across the Sahara. Within the savannah belt of the Western Sudan, the trans-Saharan gold trade had nourished one of the most highly developed political zones in all Africa from the fifth century onwards. But it was more convenient for Europe to obtain its gold on the West Coast than through North African intermediaries, and one is left to speculate on what might have occurred in the Western Sudan if there had been a steady increase in the gold trade over the seventeenth and eighteenth centuries. Nevertheless, there is something to be said in favor of African trade with Europe in this particular commodity. Gold production involved mining and an orderly system of distribution within Africa. Akan country and parts of Zimbabwe and Mozambique sustained flourishing socio-political systems up to the nineteenth century, largely because of gold production.

Certain benefits also derived from the export of ivory. The search for ivory became the most important activity in several East African societies at one time or another, sometimes in combination with the trade in captives. The Wanyamwezi of Tanzania were East Africa's best known traders —acquiring their reputation through carrying goods for hundreds of miles between Lake Tanganyika and the Indian Ocean. When the Wanyamwezi gave their attention to the export of ivory, this sparked off other beneficial developments, such as increased trading in hoes, food, and salt between themselves and their neighbors.

Yet, ivory was an asset that was rapidly exhausted in any given region, and the struggle to secure new supplies could lead to violence comparable to that which accompanied the search for human captives. Besides, the most decisive limitation of ivory trade was the fact that it did not grow logically from local needs and local production. Large quantities of ivory were not required by any society inside Africa, and no African society turned to elephant hunting and ivory collection on a big scale until the demand came from Europe or Asia. Any African society which took ivory exports seriously then had to restructure its economy so as to make ivory trade successful. That in turn led to excessive and undesirable dependence on the overseas market and an external economy. There could be growth in the volume of commerce and the rise of some positive side effects, but there was decrease in the capacity to achieve economic independence and self-sustaining social progress. Besides, at all times one must keep in mind the dialectical opposite of the trade in Africa: namely, production in Europe or in America under European control. The few socially desirable by-products of elephant hunting within Africa were chicken feed in comparison with the profits, technology, and skills associated with the product in Europe. In that way, the gap between Africa and Europe was constantly widening; and it is on the basis of that gap that we arrive at development and underdevelopment.

Continuing Politico-Military Developments in Africa—1500 to 1885

Modern African nationalist historians correctly stress that Africa had a meaningful past long before the coming of Europeans. They also stress that Africans made their own history long after coming into contact with Europe, and indeed right up to the period of colonization. That African-centered approach to the continent's past is quite compatible with one which equally emphasizes the transformatory role of external forces, such as overseas trade in slaves, gold, ivory. The reconciliation of the two approaches is facilitated by bearing in mind the following three factors:

(1) The external (and mainly European) impact up to 1885 was very uneven in geographical terms, with the coasts being obviously more exposed.

(2) Commerce with Europeans affected different aspects of African life in varying degrees, with the political, military, and ideological apparatus being virtually untouched.

(3) Dynamic features of independent African evolution and development (as illustrated in Chapter 2) *continued* to operate after 1500.

It has already been argued that it would be misleading to try to compartmentalize Africa into areas that were affected by slave trading and those which were not, for the continent as a whole had to bear the costs. However, for present purposes, it is enough to make the crude distinction between those parts of Africa which were directly caught up in European-generated activities and those parts which to all appearances continued in the traditional manner.

Developments continued in certain areas such as south Central Africa, because the population there was free to pursue a path dictated by the interplay between African people and the African environment in the particular localities. Besides, there were achievements even in those societies under the heaviest bombardment of slaving. Slave trading led to the commercial domination of Africa by Europe, within the context of international trade. In very few instances did Europeans manage to displace African political authorities in the various social systems. So African states in close contact with Europe in the pre-colonial era nevertheless had scope for political maneuver, and their evolution could and did continue.

Military conquest of Africa awaited the years of the imperialist Scramble. In pre-colonial centuries of contact with Europe, African armies were in existence, with all the socio-political implications which attach to an armed sector in society. Equally important was the fact that direct imports from Europe in the cultural and ideological spheres were virtually nil. Christianity tried sporadically and ambivalently to make an impact on some parts of the continent. But most of the few missionaries in places like the Congo, Angola, and Upper Guinea concentrated on blessing Africans as they were about to be launched across the Atlantic into slavery. As it was, Christianity continued only in Ethiopia, where it had indigenous roots. Elsewhere, there flourished Islam and other religions which had nothing to do with European trade. As before, religion continued to act as an element of the superstructure, which was crucial in the development of the state.

So long as there is political power, so long as a people can be mobilized to use weapons, and so long as a society has the opportunity to define its own ideology and culture, then the people of that society have some control over their own destinies, in spite of constraints such as those imposed as the African continent slipped into orbit as a satellite of capitalist Europe. After all, although historical development is inseparable from material conditions and the state of technology, it is also partially controlled by a people's consciousness at various stages. That is part of the interdependence of base and superstructure alluded to at the outset.

Revolution is the most dramatic appearance of a conscious people or class on the stage of history; but, to greater or lesser extent, the ruling class in any society is always engaged in the developmental process as conscious instruments of change or conservatism. Attention in this section will be focused on the political sphere and its power companion, the military. In those areas, Africans were able to excel even in the face of slave trading.

Politico-military development in Africa from 1500 to 1885 meant that African social collectives had become more capable of defending the interests of their members, as opposed to the interests of people outside the given community. It also meant that the individual in a politically mature and militarily strong state would be free from external threat of physical removal. He would have more opportunities to apply his own skill in fields as diversified as minstrelsy and bronze-working, under the protection of the state. He could also use his creativity and inventiveness to refine the religion of his people, or to work out a more manageable constitution, or to contribute to new techniques of war, or to advance agriculture and trade. Of course, it is also true that the benefits of all such contributions went mainly to a small section of African society, both within and without the zone of slaving; for, as communalism receded, the principle of egalitarian distribution was disregarded. These various points can be illustrated by concrete historical examples drawn from all over the continent during the pre-colonial period in question.

The Yoruba

In a previous discussion, the Yoruba state of Oyo was merely listed as one of the outstanding representatives of African development up to the eve of European arrival in the fifteenth century. The remarkable fourteenth- and fifteenth-century artistic achievements of Oyo, of its parent state of Ife, and of the related state of Benin have been well studied, because of the preservation of ivory, terracotta, and bronze sculptures. It is clear that the earliest bronzes were the best and that there was a deterioration in execution and sensitivity from the sixteenth through to the eighteenth century. However, politically, states such as Oyo and Benin did continue to prosper for a very long time after the arrival of Europeans on the West African coast. Since Oyo and the Yoruba people were within an intensive area of slave trading, their fate between 1500 and 1885 is of considerable significance.

The kingdom of Oyo kept fairly clear of any involvement with slave trading until the late eighteenth century. Instead, its people concentrated on local production and trade, and on the consolidation and expansion of the trade. Indeed, although the nucleus of the Oyo kingdom had already been established in the fifteenth century, it was during the next three centuries that it expanded to take control of most of what was later termed Western Nigeria, large zones north of the river Niger and the whole of what is now Dahomey. In effect, it was an empire, ruled over by an Alafin in conjunction with an aristocracy. It was in the sixteenth, seventeenth, and eighteenth centuries that the subtle constitutional mechanisms which regulated relations between the Alafin and his principal subjects and between the capital and the provinces were crystalized.

In so far as Oyo had an interest in the coast, it was as an outlet more for cloth than for slaves. Being some distance inland, the Yoruba of Oyo concentrated on relations with the hinterland, thereby connecting with the

Western Sudanic trading zone. It was from the north that Oyo got the horses which made its armies feared and respected. Oyo is a prime example of that African development which had its roots deep in the past, in the contradictions between man and environment. Its people continued to develop on the basis of forces which they did not consciously manipulate, as well as through the deliberate utilization of political techniques.

Early in the nineteenth century, Oyo and Yorubaland in general began to export captives in considerable numbers. They were obtained partly by military campaigns outside Yorubaland, but also through local slave procuring. Local slave procuring involved kidnaping, armed raids, uncertainty, and disunity. Those features, together with internal constitutional tensions and an external threat from the Islamic north, brought about the downfall of the Oyo empire by about 1830. The famous Yoruba ancestral home of Ife was also despoiled and its citizens turned into refugees, because of quarrels among the Yoruba over kidnaping for sale into slavery.

But it was testimony to the level of development in that part of Africa that within a few years the inhabitants were able to reconstruct new political states: notably those of New Oyo, Ibadan, Ajaye, Abeokuta, and Ijebu—each centered on a town, and with enough land for successful agriculture. Until the British arrived to kindly impose "order" in Nigeria, the Yoruba people kept experimenting with various political forms, with heavy emphasis on the military, and keeping to the religion of their forefathers.

Being conscious of territorial boundaries, the inhabitants and rulers of any given state invariably become involved in clashes with neighboring states. The state in the feudal epoch in Europe and Asia was particularly concerned with its military capacity. The ruling class comprised in whole or in part the professional fighting forces of the state. One rationalization by which they justified their enjoyment of the major portion of the surplus of society was that they offered armed protection to the ordinary peasant or serf. This generalization was as true of nineteenth-century Yorubaland as it was of Prussia and Japan. Without a doubt, Africans in that region were proceeding along the line of development leading to social organization comparable to feudalism in Europe, Asia, and such parts of Africa as Ethiopia and the Maghreb, which had been at that stage some centuries earlier.

In the Oyo empire, the civil power was dominant, and the military generals were servants of the king. Subsequently, however, the military took over effective political power. For instance, the Ajaye state was founded by Kurunmi, said to have been the greatest Yoruba general of those troubled times following the fall of Oyo. Kurunmi established a personal military ascendancy in Ajaye. Ibadan was slightly different, in that there it was a group of military officers who collectively formed the political elite. Efforts to put civilians back in power were half-hearted and unsuccessful. After all, the town itself grew out of a military encampment.

The city-state of Abeokuta perhaps made the most consistent effort to make the military an arm of the civil state. But, what mattered most was the defense of the townships within the fortified walls of Abeokuta. Abeokuta's fortified walls became famous as the place where many a rival army met disaster; and, under those circumstances, the *Ologun,* or war-chiefs, were the social and political powers.

While the militarization of politics was going on in Yorubaland, changes were taking place in the structure of the society, which brought about sharper class stratification. Numerous captives were taken in war, most of whom were sold to Europeans, so that Yorubaland became notorious as a slave-supplying region right up to the 1860s. But many war prisoners were retained locally, in conditions approximating either to slavery or to serfdom, depending on whether or not they were first-generation captives. Sometimes, refugees fleeing from destroyed towns also had no option other than to become clients or serfs of other free Yoruba. Such refugees were made to give service to their new overlords by farming the land, in return for armed protection. However, serfs were also used as soldiers, which means that they had access to the means of production (the land) only through meeting an obligation in military labor. That is a measure of the extent to which the principle of kinship had been weakened, and it indicates that, in contrast to the typical communal village, states such as those in nineteenth-century Yorubaland allocated roles and rewards to their citizens on the basis of reciprocal obligations characteristic of feudalism.

During the period under discussion, the division of labor among the Yoruba was extended with the rise of professional soldiers, or "war-boys," as they were called. The professional soldiers, who were sons of aristocrats, left farming disdainfully to prisoners and serfs—the large number of whom insured agricultural plenty. Other branches of economic activity also flourished, notably the making of cloth and palm oil and the trade in various products. These things were true, in spite of the fact that by that time some labor was being lost both in the form of slaves exported and in the form of labor power devoted to capturing people for export. European visitors to Yorubaland in the middle of the nineteenth century could still admire the level of its material culture, along with the highly colorful and impressive aspects of its non-material culture such as the annual "Yam Festivals" and the ritual of the religious cults of Shango, Ogboni, and others.

One item of European technology that was anxiously sought by Africans and that was fairly easily obtainable from Europeans was the firearm. From the 1820s onwards, the Yoruba acquired European firearms in large numbers, and integrated them into the pattern of trade, politics, and military strategy. On the eve of colonial rule, Yoruba generals were reaching out for breech-loading rifles and even rockets; but Europe stepped in too quickly for that move to get very far. Through a series of actions which started as early as 1860 in Lagos (and which included missionary infiltration as well as armed invasion) the British managed to bring that part of Africa under colonial rule.

Economic development is a matter of an increasing capacity to produce, and it is tied up with patterns of land tenure and class relations. These basic facts were well brought out both positively and negatively in Yoruba history, in the decades before independence was lost. So long as agricultural production was not disrupted, then for so long any given Yoruba state remained in a strong position. Ibadan was once the greatest military power in Yorubaland, selling captives as well as retaining many for use as laborers for its own benefit. But Ibadan's farming areas were hit by war, and Ibadan's rulers also started removing prisoners farming the land and selling them instead to Europeans. That became necessary because Ibadan needed firearms, and those could be obtained only by selling slaves. It was at that point that the undermining effect of the presence of European slave buyers on the coast became really paramount.

By selling its own captives and serfs, Ibadan was undermining its own socio-economic base. If the prisoners were to develop into a true serf class, then those prisoners would have had to be guaranteed the right to remain fixed on the soil and protected from sale. This was one of the reasons why slavery as a mode of production in Europe had to give way to serfdom and feudalism; and, under normal circumstances, Yoruba society did rapidly guarantee the irremovability of those captives who were integrated into the local production pattern. But, forces unleashed by the European presence as slave buyers were too great to be withstood, and any hope of solving the problem disappeared with the loss of political power under colonialism.

Too often, historians lay undue emphasis on the failure of nineteenth-century Yoruba states to unite and produce an entity as large as the former empire of Oyo. But, firstly, the size of a political unit is not the most important criterion for evaluating the achievement of its peoples. And, secondly, a given people can disintegrate politically and later integrate even more effectively. The Yoruba states of Ibadan, Abeokuta, Ajaye, had populations of up to 100,000 citizens—as large as most of the city-states, principalities, and palatinates of feudal Germany. That is a comparison which is worth bringing to light, and it is one that struck European observers who happened to visit Yorubaland in the middle years of the nineteenth century.

Germany has long had a common culture and language, and there was a form of political unity under the Holy Roman Empire from the twelfth to the fifteenth century. However, after the Reformation and the breakup of the Holy Roman Empire, the German people were divided into as many separate political entities as there are days in the year, some of them being hardly bigger than a public park. Yet, the internal class relations and productive forces continued to develop throughout Germany, and ultimately by 1870 unity was again achieved, with feudalism giving way to a powerful capitalist nation-state. Similarly, the Yoruba were a widely spread cultural entity with a single language. After the fall of the Oyo empire, the developmental processes were slowed down by both internal and external factors, but they were not stopped. It took the arrival of European colonialism to do that.

Within the sphere of West and Central African slaving, state-building continued with varying degrees of success. For instance, the Akan state system grew up in a manner as impressive as that of the Oyo empire. Fortunately for the Akan, slave exports reached alarming proportions only during the first half of the eighteenth century. By that time, a state such as Asante had sunk roots deep enough to withstand the adverse effects of slaving. It continued to be incorporated with the heartlands of the Western Sudan, and by the 1870s when the British tried to dictate to Asante, these famous African people did not give up without heroic armed struggle.

Asante's connection with the export of slaves in the eighteenth century led its rulers to concentrate on expansionism of the type which would bring in captives through wars, raids, tribute, and as articles of trade from regions where they had been made prisoner. Besides, since the fifteenth century, Akan country was building up rather than exporting its human resources. Captives were incorporated locally into the society; and on the eve of colonialism a substantial proportion of Asante society was made up of *Odonko-ba*—the descendants of one-time captives, who were the laboring population on the land. Development had come not through exporting and losing labor but by increasing and maximizing it.

Dahomey

Asante's eastern neighbor beyond the Volta River was Dahomey. Since Dahomey was more deeply involved in the European slave trade and for a much longer period, its experiences shall be cited at a greater length.

Throughout the eighteenth and nineteenth centuries, Dahomey had a stagnant if not declining population, and an economy that had virtually no props other than slave exports. What Dahomey succeeded in doing in spite of all that is a tribute to the achievements of man inside the African continent. It should be made clear that the groundwork for the socio-political development of the Aja or Fon people of Dahomey was laid down in the period preceding the influence of Europe on West Africa. By the fifteenth century, the Aja states of Allada and Whydah were already in existence, having a loose connection with the Yoruba of Ife. Dahomey was an offshoot from Allada in the sixteenth century, and by the early eighteenth century it expanded to incorporate both Allada and Whydah.

The kings of Allada and Whydah had made the mistake of either failing to protect their own citizens from enslavement or of actually conniving at their enslavement. Dahomey never followed such a policy, which was directly antagonistic to the very maintenance of the state. Instead, Dahomey eventually became the classic raiding state of West Africa, after failing to get Europeans to accept any products other than human beings. To achieve that, Dahomey had first to build up a tightly organized military state, whose monarch came much closer to an authoritarian or despot than did the Alafin of Oyo or the Asantehene of Asante. Secondly, Dahomey invested a great deal of time and ingenuity on its army, so as to protect its own citizens and wage war abroad.

Within European history, the state of Sparta stood out as one that was completely dedicated to the art of war. Europeans in Africa in the eighteenth and nineteenth centuries invariably referred to Dahomey as a black Sparta. Throughout the eighteenth century, the cavalry of Oyo was more than a match for Dahomey's foot soldiers, and Dahomey remained a tribute-paying portion of the Oyo empire. But with the fall of Oyo, Dahomey became the supreme military state in that region, and indeed wreaked vengeance on its former Yoruba overlords. Warfare was necessary for securing slaves *outside* of Dahomey and for obtaining firearms. It was in fact essential for survival.

Dahomey's profound preoccupation with militaristic activities can be illustrated in many ways. Their value system rewarded the brave and the victorious, while ruthlessly despising and even liquidating the cowardly and the unsuccessful on the battlefield. The two chief ministers of the king were the commanders of the "Left" and "Right" armies, and other military officers held political appointments. Then, too, the artistic media constantly harped upon the theme of war. Beautiful mosaics and paintings appeared on the walls of the palaces of Abomey—all dealing with military victories. Historical accounts, as rendered by professional reciters, reflected the same bias; and the cloth workers busied themselves making emblems, "colors," and umbrellas for the generals and the regiments.

Two unique innovations set Dahomey off from its African neighbors and even gives it a special claim within the context of feudal or semi-feudal military organization. Firstly, Dahomey encouraged young boys to become apprentices of war. By the age of eleven or twelve, a boy would be attached to a veteran soldier—helping to carry his supplies and observing battle. The second innovation (and the one that was more widely commented upon) was Dahomey's utilization of its female population within the army. Apparently, the wives in the royal palace started off as a ceremonial guard in the eighteenth century, and then progressed to become an integral part of Dahomey's fighting machine, on terms of complete equality of hardship and reward. Dahomey's population in the nineteenth century was probably no more than two hundred thousand; and the state consistently managed to send twelve to fifteen thousand actives on its annual campaigns. Of those, it was estimated in 1845 that some five thousand were women—the so-called Amazons of Dahomey, who were feared for their ferocity in battle.

In the long run, the trade in slaves cast a blight on Dahomey. Slaving campaigns were costly and not always rewarding in terms of captives. European buyers failed to turn up during certain years, depending on European conditions (e.g., during the American War of Independence, the French Revolution, and the subsequent revolutionary wars, there was a lull in Dahomean slave exports, because far fewer European ships could be spared for the trade in slaves). Without selling captives to get firearms to carry on more warfare for slaves, Dahomey felt its glory and military honor was slipping. Resort to human sacrifice was one attempt to compensate for the diminishing reputation of the state and its monarch, as was the case with the *Oba* of Benin in the nineteenth century.

Even so, the story of the reputed savagery of Dahomey was exaggerated incredibly. The Dahomean state created such refinements as a population census; it conducted diplomacy far and wide, with all the niceties and the protocol that one usually hears of only in connection with "civilized" European states; and it built up a system of espionage and intelligence as an essential ingredient in its own security. Above all, attention should be focused at least briefly on the role of the artist in Dahomean society. Much of African art springs from elaboration of things functional, such as pottery and cloth. However, both religion and the state power also stimulated art. For instance, the brasses and bronzes of Ife were executed on behalf of the religious cults and were associated with the *Oni* of Ife and the royal family. Indeed, it is a most widespread phenomenon that the feudal ruling class gave its protection to artists, along with sustenance and recognition. This was true in Mandarin China with pottery-makers and theatre artists; it was true of sixteenth-century Italy of the Renaissance; and it was true of Dahomey from the seventeenth to the nineteenth centuries.

No one now knows which Dahomean is to be credited with any given artistic achievement of the independent pre-colonial period. However, in that time, particular individuals were being given the opportunity for self-discovery and self-development and of serving the society as a whole. Their task was to give pleasure and to capture the hopes and ambitions of the people in palace wall-paintings, in wrought-iron sculptures, in the stamped patterns of handwoven cloths designed for royalty, in the intricately carved heads of the safe-conduct staffs of the king's ambassadors, and in the lively tales of how the founder of the Dahomean kingdom came out of the belly of a leopard. It was art that centered around royalty and noble families, but it was also a national product and a point of identification for the people as a whole. Subsequently, such artistic skills either disappeared or became debased to serve the curiosity of philistine colonialists.

It is still held in some quarters that Dahomey's development in certain spheres must be credited to slave trading. To demonstrate conclusively that African political and military development through to the nineteenth century was an extension of groundwork already laid in an earlier epoch, it is best to turn to zones where foreign influence was non-existent. The interlacustrine zone of East Africa is one such.

The Eastern Interlacustrine States

In an earlier discussion, attention was directed to Bunyoro-Kitara as the most advanced socio-political formation in East Africa up to the fifteenth century. Its ruling dynasty, the Bachwezi, declined for reasons that are not clear, and they were overwhelmed by new immigrants from the north. While there is some doubt as to whether the Bachwezi had an Ethiopian origin, it is clearly established that the sixteenth-century immigrants were Luo peoples from a section of the Nile that flows through the Sudan.

Following upon Luo migrations, a new line known as the Babito dynasty was placed in power over Bunyoro proper. Other branches of the same dynasty were enthroned in several places, sometimes breaking off from the main line. As late as the nineteenth century, a separate Babito kingdom was carved out in Toro. Meanwhile, the Bachwezi or Bahima had staged a comeback in regions to the south, in the form of a clan known as the Bahinda. The Bahinda were one of the pastoralist clans of the old Bunyoro-

Kitara state, and in the period from the sixteenth century onwards their stronghold was in Ankole and Karagwe.

Obviously, the new Babito ruling class immediately sought to take control of the land, but in accordance with settled African customs, they later tried to project themselves as the original owners of the land, rather than usurpers. In Busoga, where there were several small Babito kings, a researcher reported the following dialogue about land between a member of a royal clan and a commoner:

> *Royal clan member*—We found this place empty and made something of it. You fellows later came round begging for land, so we were generous and gave you some. Naturally you're now our slaves.
>
> *Commoner*—Oho! What a lie! We were here *long* before you. You took your power by trickery. You princes have always been scoundrels!

At no stage in the independent history of these interlacustrine states did land become purely a personal possession, to be monopolized by a given class, as in the classic European feudal model. Scholars frequently demand this feature before they concede that feudalism has arrived; but they fail to take into account the reality of the fact that distribution and usufruct (or produce) of the land may be in the hands of a few, and they fail to realize that where cattle were a dominant form of wealth, then private ownership of herds was also part of a process by which producers were separated from the means of production. To be specific, those who owned the herds were usually the Bahinda or other Bahima or the new Babito families, while those who tended them were clients and virtually serfs of the owners. As far as land was concerned, the peasant who farmed it paid a heavy tax in crops to the clan heads and ruling authorities to allow the latter to live without resort to agricultural work.

It is necessary to recall that in the process of independent evolution on all continents, the increase in productive capacity was accompanied by increasing inequality at all stages except socialism. To say that the interlacustrine zone continued developing uninterruptedly up to the eve of colonialism is to highlight the expanded productive capacity of the states and at the same time to recognize frankly that it was the result of increased exploitation not only of natural resources but also of the labor of the majority. The latter were disenfranchised and oppressed to get them to toil in the interests of a few who lived in palaces.

The interlacustrine kingdoms fell mainly in what is now Uganda, Rwanda, and Burundi. Only in the northeast of Tanzania are there representatives of the interlacustrine complex of states. Northeast Tanzania was the most developed portion of the country in the pre-colonial epoch, because the rest of mainland Tanzania comprised numerous small kingdoms that had not decisively left behind the communal stage. But northeast Tanzania was also the corner of the country in which problems arose when a new ideology of egalitarianism was being preached after the end of the colonial era, because there was already a regime of inequality in the distribution of land and produce and in the rights granted to individuals. In fact, in any meaningful political sense, the area was feudal.

There is some disagreement as to the origins of the important interlacustrine state of Buganda. Some traditions give it the same Luo origin as Bunyoro, while others tend to hold that it was a Bachwezi survival. Its social structure certainly paralleled that of Babito Bunyoro closely. Contrary to the situation in Ankole, in Buganda the Bahima did not have the reins of political power. They were only associated with the cattle-owning ruling class, very often in the junior capacity of herdsmen. In any event, Buganda's history was one of gradual expansion and consolidation at the expense of Bunyoro and other neighbors. By the eighteenth century, it had become the dominant power in the whole region.

The Baganda state had a sound agricultural base, with bananas as a staple and with cattle products being available. Their craftsmen manufactured barkcloth for export, and local production of iron and pots was supplemented by imports from neighboring African communities. Their lack of salt was a big stimulus to the extending of their trade network to obtain necessary supplies; and, as was true of the Western Sudan, such an extension of the network of commerce was in effect integrating the productive resources of a large area. Carl Peters, the advance agent of German colonialism in East Africa, remarked that "in estimating the political and commercial affairs of East Africa too little stress is laid on this internal trade among the tribes. The barter trade of Buganda defies all direct calculation." In Buganda's case, the absence of slave trading must have been important in expanding internal production and trade, and therefore providing a sound base for the political superstructure.

The kings of Buganda set up a small permanent armed force, which served as a bodyguard; and the rest of the national army was raised when necessary. The political administration was centralized under the Kabaka, and district rulers were appointed by the Kabaka and his council, rather than left to be provided by the clans on a hereditary family basis. Great ingenuity went into devising plans for administering this large kingdom through a network of local officials. Perhaps the best tributes to the political sophistication of Buganda came from the British, when they found Buganda and other East African feudalities in the nineteenth century. They were the best tributes because they were reluctantly extracted from white racists and culturally arrogant colonialists, who did not want to admit that Africans were capable of anything.

Actually, Europeans were so impressed with what they saw in the inter-lacustrine zone that they invented the thesis that those political states could not possibly have been the work of Africans and must have been built at an earlier date by white "Hamites" from Ethiopia. This myth seemed to get some support from the fact that the Bachwezi were said to have been light-skinned. However, in the first place, had the Bachwezi come from Ethiopia they would have been black or brown Africans. And secondly, as noted earlier, the cultures of East Africa were syntheses of local developments, plus African contributions from outside the specific localities. They were certainly not foreign imports.

Assuming that the Bachwezi or Bahima were from Ethiopia, then they lost their language and became Bantu-speaking like their subjects. The same thing happened to the Babito dynasty of Luo extraction, indicating that they had been absorbed by the local culture. Furthermore, the Babito and the Bahima/Bahinda also forged close connections from the sixteenth to the nineteenth centuries. In effect, out of different ethnic groups, castes, and classes, a number of "nationalities" were emerging. The "nationality" group is held to be that social formation which immediately precedes the nation-state, and the definition applies to the peoples of Buganda, Bunyoro, Ankole, Karagwe, and Toro, as well as to those in Rwanda and Burundi.

Rwanda

The westernmost portion of the interlacustrine zone comprised the king-doms of Rwanda and Burundi. The two countries which today bear those names are centered around the old kingdoms. The experiences of Rwanda will be cited here.

Like the old Bunyoro-Kitara kingdom and like its northeastern neighbor state in Ankole, Rwanda was split into two major social groups. Though the great majority of the population were cultivators known as the Bahutu, political power was in the hands of Batutsi pastoralists, comprising about 10 per cent of the population. An even smaller minority were the Batwa (about 1 per cent), who were at a very low level of pre-agricultural social organization.

The relative physiques of the three social segments in Rwanda offer an interesting commentary on the development of human beings as a species. The Batutsi are one of the tallest human groups in the world; the Bahutu are short and stocky; and the Batwa are pygmies. The differences can be explained largely in terms of social occupation and diet. The Batwa were not living in settled agricultural communities; instead, they wandered around in small bands, hunting and digging roots, thereby failing to assure themselves of plentiful or rich food. At the other extreme, the Batutsi pastoralists were subsisting on a constantly accessible and rich diet of milk and meat. The Bahutu were more socially advanced than the Batwa; they ate more, and more regularly, than the latter because Bahutu agriculture meant that they did not live entirely on the whims of nature, following scarce game like the Batwa. However, the quality of their food fell short of the protein-rich Batutsi diet. Thus, the development of man as physical being is also linked in a broad sense to the expansion of productive capacity and the distribution of food.

In any event, it was their political and military achievements rather than their height which distinguished the Batutsi from a historical viewpoint. Their contribution to the kingdom of Rwanda goes back to the fourteenth century, to a period contemporaneous with the Bachwezi. There were indeed striking parallels and actual links between Rwanda and Ankole and between Karagwe and Burundi. But unlike Bunyoro-Kitara, Rwanda in the fourteenth and fifteenth centuries was far from being a single political entity. There were several small chiefdoms, and it was the expansion of a central Rwanda Tutsi clan which gradually created a small compact state in the seventeenth century. Later still, that central Rwanda state extended its frontiers; and it was still doing so when the colonialists arrived. For instance, rulers in Mpororo (Ankole) were already paying tribute to Rwanda, which was growing at Ankole's expense.

At the head of the Rwanda kingdom was the Mwami. As with so many other African rulers, his powers were sanctioned by religious beliefs and his person surrounded by religious ritual. Feudal kings in Europe often tried to get their subjects to believe that royal authority emanated from God and that the king therefore ruled by "divine right." Subjects of African kings like those of the Mwami of Rwanda often accepted something quite close to that proposition. Of course, in addition, the authority of the king had to be based on real power, and the Mwami of Rwanda did not overlook that fact.

Rujugira was a famous Mwami of the eighteenth century, and the last of the independent line was Rwaabugiri (known also as Kigeri IV), who died in 1895. Gahindiro is another whose praises were sung by the court musicians and historians. Each of them was associated with one or more contributions to refining and elaborating the power structure of the state, which meant that they each embodied certain historical, class, and national forces.

The Mwami Rujugira in the eighteenth century took the step of placing his frontier zones under the exclusive authority of a military commander, and stationing strong contingents of soldiers there. The move was significant because in any young and growing state the most uncertain areas are those on the frontiers, known as the "marches provinces" in European feudal terminology. Rujugira was in effect placing the marches provinces under military law, and he also put permanent military camps at strategic places.

Early in the nineteenth century, Mwami Gahindiro overhauled the civil administration. In each province, there was created both a land chief and a cattle chief—one being responsible for farm rents and the other for cattle dues. Besides, there were smaller district authorities or "hill chiefs" within all the provinces, all members of the Batutsi aristocracy. Whether by accident or design, it turned out that administrators responsible for different areas and different matters were jealous of each other, and that kept them from uniting to conspire against the Mwami. The "hill chiefs" were for a long time hereditary within given Batutsi clans or lineages; but under Rwaabugiri they became appointive—another move which strengthened central government. Meanwhile, the civil servants and councilors (collectively known as Biru) were given grants of land which were free from the intervention of the land and cattle chiefs, thereby cementing the loyalty of the Biru to the throne.

The system of social relations which emerged in Rwanda was more completely hierarchical and feudal than in most other parts of Africa. Hierarchy and socio-legal interdependence of classes and individuals were features found in the army, in the civil administration, and in the social fabric itself. The key to everything else was the control over cattle, through an institution known as *ubuhake*. This meant that the poor (in cattle) and those of low status (by birth) could approach anyone with more cattle and more respected status, and offer his physical labor services in return for cattle and protection. The cattle were never given as outright property, but only the usufruct was handed over to a client. Therefore, the client could have the use of the cattle for so long as he reciprocated by handing over milk and meat to his overlord, and for so long as he remained loyal. Of course, the peasant on the land also had to perform labor services and provide tribute in the form of food.

The Batutsi aristocracy fulfilled their function of offering "protection" partly by making representations at the Mwami's court or by defending their dependents in legal cases. Above all, however, the protection came through specialization in the military art. Ever since the fifteenth century, there had been compulsory military service for certain Batutsi lineages. Sons of the Batutsi aristocracy became royal pages, receiving all their educational training within a military context. Each new Mwami made a fresh recruitment to add to existing forces. Some Bahutu were associated with particular regiments to provide supplies, and the Batwa were also incorporated as specialist archers (with poisoned arrows).

Of course, the protection which the Batutsi gave the Bahutu was a myth, in the sense that what they were guarding was their exploitation of the Bahutu. They defended them from external enemies, so that the population became dense and plentiful. They conserved the Bahutu, so that the latter could exercise their highly developed agronomical knowledge to produce surplus. Furthermore, the top stratum of Batutsi were the cattle owners, and they left their cattle to the lesser Batutsi to tend, thereby exploiting the labor and profound empirical knowledge which the common cattle herders possessed. As in Europe and Asia, such was the socio-economic base which supported a life of leisure and intrigue among the Batutsi aristocracy.

There was little intermarriage between Batutsi and Bahutu, and hence they are regarded as castes. The Batwa, too, can be similarly categorized; but since the castes were hierarchically placed one over the other, it was also a situation of class, and there was upward and downward mobility from one class to another to a certain extent. At the same time, Batutsi, Bahutu, and Batwa together evolved as the Rwanda nation, having common interests to defend against even the Batutsi, Bahutu, and Batwa who comprised the kingdom of Burundi. The people of Rwanda were not unique in developing a state and a sense of national consciousness, while at the same time experiencing the rise of more sharply differentiated classes and castes in society. The important thing is that they were free to develop relatively unaffected by alien influence, and certainly free from direct ravages of slave trading.

Ama-Zulu

The same freedom from slave trading was operational in South Africa, for West African exports of captives began in Angola and East African exports came from Mozambique and zones farther north. The area south of the Limpopo was one that had some of the simpler social formations in Africa up to the fifteenth century. The eastern side was sparsely peopled up to a late date by the Khoi Khoi herdsmen, who were slowly edged out by Bantu speakers. When European ships touched on the Natal coast in the sixteenth century, it was still a region of widely scattered homesteads; but in the years to come the population became denser and important politico-military development took place.

Anyone with a nodding acquaintance with the African past would have heard the name of Shaka, the Zulu leader who most embodied the social and political changes which took place in the eastern portion of South Africa. One biographer (a European) had this to say of Shaka:

> Napoleon, Julius Caesar, Hannibal, Charlemagne . . . such men as these have arisen periodically throughout the history of the world to blaze a trail of glory that has raised them high above the common level. Such a man was Shaka, perhaps the greatest of them all.

The above praise-song appeared on the back cover of the biography in question; and, since capitalist publishers treat books just like boxes of soap powder, one has admittedly to be suspicious of any advertisement designed to sell the book. Nevertheless, all commentators on Shaka (both African and European) frequently compare him favorably with the "Great Men" of European history. It is therefore appropriate to examine Ama-Zulu society up to the nineteenth century with a view to understanding the role of the leader in relationship to the development of society as a whole.

Shaka was born about the year 1787, and the impressive achievements attributed to him in his forty-year life span can only be briefly enumerated here. By 1816, he was head of a small Ama-Ngoni clan, the Ama-Zulu. Within a few years, he had reorganized it militarily—both in terms of weapons and the tactics and strategy of war—so that the Ama-Zulu clan became a feared fighting force. Through warfare and political maneuvering, he united and commanded the Ama-Ngoni who had previously been divided into dozens of independent or semi-independent clans. At one point, it seemed as though Shaka was about to unite under one rule the whole of the region that is now Natal, Lesotho, and Swaziland. That task was not accomplished when he met his death in 1828, nor were his successors able to maintain Shaka's sway. But the territory belonging to the Ama-Zulu nation in the late nineteenth century was a hundred times greater than the 100 square miles of the original patrimony of the Ama-Zulu clan as inherited by Shaka in 1816. It was a diminished and less powerful Ama-Zulu that was still capable in 1876 of inflicting upon the British one of the most crushing defeats in their history of overseas adventuring—at the battle of Isandhlwana.

Shaka grew up at a time when the questions of unity and of effective armies were being posed seriously for the first time among the Ama-Ngoni. Previously, the clans (which generally coincided with chiefdoms) displayed a tendency to segment or break into smaller and smaller units. As the eldest son of a clan head grew to adulthood, he went off to settle his own kraal; and a new junior clan was born, for his father's clan remained senior and its headship passed to the eldest son of the "great wife." That pattern of segmentation was possible so long as population density was low and land was plentiful for farming and grazing. Under those circumstances, there was little competition for resources or political power; and wars were hardly any more dangerous than a game of football in Latin America. Usually a clan had traditional rivalry with another given clan. They knew each other well, and their champions fought in a spirit of festivity. One or two might have been killed, but then everyone went home until the re-match.

Early in the nineteenth century, the casual tempo of Ama-Zulu life and politics had changed considerably. A greater population meant less and less room for junior members to "hive off" on their own. It meant less grazing land for cattle, and disputes over cattle and land. As the Ama-Zulu began to fight more frequently, so they began to feel the necessity to fight more effectively. At the same time, senior clan heads began to recognize the need for a political structure to insure unity, the maximization of resources and the minimization of internecine conflict.

Shaka addressed himself to both the military and the political problems of Zululand, which he saw as two sides of the same coin. He thought that the centralizing political nucleus should achieve military superiority and demonstrate it to other sectors. That would generally lead to peaceful ac-ceptance of the greater political state, or else the dissidents would be thoroughly crushed.

The era of conflict and warfare in Zululand in the early nineteenth cen-tury brought troops face to face much more often, but the pattern of military encounter still remained that of the long-distance hurling of light umkhonto, or spears. For close fighting, a weapon grasped in the hands is much more damaging—as feudal armies discovered in Europe and Asia and therefore resorted to sword and pike. Shaka, while serving as a young soldier, came up with the solution of devising a heavy short assegai, which was used purely for stabbing rather than throwing. In addition, he dis-carded the loose sandals so as to achieve more speed in closing with the enemy and more dexterity at close quarters. Through experience, Shaka and his fellow youths then discovered the specific techniques of using their shields and assegais to best effect.

Of course, warfare comprises not just the encounter of individual soldiers, but (more importantly) a pattern of tactics and strategy in rela-tionship to the opposing forces taken as a whole. This aspect of war also attracted Shaka's attention, and his outstanding innovation came in the form of izimpi (regiments) deployed so as to allow for a reserve behind the fighting vanguard and for two wings or "horns" capable of encircling the enemy's flanks. Finally (and most importantly), an army has to be trained, disciplined, and organized so that it is a meaningful unit in peace and in war. Shaka created new regiments to include men up to forty years of age. He kept his izimpi on constant exercises and "fatigues," so that the individual soldier was fit and proficient, while the army as a whole synchronized in accordance with the wishes of its commanders.

The Zulu army was more than a fighting force. It was an educational institution for the young, and an instrument for building loyalties that cut across clans and could be considered as national. Promotion came through merit, and not through clan or regional origin. The enforced use of the Zulu branch of the family of Ngoni languages also worked in the direction of national consciousness. Over an area of twelve thousand square miles, citizens came to call themselves Ama-Zulu, and to relegate their clan names to second place. Over a much larger area still, Zulu influence was profoundly felt. Policies such as curbing the excesses of witchcraft diviners (izanusi) and the fact that Zululand became free of internal struggles led to an influx of population from outside its boundaries—a positive contribution to the resources of the Zulu state.

European travelers who have left written accounts of Zululand in Shaka's time were impressed by the cleanliness (as they were in Benin in the fifteenth century) and they were equally struck by the social order, absence of theft, sense of security (just as were the Arabs who traveled in the Western Sudan during its period of imperial greatness). In actual fact, both the cleanliness and the security of life and property were part of Zulu life from long before, and under Shaka what was impressive was the scale on which these things extended, owing to the protective umbrella of the state. The people being impressed were Europeans; and European evidence is the best evidence in that it can scarcely be said to have been pro-African propaganda. One white visitor who saw a march-past of fifteen of Shaka's regiments wrote that "it was a most exciting scene, surprising to us, who could not have imagined that a nation termed 'savages' could be so disciplined and kept in order."

A great deal more could be added concerning Ama-Zulu political institutions and its army. But what is relevant here is to understand why a Shaka was possible in Africa in the nineteenth century, before the coming of colonial rule.

Had Shaka been a slave to some cotton planter in Mississippi or some sugar planter in Jamaica, he might have had an ear or a hand chopped off for being a "recalcitrant nigger," or at best he might have distinguished himself in leading a slave revolt. For the only great men among the *unfree* and the oppressed are those who struggle to *destroy* the oppressor. On a slave plantation, Shaka would not have built a Zulu army and a Zulu state —that much is certain. Nor could any African *build* anything during the colonial period, however much a genius he may have been. As it was,

Shaka was a herdsman and a warrior. As a youth, he tended cattle on the open plains—*free* to develop his own potential and apply it to his environment.

Shaka was able to invest his talents and creative energies in a worthwhile endeavor of construction. He was not concerned with fighting for or against slave traders; he was not concerned with the problem of how to resell goods made in Sweden and France. He was concerned with how to develop the Zulu area within the limits imposed by his people's resources.

It must be recognized that things such as military techniques were responses to real needs, that the work of the individual originates in and is backed by the action of society as a whole, and that whatever was achieved by any one leader must have been bounded by historical circumstances and the level of development, which determine the extent to which an individual can first discover, then augment, and then display his potential.

To substantiate the above points, it can be noted that Shaka was challenged to create the heavy stabbing assegai when he realized that the throwing spear broke when used as a stabbing weapon. More important still, what Shaka came up with depended upon the collective effort of the Ama-Zulu. Shaka could ask that a better assegai be forged, because the Ama-Ngoni had been working iron for a long time, and specialist blacksmiths had arisen within certain clans. It was a tribute to the organizational and agricultural capacity of the society as a whole that it could feed and maintain a standing army of thirty thousand men, re-equip them with iron weapons, and issue each soldier with the full-length Zulu shield made from cattle hide.

Because the scientific basis and experimental preconditions were lacking in Zulu society, Shaka could not have devised a firearm—no matter how much genius he possessed. But, he could get his people to forge better weapons, as explained above; and he found them receptive to better selective breeding practices when he set up special royal herds, because the people already had a vast fund of empirical knowledge about cattle and a love of the cattle-herding profession.

In the politico-military sphere, Shaka was following in the footsteps of his original protector, Dingizwayo, and to some extent in the footsteps of Zwide, who was a rival to both Dingizwayo and Shaka. Dingizwayo opened up trade with the Portuguese at Delagoa Bay in 1797 (mainly in ivory), and he stimulated arts and crafts. His most distinguished innovation was in the army, when he instituted a system of recruiting regiments according to age-grades. Previously, each locality tended to dominate within a given regiment; and, in any event, people were accustomed to fighting side by side with members of their own kraal, locality, and clan. However, when all men in a given age-grade were brought into the same regiment, this emphasized a greater national feeling and also increased Dingizwayo's power vis-à-vis the smaller clan heads.

Dingizwayo was head of the important Ama-Mthethwa clan, and he succeeded in establishing his paramountcy in what later became the southern portion of Zululand. In the north, Zwide of the Ama-Ndwandwe was also engaging in political consolidation. Shaka served in one of the junior age-grade regiments of Dingizwayo, and remained faithful to the latter's centralizing power, until Dingizwayo met his death at the hands of Zwide in 1818. Thereafter, Shaka took up many of the military and political techniques of Dingizwayo and greatly improved them. That is development. It is a matter of building upon what is inherited and advancing slowly, provided that no one comes to "civilize" you.

The regions of Yorubaland, Dahomey, the interlacustrine kingdoms, and Zululand, which have so far been discussed, are examples of leading forces in the political development which was taking place in Africa right up to the eve of colonization. They were not the only leading forces, and even where the states were territorially much smaller, there were observable advances in political organization.

Areas of Africa that were most advanced by the fifteenth century generally maintained their standards, with few exceptions such as Kongo. In North Africa and Ethiopia, for example, feudal structures remained intact, though there was a noticeable lack of continued growth. In the Western Sudan, the Hausa states were heirs to the political and commercial tradition of the great empires after the fall of Songhai in the seventeenth century; and early in the nineteenth century there arose the Islamic Caliphate of Sokoto with its center in Hausaland. The Sokoto empire was one of the largest political units ever established on the African continent, and it suffered from many internal schisms through lack of adequate mechanisms for integrating so vast a territory. Experiments to deal with the problem of unity were continued in the Western Sudan, with Islam as the hoped-for unifying factor. An Islamic theocratic state was established across the Niger bend by Ahmadu Ahmadu in the middle of the nineteenth century, while another was created by Al Haj Omar on the upper Niger. Most outstanding of all was the Mandinga state carved out under the leadership of Samori Toure by the 1880s. Samori Toure was not scholarly like the renowned Uthman dan Fodio and Al Haj Omar, who before him had been creators of Islamic states; but Samori Toure was a military genius and a political innovator, who went further than the others in setting up a political administration where a sense of loyalty could prevail over the above clans, localities, and ethnic groups.

Zimbabwe, too, progressed, with only slight interference from Europeans. Locally, the center of power shifted from Mutapa to Changamire; and eventually in the nineteenth century Nguni groups (fleeing from the power of the Zulu) overran Zimbabwe. So long as the Nguni were warrior bands on the march, they obviously proved destructive; but by the middle of the nineteenth century the Nguni had already spread their own *state-building* techniques to Mozambique and to what is now Southern Rhodesia, and had joined with the local population to establish new and larger kingdoms—infused with a sense of nationality, as was the case in Zululand.

Meanwhile, across vast areas of Central Africa, striking political change was also taking place. Up to the fifteenth century, the level of social organization was low in the area between Kongo and Zimbabwe. Precisely in that area, there arose the group of states known as the Luba-Lunda complex. Their political structures rather than their territorial size made them significant; and their achievements were registered in the face of constantly encroaching slaving activities.

On the large island of Madagascar, the several small states of an earlier epoch had by the late eighteenth century given way to the powerful feudal Merina kingdom. More often than not, Madagascar is ignored in general assessments of the African continent, although (both in the physical and the cultural sense) Africa is writ large on the Malagasy people. They, too, suffered from loss of population through slave exports; but the Merina kingdom did better than most slaving states, because more intensive cultivation of high-yielding swamp rice and the breeding of cattle offset the loss of labor. This situation should serve as a reminder that development *accompanied by* slave trading must not be superficially and illogically *attributed to* the export of the population and the dislocation attendant upon slave raiding. The bases of the political development of the Merina kingdom and of all others (whether or not engaged in slaving) lay in their own environment—in the material resources, human resources, technology, and social relations. So long as any African society could at least maintain its inherited advantages springing from many centuries of evolutionary change, then for so long could the superstructure continue to expand and give further opportunities to whole groups of people, to classes, and to individuals.

At the beginning of this section, attention was drawn to the necessity for reconciling a recognition of African development up to 1885 with an awareness of the losses simultaneously incurred by the continent in that epoch, due to the nature of the contact with capitalist Europe. That issue must also be explicitly alluded to at this point. It is clearly ridiculous to assert that contacts with Europe built or benefited Africa in the pre-colonial period. Nor does it represent reality to suggest (as President Leopold Senghor once did) that the slave trade swept Africa like a bush fire, leaving nothing standing. The truth is that a developing Africa went into slave trading and European commercial relations as into a gale-force wind, which shipwrecked a few societies, set many others off course, and generally slowed down the rate of advance. However, (pursuing the metaphor further) it must be noted that African captains were still making decisions before 1885, though already forces were at work which caused European capitalists to insist on, and succeed in taking over, command.

The Coming of Imperialism and Colonialism

In the centuries before colonial rule, Europe increased its economic capacity by leaps and bounds, while Africa appeared to have been almost static. Africa in the late nineteenth century could still be described as part communal and part feudal, although Western Europe had moved completely from feudalism to capitalism. To elucidate the main thesis of this study, it is necessary to follow not only the development of Europe and the underdevelopment of Africa, but also to understand how those two combined in a single system—that of capitalist imperialism.

The European economy was producing far more goods by making use of their own resources and labor, as well as the resources and labor of the rest of the world. There were many qualitative changes in the European economy, which accompanied and made possible the increase in the quantity of goods. For example, machines and factories rather than land provided the main source of wealth; and labor had long since ceased to be organized on a restricted family basis. The peasantry had been brutally destroyed and the labor of men, women, and children was ruthlessly exploited. Those were the great social evils of the capitalist system, which must not be forgotten; but, on the issue of comparative economics, the relevant fact is that what was a slight difference when the Portuguese sailed to West Africa in 1444 was a huge gap by the time that European robber statesmen sat down in Berlin 440 years later to decide who should steal which parts of Africa. It was that gap which provided both the necessity and the opportunity for Europe to move into the imperialist epoch, and to colonize and further underdevelop Africa.

The growing technological and economic gap between Western Europe and Africa was part of the trend within capitalism to concentrate or polarize wealth and poverty at two opposite extremes.

Inside Western Europe itself, some nations grew rich at the expense of others. Britain, France, and Germany were the most prosperous nations. Poverty prevailed in Ireland, Portugal, Spain, and southern Italy. Inside the British, French, and German economies, the polarization of wealth was between the capitalists on the one hand and the workers and a few peasants on the other. The big capitalists got bigger and the little ones were eliminated. In many important fields, such as iron and steel manufacture, textiles, and particularly banking, it was noticeable that two or three firms monopolized most of the business. The banks were also in a commanding position within the economy as a whole, providing capital to the big monopoly industrial firms.

European monopoly firms operated by constantly fighting to gain control over raw materials, markets, and means of communications. They also fought to be the first to invest in new profitable undertakings related to their line of business—whether it be inside or outside their countries. Indeed, after the scope for expansion became limited inside their national economies, their main attention was turned to those countries whose economies were less developed and who would therefore offer little or no opposition to the penetration of foreign capitalism. That penetration of foreign capitalism on a world-wide scale from the late nineteenth century onwards is what we call "imperialism."

Imperialism meant capitalist expansion. It meant that European (and North American and Japanese) capitalists were forced by the internal logic of their competitive system to seek abroad in less developed countries opportunities to control raw material supplies, to find markets, and to find profitable fields of investment. The centuries of trade with Africa contributed greatly to that state of affairs where European capitalists were faced with the *necessity* to expand in a big way outside their national economies.

There were certain areas of Africa in which European investment was meant to get immediate superprofits. The mines of South Africa, the loans to North African governments, and the building of the Suez Canal also insured the greater profitability of European investment in and trade with India. However, Africa's greatest value to Europe at the beginning of the imperialist era was as a source of raw materials such as palm products, groundnuts, cotton, and rubber. The need for those materials arose out of Europe's expanded economic capacity, its new and larger machines, and its increasing wage-earning population in towns. All of those things had developed over the previous four centuries; and again it needs to be repeated that one of the important factors in that process was the unequal trade with Africa.

Imperialism is essentially an economic phenomenon, and it does not necessarily lead to direct political control or colonization. However, Africa was the victim of colonization. In the period of the notorious "Scramble for Africa," Europeans made a grab for whatever they thought spelled profits in Africa, and they even consciously acquired many areas not for immediate exploitation but with an eye to the future. Each European nation that had these short-term and long-term economic interests ran up its own flag in different parts of Africa and established colonial rule. The gap that had arisen during the period of pre-colonial trade gave Europe the *power* to impose political domination on Africa.

Pre-colonial trade in slaves, ivory, gold, and other things was conducted from the coasts of Africa. On the coasts, European ships could dominate the scene, and if necessary forts could be built. Before the nineteenth century, Europe was incapable of penetrating the African continent, because the balance of force at their disposal was inadequate. But the same technological changes which created the need to penetrate Africa also created the power to conquer Africa. The firearms of the imperialist epoch marked a qualitative leap forward. Breech-loading rifles and machine guns were a far cry from the smooth-bored muzzle loaders and flintlocks of the previous era. European imperialists in Africa boasted that what counted was the fact that they had the Maxim machine gun and Africans did not.

Curiously, Europeans often derived the moral justification for imperialism and colonialism from features of the international trade as conducted up to the eve of colonial rule in Africa. The British were the chief spokesmen for the view that the desire to colonize was largely based on their good intentions in wanting to put a stop to the slave trade. True enough, the British in the nineteenth century were as opposed to slave trading as they were once in favor of it. Many changes inside Britain had transformed the seventeenth-century necessity for slaves into the nineteenth-century necessity to clear the remnants of slaving from Africa so as to organize the local exploitation of land and labor. Therefore, slaving was rejected in so far as it had become a fetter on further capitalist development; and it was particularly true of East Africa, where Arab slaving persisted until late in the nineteenth century. The British took special self-righteous delight in putting an end to Arab slave trading, and in deposing rulers on the grounds that they were slave traders. However, in those very years, the British were crushing political leaders in Nigeria, like Jaja and Nana, who had by then ceased the export of slaves, and were concentrating instead on products like palm oil and rubber. Similarly, the Germans in

East Africa made a pretense of being most opposed to rulers like Bushiri who were engaged in slave trading, but the Germans were equally hostile to African rulers with little interest in slaving. The common factor underlying the overthrow of African rulers in East, West, Central, North, and South Africa was that they stood in the way of Europe's imperial needs. It was the only factor that mattered, with anti-slaving sentiments being at best superfluous and at worst calculated hypocrisy.

King Leopold II of Belgium also used the anti-slavery excuse to introduce into Congo forced labor and modern slavery. Besides, all Europeans had derived ideas of racial and cultural superiority between the fifteenth and nineteenth centuries, while engaged in genocide and the enslavement of non-white peoples. Even Portugal, an impoverished and backward European nation in the imperialist era, could still presume that it had a destiny to civilize the natives in Africa!

There is a curious interpretation of the Scramble and African partition which virtually amounts to saying that colonialism came about because of Africa's needs rather than those of Europe. Africa, they say, required European colonization if it were to advance beyond the stage it had reached in the late nineteenth century. Clearly, they do not appreciate that such a line of reasoning was suggesting that Africa would develop if it were given bigger doses of the European concoction that had already started its underdevelopment—that it would develop if it lost the last remnants of its freedom of choice, which had clearly been seriously undermined by the pre-colonial trade—that it would develop if its economy became more integrated with Europe's on terms that were entirely dictated by Europe. Those implications and their fallacies would be plain to anyone who tries to understand the development process before making pronouncements on any particular epoch of human development in Africa.

Throughout the fourteenth century, African rulers were displaying great initiative in pursuit of the broadest forms of cultural contact with Europe. In the case of West Africa, that meant seeking substitutes for trade in slaves. Dahomey, one of the most embroiled in slave trading, was among those states that used many of the last years of its independence to find a healthy basis for cultural exchange with Europeans.

In 1850, the reigning Dahomean king, Gezo, proclaimed an edict whereby all young oil palms were to be freed from parasites surrounding them, and severe penalties were to be imposed for cutting palm trees. Gezo, who ruled from 1818 to 1857, was a reformer, and he made sincere efforts to meet criticisms of his policies by groups such as missionaries and anti-slavery campaigners; but it soon became clear that Europeans were not bent on seeing Dahomey re-emerge as a strong state, but were rather creating excuses and the subjective conditions to justify their proposed colonization of the people of Dahomey. Under those circumstances, the last Dahomean monarch, Glele, fell back on his capital at Abomey, and pursued the policies which he considered most consistent with the dignity and independence of Dahomey. Glele raided Abeokuta, which contained converts who were already "British protected persons"; he told the French to get the hell out of Porto-Novo; and he generally resisted until defeated militarily by the French in 1889.

African groups who had little or nothing to do with slave exports also intensified their efforts to integrate into a wider world in the nineteenth century. Gungunhana, the Nguni ruler of Gaza in Mozambique, asked for a Swiss missionary doctor and maintained him at his court for several years until the Portuguese conquered his kingdom in 1895. After the Portuguese imposed colonial rule, it was a long time before Africans saw another doctor!

It is particularly instructive to turn to the example of Egypt under Mohammed Ali, who ruled from 1805 to 1849. Capitalist Europe had left feudal North Africa behind over the course of the seventeenth and eighteenth centuries. Mohammed Ali was aware of that, and consciously aimed at catching up with Europe. He instituted a series of reforms, the most important of which were of an economic nature. Egypt grew and manufactured its own cotton, and it made glass, paper, and other industrial goods. Egypt was not to be used as a dumping ground for European goods which would undermine local industry, so that protective tariff walls were set up around Egypt's "infant industries." That did not mean that Egypt became isolated from the rest of the world. On the contrary, Mohammed Ali borrowed experts from Europe, and he increased Egypt's foreign trade.

The ideals of Mohammed Ali could be related in the idiom of modern social science as being the creation of a viable, self-propelling economy to provide the basis for national independence. Such ideals were diametrically opposed to the needs of European capitalism. British and French industrialists wanted to see Egypt not as a textile manufacturer but as a producer of raw cotton for export, and an importer of European manufactures. European financiers wanted Egypt to be a source of investment, and in the second half of the eighteenth century they turned the sultan of Egypt into an international beggar, who mortgaged the whole of Egypt to international monopoly financiers. Finally, European statesmen wanted Egyptian soil to serve as a base for exploiting India and Arabia. Therefore, the Suez Canal was dug out of Egyptian soil by Egyptians, but it was owned by Britain and France, who then extended political domination over Egypt and Sudan.

Education is undeniably one of the facets of European life which had grown most appreciably during the capitalist epoch. Through education and extensive use of the written word, Europeans were in a position to pass on to the others the scientific principles of the material world which they had discovered, as well as a body of varied philosophical reflections on man and society. Africans were quick to appreciate advantages deriving from a literate education. In Madagascar, the Merina kingdom did a great deal to sponsor reading and writing. They used their own language and an Arabic script, and they welcomed the aid of European missionaries. That conscious borrowing from all relevant sources was only possible when they had the freedom to choose. Colonization, far from springing from Malagasy needs, actually erected a barrier to the attainment of the "modernization" initiated by the Merina kings in the 1860s and 1870s. A similar example can be found in the history of Tunisia before the ax of partition fell.

In many parts of the world, capitalism in its imperialist form accepted that some measure of political sovereignty should be left in the hands of the local population. This was so in Eastern Europe, in Latin America, and to a more limited extent in China. However, European capitalists came to the decision that Africa should be directly colonized. There is evidence to suggest that such a course of action was not entirely planned. Britain and France up to the 1850s and 1860s would have preferred to divide Africa into informal "spheres of influence." That means that there would have been a gentlemen's agreement that (say) Nigeria would be exploited by the British merchants while Senegal would be exploited by Frenchmen. At the same time both Englishmen and Frenchmen would trade in a minor way in each other's informal empire. But, firstly, there was disagreement over who should suck which pieces of Africa (especially since Germany wanted to join the grabbing); and, secondly, the moment that one European power declared an area of Africa as a protectorate or a colony, it put up tariffs against European traders of other nationalities, and in turn forced their rivals to have colonies and discriminatory tariffs. One thing led to another, and soon six European capitalist nations were falling over each other to establish direct political rule over particular sections of Africa. Make no mistake about it, gentlemen like Carl Peters, Livingstone, Stanley, Harry Johnston, De Brazza, General Gordon, and their masters in Europe were literally scrambling for Africa. They barely avoided a major military conflagration.

In addition to the factors that caused the chain reaction of the Scramble as described above, Europeans were also racially motivated to seek political domination over Africa. The nineteenth century was one in which white racism was most violently and openly expressed in capitalist societies, with the U.S.A. as a focal point, and with Britain taking the lead among the Western European capitalist nations. Britain accepted granting dominion status to its old colonies of white settlers in Canada, Australia, and New Zealand; but it withdrew self-government from the West Indies when the white planters were ousted from the legislative assemblies by black (or brown) people. As far as Africa is concerned, Englishmen violently opposed black self-government such as the Fante Confederation on the Gold Coast in the 1860s. They also tried to erode the authority of black Creoles in Sierra Leone. In 1874, when Fourah Bay College sought and obtained affiliation with Durham University, the *Times* newspaper declared that Durham should next affiliate with the London Zoo! Pervasive and vicious racism was present in imperialism as a variant independent of the economic rationality that initially gave birth to racism. It was economics that determined that Europe should invest in Africa and control the continent's raw materials and labor. It was racism which confirmed the decision that the form of control should be direct colonial rule.

Africans everywhere fought against alien political rule, and had to be subdued by superior force. But a sizable minority did insist that their trade connections with Europe should remain unbroken, for that was a measure of the extent to which they were already dependent on Europe. The most dramatic illustration of that dependence was the determination with which some Africans fought the end of the European slave trade.

For most European capitalist states, the enslavement of Africans had served its purpose by the middle of the nineteenth century; but for those Africans who dealt in captives the abrupt termination of the trade at any given point was a crisis of the greatest magnitude. In many areas, major social changes had taken place to bring the particular regions effectively into the service of the European slave trade—one of the most significant being the rise of "domestic slavery" and various forms of class and caste subjugation. African rulers and traders who found their social existence threatened by the earliest legal edicts such as the 1807 British act against the trade in slaves found ways of making contact with Europeans who still wanted slaves.

In sub-Saharan Africa and especially in West Africa, the export of slaves declined most rapidly where Europeans were prepared to buy other commodities. As soon as inhabitants of any region found that they had a product which Europeans were accepting in place of the former slave trade, those inhabitants put tremendous effort into organizing the alternatives: namely, ivory, rubber, palm products, groundnuts. Once more, those efforts demonstrated the determination of a small but decisive proportion of Africans. It was a determination based on the desire to obtain European trade goods, many of which had ceased to be mere curiosities or luxuries, and were regarded instead as necessities.

The first four centuries of Afro-European trade in a very real sense represent the roots of African underdevelopment. Colonialism flourished rapidly from a European viewpoint, because several of its features were already rooted in Africa in the preceding period. One of the most decisive features of the colonial system was the presence of Africans serving as economic, political, and cultural agents of the European colonialists. Those agents, or "compradors," were already serving European interests in the pre-colonial period. The impact of trade with Europe had reduced many African rulers to the status of middlemen for European trade; it had raised ordinary Africans to that same middleman commercial role; and it had created a new trading group of mixed blood—the children of European or Arab fathers. Those types can all be referred to as "compradors," and they played a key role in extending European activity from the coast into the hinterland, as soon as Europeans thought of taking over political power. One outstanding example of the above is the way that the French colonialists used Africans and mulattos on the Senegalese coast as agents for the spread of French control for thousands of miles into areas now covered by Senegal, Mali, Chad, Upper Volta, and Niger. Those particular blacks and mulattos were living in the trading ports of Gorée, Dakar, St. Louis, and Rufisque; and they had had long-standing links with Atlantic trade.

Africans conducting trade on behalf of Europeans were not merely commercial agents, but also cultural agents, since inevitably they were heavily influenced by European thought and values. The search for European education began in Africa before the colonial period. Coastal rulers and traders recognized the necessity to penetrate more deeply into the way of life of the white man who came across the sea. The mulatto sons of white traders and the sons of African rulers were the ones who made the greatest effort to learn the white man's ways. This helped them to conduct business more efficiently. One Sierra Leone ruler in the eighteenth century explained that he wished "to learn book to be rogue as good as white man"; and there were many others who saw the practical advantages of literacy. However, the educational process also meant imbibing values which led to further African subjugation. One West African educated in this early period wrote a Ph.D. thesis in Latin justifying slavery. That was not surprising. The Reverend Thomas Thompson was the first European educator on the Gold Coast, and he wrote in 1778 a pamphlet entitled, *The African Trade for Negro Slaves Shown to be Consistent with the Principles of Humanity and the Laws of Revealed Religion.*

One of the most striking features of nineteenth-century West African history is the manner in which Africans returned from slavery under European masters and helped in the establishment of colonial rule. This was especially true of Africans who returned from the West Indies and North America to Sierra Leone or who were released from slave ships and landed in Sierra Leone. To a lesser extent, it also applied to Africans who were once in Brazil. Such individuals had assimilated capitalist values, and like most European missionaries, promoted the kinds of activity that went along with colonial rule. In a rather different context, it can be argued that the Arabs of Zanzibar and the East African coast were also transformed into agents of European colonialism. At first, they resisted because European colonialism affected their own expansionist ambitions on the East African mainland, but they soon came to an arrangement which gave Europeans the ultimate powers. The Europeans reduced the small Arab clique into political and economic instruments of imperialism.

European superiority over the Arabs in East and North Africa and in the Middle East demonstrates conclusively that modern imperialism is inseparable from capitalism, and underlines the role of slavery in the context of capitalism. The Arabs had acquired Africans as slaves for centuries, but they were exploited in a feudal context. African slaves in Arab hands became domestics, soldiers, and agricultural serfs. Whatever surplus they produced was not for reinvestment and multiplication of capital, as in the West Indian or North American slave systems but for consumption by the feudal elite. Indeed, slaves were often maintained more for social prestige than for economic benefit.

The major exceptions to that rule were nineteenth-century Zanzibar and Egypt under Mohammed Ali. In both those instances, African labor was being exploited to produce profit on a plantation basis; and this may also have applied to date-palm production in Arabia. But, Europe had already been exploiting African labor to maximize surplus for three centuries previously, and the contribution which the plantation system made to the European capitalist development was so great that Western Europe in the nineteenth century had engulfed the lesser exploitation of Zanzibar and Arabia, and it secured a firm grasp on Egypt's economy after the death of Mohammed Ali in 1849. In other words, the cloves, cotton, and dates produced in Zanzibar, Egypt, and Arabia, respectively, previous to colonization were already going to strengthen European trade and production. Eventually, it was no problem for the capitalist slave traders of Europe to extend political domination over the feudalist Arab slave traders and to use the latter as agents of colonialism in East Africa.

Returning to the question of indigenous African agents of European colonial rule in Africa, it should be recognized that Europeans recruited Africans to serve in the armies that actually conquered Africa in the bloody period from the 1880s through the First World War started by Europeans in 1914. It is a widespread characteristic of colonialism to find agents of repression from among the colonial victims themselves. Yet, without the previous centuries of trade between Africa and Europe, it would have been impossible for Europeans to have so easily recruited the askaris, porters, and others, who made their colonial conquest possible.

African residents of the Senegalese ports already referred to were the ones who were put in French army uniform and fought to establish French rule in the interior and other parts of the coast such as Dahomey. When the British defeated Asante in 1874, they had in their forces African troops from the coastal towns around the Gold Coast forts. Those Africans had been in contact with Europeans for so long that from the seventeenth century they identified themselves as "Dutch," "Danish," or "English," depending upon whose fort gave them employment. They had fought battles for one European nation against another, and by the late nineteenth century it was an easy matter to get them to fight against fellow Africans on behalf of the conquering colonial power of Britain.

In the Portuguese territories, the origins of the black colonial police and army also went back into the "pre-colonial" trade period. Around the forts of Luanda and Benguela in Angola and Lourenço Marques and Beira in Mozambique, there grew up communities of Africans, mulattos, and even Indians who helped "pacify" large areas for the Portuguese after the Berlin Conference. Traders in Mozambique and in the rest of East, West, and Central Africa who had experience with Europeans previous to colonialism were the ones to provide porters to carry the heavy machine guns, cannons, and the support equipment; they were the ones who provided the would-be European colonialist with the information and military intelligence that facilitated conquest; and they were the interpreters who were the voice of the Europeans on African soil.

Of course, it is true that many Africans who had little or nothing to do with pre-colonial trade also allied themselves with European newcomers. In that respect, the gap in levels of political organization between Europe and Africa was very crucial. The development of political unity in the form of large states was proceeding steadily in Africa. But even so, at the time of the Berlin Conference, Africa was still a continent of a large number of socio-political groupings who had not arrived at a common purpose. Therefore, it was easy for the European intruder to play the classic game of divide and conquer. In that way, certain Africans became *unwitting* allies of Europe.

Many African rulers sought a European "alliance" to deal with their own African neighbor, with whom they were in conflict. Few of those rulers appreciated the implications of their actions. They could not know that Europeans had come to stay permanently; they could not know that Europeans were out to conquer not some but all Africans. This partial and inadequate view of the world was itself a testimony of African underdevelopment *relative* to Europe, which in the nineteenth century was self-confidently seeking dominion in every part of the globe.

Political divisions in Africa were no evidence of innate inferiority or backwardness. That was the state in which the continent then found itself —a point along a long road that others had traversed and along which Africa was moving. Commercial impact of Europe slowed down the process of political amalgamation and expansion, in contrast to the way trade with Africa strengthened Europe's nation-states. When European capitalism took the form of imperialism and started to subjugate Africa politically, the *normal* political conflicts of the pre-capitalist African situation were transformed into *weakness* which allowed the Europeans to set up their colonial domination.

Altogether, it is very clear that to understand the coming of colonialism into Africa, one has to consider the previous historical evolution of both Africa and Europe and in particular one has to consider ways in which their trade contacts influenced the two continents mutually, so that what was called "pre-colonial" trade proved to be a preparatory stage for the era of colonial rule.

It is widely accepted that Africa was colonized because of its weakness. The concept of weakness should be understood to embrace military weakness and inadequate economic capacity, as well as certain political weaknesses: namely, the incompleteness of the establishment of nation-states, which left the continent divided, and the low level of consciousness concerning the world at large, which had already been transformed into a single system by the expansion of capitalist relations.

Brief Guide to Reading

The section of this chapter dealing with African society is a continuation of Chapter 2; and general books cited there are also relevant to this context. More African writers are involved in this recent pre-colonial period, which is of course one aspect of a national struggle. There are also more and better monographs on given areas and subjects. But, the coming of imperialism has not yet been seriously pursued from an African viewpoint, and there is a marked absence of theory linking together the numerous facts that are now well established about events taking place in Africa between 1500 and 1885.

J. B. WEBSTER and A. A. BOAHEN, *History of West Africa; the Revolutionary Years—1815 to Independence.* New York: Praeger, 1967.

BASIL DAVIDSON with J. E. MHINA, *History of East and Central Africa to the Late Nineteenth Century.* New York: Doubleday Anchor Book A 677.

These two should be added to the list of general texts which provide regional surveys over a long period of time. They have the advantage of being coherent interpretations and not just collected essays.

WALTER RODNEY, *West Africa and the Atlantic Slave Trade.* Nairobi: Published for the Historical Association of Tanzania by the East African Publishing House, 1969.

E. ALPERS, *The East African Slave Trade.*

I. A. AKINJOGBIN, *Dahomey and Its Neighbours.* Cambridge: Cambridge University Press, 1967.

The first two are short accounts of the impact of slave exports on the African regions concerned. The third is a detailed account by a Nigerian scholar of Dahomey's involvement with Europeans.

JACOB U. EGHAREVBA, *A Short History of Benin.* Ibadan: Ibadan University Press, 1968.

B. A. OGOT, *History of the Southern Luo.* Nairobi: East Africa Publishing House, 1967.

ISARIA KIMAMBO, *A Political History of the Pare of Tanzania.* New York: International Publications, 1971.

JAN VANSINA, *Kingdoms of the Savanna.* Madison: University of Wisconsin Press, 1966.

The first three are good examples of scholarship by Africans concerning historical developments starting before contact with Europe. They are characterized by the use of African oral traditions as a basis for interpretation. The fourth (by a European) was a pioneering work which drew heavily on oral traditions in reconstructing Central African history.

J. ADE AJAYI, *Christian Missions in Nigeria, 1845–1891.* New York: International Publications, 1971.

E. A. AYANDELE, *The Missionary Impact on Modern Nigeria.* New York: Humanities Press, 1967.

One aspect of the imperialist epoch that has been probed by African historians (and many non-Africans) is that of the Christian missionaries, as evidenced by the above works.

CHAPTER
V

*Africa's Contribution to the Capitalist
Development of Europe—The Colonial Period*

· Expatriation of African Surplus under Colonialism
· The Strengthening of the Technological and Military Aspects of
Capitalism

THE COLONIES HAVE BEEN CREATED FOR THE METROPOLE BY THE METRO-
pole.

—FRENCH SAYING

Sales operations in the United States and management of the fourteen
(Unilever) plants are directed from Lever House on New York's fashionable Park Avenue. You look at this tall, striking, glass-and-steel structure
and you wonder how many hours of underpaid black labour and how
many thousands of tons of underpriced palm oil and peanuts and cocoa
it cost to build it.

—W. ALPHEUS HUNTON

Expatriation of African Surplus under Colonialism

Capital and African Wage Labor

Colonial Africa fell within that part of the international capitalist economy
from which surplus was drawn to feed the metropolitan sector. As seen
earlier, exploitation of land and labor is essential for human social advance, but only on the assumption that the product is made available
within the area where the exploitation takes place. Colonialism was not
merely a system of exploitation, but one whose essential purpose was to
repatriate the profits to the so-called mother country. From an African
viewpoint, that amounted to consistent expatriation of surplus produced
by African labor out of African resources. It meant the development of
Europe as part of the same dialectical process in which Africa was underdeveloped.

By any standards, labor was cheap in Africa, and the amount of surplus
extracted from the African laborer was great. The employer under colonialism paid an extremely small wage—a wage usually insufficient to keep
the worker physically alive—and, therefore, he had to grow food to
survive. This applied in particular to farm labor of the plantation type,
to work in mines, and to certain forms of urban employment. At the time
of the imposition of European colonial rule, Africans were able to gain a
livelihood from the land. Many retained some contact with the land in the
years ahead, and they worked away from their *shambas* in order to pay
taxes or because they were forced to do so. After feudalism in Europe had
ended, the worker had absolutely no means of sustenance other than

149

through the sale of his labor to capitalists. Therefore, to some extent the employer was responsible for insuring the physical survival of the worker by giving him a "living wage." In Africa, this was not the case. Europeans offered the lowest possible wages and relied on legislation backed by force to do the rest.

There were several reasons why the African worker was more crudely exploited than his European counterpart in the present century. Firstly, the alien colonial state had a monopoly of political power, after crushing all opposition by superior armed force. Secondly, the African working class was small, very dispersed, and very unstable owing to migratory practices. Thirdly, while capitalism was willing to exploit all workers everywhere, European capitalists in Africa had additional racial justifications for dealing unjustly with the African worker. The racist theory that the black man was inferior led to the conclusion that he deserved lower wages; and interestingly enough, the light-skinned Arab and Berber populations of North Africa were treated as "blacks" by the white racist French. The combination of the above factors in turn made it extremely difficult for African workers to organize themselves. It is only the organization and resoluteness of the working class which protects it from the natural tendency of the capitalist to exploit to the utmost. That is why in all colonial territories, when African workers realized the necessity for trade union solidarity, numerous obstacles were placed in their paths by the colonial regimes.

Wages paid to workers in Europe and North America were much higher than wages paid to African workers in comparable categories. The Nigerian coal miner at Enugu earned one shilling per day for working underground and nine pence per day for jobs on the surface. Such a miserable wage would be beyond the comprehension of a Scottish or German coal miner, who could virtually earn in an hour what the Enugu miner was paid for a six-day week. The same disparity existed with port workers. The records of the large American shipping company, Farrell Lines, show that in 1955, of the total amount spent on loading and discharging cargo moving between Africa and America, five-sixths went to American workers and one-sixth to Africans. Yet, it was the same amount of cargo loaded and unloaded at both ends. The wages paid to the American stevedore and the European coal miners were still such as to insure that the capitalists made a profit. The point here is merely to illustrate how much greater was the rate of exploitation of African workers.

When discrepancies such as the above were pointed out during the colonial period and subsequently, those who justified colonialism were quick to reply that the standard and cost of living was higher in capitalist countries. The fact is that the higher standard was made possible by the exploitation of colonies, and there was no justification for keeping African living standards so depressed in an age where better was possible and in a situation where a higher standard was possible because of the work output of Africans themselves. The kind of living standard supportable by African labor within the continent is readily illustrated by the salaries and the life-style of the whites inside Africa.

Colonial governments discriminated against the employment of Africans in senior categories; and, whenever it happened that a white and a black filled the same post, the white man was sure to be paid considerably more. This was true at all levels, ranging from civil service posts to mine workers. African salaried workers in the British colonies of Gold Coast and Nigeria were better off than their brothers in many other parts of the continent, but they were restricted to the "junior staff" level in the civil service. In the period before the last world war, European civil servants in the Gold Coast received an average of 40 pounds per month, with quarters and other privileges. Africans got an average salary of 4 pounds. There were instances where one European in an establishment earned as much as his twenty-five African assistants put together. Outside the civil service, Africans obtained work in building projects, in mines, and as domestics— all low-paying jobs. It was exploitation without responsibility and without redress. In 1934, forty-one Africans were killed in a gold mine disaster in the Gold Coast, and the capitalist company offered only 3 pounds to the dependents of each of these men as compensation.

Where European settlers were found in considerable numbers, the wage differential was readily perceived. In North Africa, the wages of Moroccans and Algerians were from 16 percent to 25 percent those of Europeans. In East Africa, the position was much worse, notably in Kenya and Tanganyika. A comparison with white settler earnings and standards brings out by sharp contrast how incredibly low African wages were. While Lord Delamere controlled 100,000 acres of Kenya's land, the Kenyan had to carry a *kipande* pass in his own country to beg for a wage of 15 or 20 shillings per month. The absolute limit of brutal exploitation was found in the southern parts of the continent; and in Southern Rhodesia, for example, agricultural laborers rarely received more than 15 shillings per month. Workers in mines got a little more if they were semi-skilled, but they also had more intolerable working conditions. Unskilled laborers in the mines of Northern Rhodesia often got as little as 7 shillings per month. A truck driver on the famous copper belt was in a semi-skilled grade. In one mine, Europeans performed that job for 30 pounds per month, while in another, Africans did it for 3 pounds per month.

In all colonial territories, wages were reduced during the period of crisis which shook the capitalist world during the 1930s, and they were not restored or increased until after the last capitalist world war. In Southern Rhodesia in 1949, Africans employed in municipal areas were awarded minimum wages from 35 to 75 shillings per month. That was a considerable improvement over previous years, but white workers (on the job for 8 hours per day compared to the Africans' 10 or 14 hours) received a minimum wage of 20 shillings *per day* plus free quarters and other benefits.

The Rhodesians offered a miniature version of South Africa's apartheid system, which oppressed the largest industrial working class on the continent. In the Union of South Africa, African laborers worked deep underground, under inhuman conditions which would not have been tolerated by miners in Europe. Consequently, black South African workers recovered gold from deposits which elsewhere would be regarded as noncommercial. And yet it is the white section of the working class which received whatever benefits were available in terms of wages and salaries. Officials have admitted that the mining companies could pay whites higher than miners in any other part of the world because of the superprofits made by paying black workers a mere pittance.*

In the final analysis, the shareholders of the mining companies were the ones who benefited most of all. They remained in Europe and North America and collected fabulous dividends every year from the gold, diamonds, manganese, uranium, etc., which were brought out of the South African subsoil by African labor. For years, the capitalist press itself praised Southern Africa as an investment outlet returning superprofits on capital invested. From the very beginning of the Scramble for Africa, huge fortunes were made from gold and diamonds in Southern Africa by people like Cecil Rhodes. In the present century, both the investment and the outflow of surplus have increased. Investment was mainly concentrated in mining and finance where the profits were greatest. In the mid-1950s, British investments in South Africa were estimated at 860 million pounds and yielded a stable profit of 15 percent, or 129 million pounds every year. Most mining companies had returns well above that average. De Beers Consolidated Mines made a profit that was both phenomenal and consistently high—between $26 million and $29 million throughout the 1950s.

The complex of Southern African mining concerns operated not just in South Africa itself, but also in South-West Africa, Angola, Mozambique,

---

* As is well known, those conditions still operate. However, this chapter presents matters in the past tense to picture the colonial epoch.

Northern Rhodesia, Southern Rhodesia, and the Congo. Congo was consistently a source of immense wealth for Europe, because from the time of colonization until 1906, King Leopold II of Belgium made at least $20 million from rubber and ivory. The period of mineral exploitation started quite early, and then gained momentum after political control passed from King Leopold to the Belgium state in 1908. Total foreign capital inflow into the Congo between 1887 and 1953 was estimated by the Belgians to have been 5,700 million pounds. The value of the outflow in the same period was said to have been 4,300 million pounds, exclusive of profits retained within the Congo. As was true everywhere else on the continent, the expatriation of surplus from Congo increased as the colonial period wore on. In the five years preceding independence the net outflow of capital from Congo to Belgium reached massive proportions. Most of the expatriation of surplus was handled by a major European finance monopoly, the *Société Générale*. The *Société Générale* had as its most important subsidiary the *Union Minière de Haute-Katanga,* which has monopolized Congolese copper production since 1889 (when it was known as the *Compagnie de Katanga*) : *Union Minière* has been known to make a profit of 27 million pounds in a single year.

It is no wonder that of the total wealth produced in Congo in any given year during the colonial period, more than one-third went out in the form of profits for big business and salaries for their expatriate staffs. But the comparable figure for Northern Rhodesia under the British was one-half. In Katanga, *Union Minière* at least had a reputation for leaving some of the profits behind in the form of things like housing and maternity services for African workers. The Rhodesian Copper Belt Companies expatriated profits without compunction.

It should not be forgotten that outside Southern Africa there were also significant mining operations during the colonial period. In North Africa, foreign capital exploited natural resources of phosphates, oil, lead, zinc, manganese, and iron ore. In Guinea, Sierra Leone, and Liberia, there were important workings of gold, diamonds, iron ore, and bauxite. To all that should be added the tin of Nigeria, the gold and manganese of Ghana, the gold and diamonds of Tanganyika, and the copper of Uganda and Congo Brazzaville. In each case, an understanding of the situation must begin with an inquiry into the degree of exploitation of African resources and labor, and then must proceed to follow the surplus to its destination outside Africa—into the bank accounts of the capitalists who control the majority shares in the huge multinational mining combines.

The African working class produced a less spectacular surplus for export with regard to companies engaged in agriculture. Agricultural plantations were widespread in North, East, and South Africa; and they also appeared in West Africa to a lesser extent. Their profits depended on the incredibly low wages and harsh working conditions imposed on African agricultural laborers and on the fact that they invested very little capital in obtaining the land, which was robbed wholesale from Africans by colonial powers and then sold to whites at nominal prices. For instance, after the Kenya highlands had been declared "Crown Land," the British handed over to Lord Delamere 100,000 acres of the best land at a cost of a penny per acre. Lord Francis Scott purchased 350,000 acres, the East African Estates Ltd. got another 350,000 acres, and the East African Syndicate took 100,000 acres adjoining Lord Delamere's estate—all at giveaway prices. Needless to say, such plantations made huge profits, even if the rate was lower than in a South African gold mine or an Angolan diamond mine.

During the colonial era, Liberia was supposedly independent; but to all intents and purposes, it was a colony of the U.S.A. In 1926, the Firestone Rubber Company of the U.S.A. was able to acquire one million acres of forest land in Liberia at a cost of 6 cents per acre and 1 percent of the value of the exported rubber. Because of the demand for and the strategic importance of rubber, Firestone's profits from Liberia's land and labor carried them to 25th position among the giant companies of the U.S.A.

European Trading Companies versus the African Peasant

So far, this section has been dealing with that part of the surplus produced by African wage earners in mines and plantations. But the African working class under colonialism was extremely small and the vast majority of Africans engaged in the colonial money economy were independent peasants. How then can it be said that these self-employed peasants were contributing to the expatriation of African surplus? Apologists for colonialism argue that it was a positive benefit for such farmers to have been given the opportunity to create surplus by growing or collecting produce such as cocoa, coffee, palm oil. It is essential that this misrepresentation be clarified.

A peasant growing a cash crop or collecting produce had his labor exploited by a long chain of individuals, starting with local businessmen. Sometimes, those local businessmen were Europeans. Very rarely were they Africans, and more usually they were a minority group brought in from outside and serving as intermediaries between the white colonialists and the exploited African peasant. In West Africa, the Lebanese and Syrians played this role; while in East Africa the Indians rose to this position. Arabs were also in the middleman category in Zanzibar and a few other places on the East African coast.

Cash-crop peasants never had any capital of their own. They existed from one crop to another, depending on good harvests and good prices. Any bad harvest or fall of prices caused the peasants to borrow in order to find money to pay taxes and buy certain necessities. As security, they mortgaged their future crops to moneylenders in the middleman category. Non-payment of debts could and did lead to their farms' being taken away by the moneylenders. The rate of interest on the loans was always fantastically high, amounting to what is known as "usury." In East Africa, things were so bad that even the British colonial government had to step in and enact a "Native Credit Ordinance" to protect Africans from Asian businessmen.

However, in spite of some minor clashes between the colonialists and the middlemen, the two were part and parcel of the same apparatus of exploitation. On the whole, the Lebanese and Indians did the smaller jobs which Europeans could not be bothered with. They owned things such as cotton gins which separated the seed from the lint; while of course Europeans concentrated on the cotton mills in Europe. The middlemen also went out to the villages, while Europeans liked to stay in towns. In the villages, the Indians and Lebanese took over virtually all buying and selling, channeling most of the profits back to Europeans in the towns and those overseas.

The share of profits which went to middlemen was insignificant in comparison to those profits reaped by big European business interests and by the European governments themselves. The capitalist institution which came into most direct contact with African peasants was the colonial trading company: that is to say, a company specializing in moving goods to and from the colonies. The most notorious were the French concerns, *Compagnie Française d'Afrique Occidentale* (CFAO) and *Société Commerciale Ouest Africaine* (SCOA), and the British-controlled United Africa Company (UAC). These were responsible for expatriating a great proportion of Africa's wealth produced by peasant toil.

Several of the colonial trading companies already had African blood on their hands from participation in the slave trade. Thus, after French merchants in Bordeaux made fortunes from the European slave trade, they transferred that capital to the trade in groundnuts from Senegal and Gambia in the middle of the nineteenth century. The firms concerned continued to operate in the colonial period, although they changed hands and there were a lot of mergers. In Senegal, Mauritania, and Mali, the names of Maurel & Prom, Maurel Brothers, Buhan & Teyssere, Delmas &

Clastre, were all well known. Several of them were eventually incorporated into SCOA, which was dominated by a consortium of French and Swiss financiers. A parallel process in the French port of Marseilles led to the transfer of slave-trade capital into direct trade between Africa and France. After the end of the First World War, most of the small Marseilles firms were absorbed into the massive CFAO, which imported into French West Africa whatever European goods the market would take, and exported in turn the agricultural produce that was largely the consequence of peasant labor. CFAO also had British and Dutch capital, and its activities extended into Liberia and into British and Belgian colonies. It is said that SCOA and CFAO made a profit of up to 90 per cent in good years and 25 per cent in bad years.

In Britain, the notorious slave trading port of Liverpool was the first to switch to palm oil early in the nineteenth century when the trade in slaves became difficult or impossible. This meant that Liverpool firms were no longer exploiting Africa by removing its labor physically to another part of the world. Instead, they were exploiting the labor and raw materials of Africa *inside* Africa. Throughout the nineteenth century and right into the colonial era, Liverpool concentrated largely on importing African peasant produce. Backed by the industrial districts of Manchester and Cheshire, this British port was in control of a great proportion of Britain's and Europe's trade with Africa in the colonial period—just as it had done in the slave trade period. Glasgow also had a keen interest in the colonial trade, and so did the merchants and big business interests of London. By 1929, London replaced Liverpool as the chief port dealing with African import and export.

As indicated, the UAC was the British company which was best known among the commercial concerns. It was a subsidiary of the giant Anglo-Dutch monopoly, Unilever; and its agencies were found in all the British colonies of West Africa and on a smaller scale in East Africa. Unilever also controlled the *Compagnie du Niger Français,* the *Compagnie Française de la Côte d'Ivoire,* SCKN in Chad, NOSOCO in Senegal, NSCA in Portuguese Guinea, and John Walken & Co. Ltd. in Dahomey. Certain other British and French firms were not found in every colony, but they did well in the particular area in which they were entrenched. For example, there was John Holt in Nigeria.

In East Africa, the import-export business tended to have smaller firms than in West Africa, but even so there were five or six which were much larger than the rest and appropriated the largest amounts. One of the oldest was Smith Mackenzie, which was an offshoot of the Scottish company of Mackinnon and Mackenzie which had spearheaded British colonization in East Africa and which also had interests in India. Other notable commercial firms were those of A. Baumann, Wigglesworth and Company, Dalgetty, Leslie & Anderson, Ralli Bros., Michael Cotts, Jos. Hansen, the African Mercantile and Twentsche Overseas Trading Co. Some of them amalgamated before colonial rule was over, and they all had several other subsidiaries, as well as themselves being related to bigger companies in the metropoles. The UAC also had a slice of the East African import trade, having brought up the firm of Gailey and Roberts which was started by white settlers in 1904.

The pattern of appropriation of surplus in East Africa was easy to follow, in that there was centralization of the extractive mechanisms in Nairobi and the port of Mombasa. All the big firms operated from Nairobi, with important offices in Mombasa to deal with warehousing, shipping, insuring. Uganda and Tanganyika were then brought into the picture via their capital cities of Kampala and Dar es Salaam, where the big firms had branches. Up to the start of the last war, the volume of trade from East Africa was fairly small, but it jumped rapidly after that. For instance, the value of Kenya imports rose from 4 million pounds in 1938 to 34 million in 1950 and to 70 million in 1960. The value of exports was of course rising at the same time, and the commercial firms were among the principal beneficiaries of the growth in foreign trade.

Trading companies made huge fortunes on relatively small investments in those parts of Africa where peasant cash-crop farming was widespread. The companies did not have to spend a penny to grow the agricultural raw materials. The African peasant went in for cash-crop farming for many reasons. A minority eagerly took up the opportunity to continue to acquire European goods, which they had become accustomed to during the pre-colonial period. Many others in every section of the continent took to earning cash because they had to pay various taxes in money or because they were forced to work. Good examples of Africans literally being forced to grow cash crops by gun and whip were to be found in Tanganyika under German rule, in Portuguese colonies, and in French Equatorial Africa and the French Sudan in the 1930s.* In any event, there were very few cases where the peasant was wholly dependent on the cash for his actual sustenance. The trading companies took full advantage of that fact. Knowing that an African peasant and his family would keep alive by their own food *shambas,* the companies had no obligation to pay prices sufficient

---

* These facts came most dramatically to the attention of the outside world when Africans resorted to violence. For example, forced cultivation of cotton was a major grievance behind the outbreak of Maji Maji wars in Tanganyika and behind the nationalist revolt in Angola as late as 1960.

for the maintenance of a peasant and his family. In a way, the companies were simply receiving tribute from a conquered people, without even the necessity to trouble themselves as to how the tributary goods were produced.

Trading companies also had their own means of transport inside Africa, such as motor vessels and trucks. But, usually they transferred the burden of transport costs on to the peasant via the Lebanese or Indian middlemen. Those capitalist companies held the African farmer in a double squeeze, by controlling the price paid for the crop and by controlling the price of imported goods such as tools, clothing, and bicycles to which peasants aspired. For example, prices of palm products were severely reduced by the UAC and other trading companies in Nigeria in 1929, while the cost of living was rising owing to increased charges for imported goods. In 1924, the price for palm oil had been 14 shillings per gallon. This fell to 7 in 1928 and to slightly over one shilling in the following year. Although the trading companies received less for every ton of palm oil during the depression years, their profit margin increased—showing how brazenly surplus was being pounded out of the peasant. In the midst of the depression the UAC was showing a handsome profit. The profits in 1934 were 6,302,875 pounds and a dividend of 15 per cent was paid on ordinary shares.

In every part of colonial Africa, the depression years followed the same pattern. In Sukumaland (Tanganyika) the price of cotton dropped in 1930 from 50 cents to 10 cents per pound. The French colonies were hit a little later, because the depression did not make its impact on the French monetary zone until after 1931. Then, prices of Senegalese groundnuts were cut by more than half. Coffee and cocoa dropped even further, since they were relative luxuries to the European buyer. Again, it can be noted that French firms such as CFAO and SCOA faced lower prices when they sold the raw materials in Europe, but they never absorbed any losses. Instead, African peasants and workers bore the pressure, even if it meant forced labor. African peasants in French territories were forced to join so-called cooperative societies which made them grow certain crops like cotton and made them accept whatever price was offered.

Hardly had the depression ended when Europe was at war. The Western powers dragged in the African people to fight for freedom! The trading firms stepped up the rate of plunder in the name of God and country. On the Gold Coast, they paid 10 pounds per ton for cocoa beans as compared to 50 pounds before the war. At the same time, the price of imported goods doubled or trebled. Many necessities passed beyond the reach of the ordinary man. On the Gold Coast, a piece of cotton print which had sold before the war for 12½ shillings was 90 shillings in 1945. In Nigeria, a yard of khaki which was 3 shillings in prewar days went up to 16; a bundle of iron sheets formerly costing 30 went up to 100.

Urban workers were hardest hit by rising prices, since they had to purchase everyday necessities with money, and part of their food was imported. Worker dissatisfaction highlighted this exploitative postwar situation. There were several strikes, and in the Gold Coast, the boycott of imported goods in 1948 is famous as the prelude to self-government under Nkrumah. However, peasants were also restless under low prices and expensive imports. In Uganda, the cotton-growing peasants could stand things no longer by 1947. They could not get their hands on the big British import-export firms, but they could at least deal with the Indian and African middlemen. So they marched against the Indian-owned cotton gins and demonstrated outside the palace of the Kabaka—the hereditary ruler who often functioned as a British agent in Uganda.

To insure that at all times the profit margin was kept as high as possible, the trading firms found it convenient to form "pools." The pools fixed the price to be paid to the African cultivator, and kept the price down to the minimum. In addition, the trading companies spread into several other aspects of the economic life of the colonies, in such a way as to introduce several straws for the sucking out of surplus. In Morocco, to give one example, the *Compagnie Générale du Maroc* owned large estates, livestock farms, timber workings, mines, fisheries, railways, ports, and power stations. The giants like CFAO and UAC also had their fingers in everything. CFAO's interests ranged from groundnut plantations to shares in the Fabre & Frassinet shipping line. The people of Ghana and Nigeria met the UAC everywhere they turned. It controlled wholesale and retail trade, owned butter factories, sawmills, soap factories, singlet factories, cold storage plants, engineering and motor repair shops, tugs, coastal boats. Some of those businesses directly exploited African wage labor, while in one way or another all operations skimmed the cream produced by peasant efforts in the cash-crop sector.

Sometimes, the firms which purchased agricultural products in Africa were the same concerns which manufactured goods based on those agricultural raw materials. For instance, Cadbury and Fry, the two foremost English manufacturers of cocoa and chocolate, were buyers on the West African coast, while in East Africa the tea manufacturing concern of Brooke Bond both grew and exported tea. Many of the Marseilles, Bordeaux, and Liverpool trading companies were also engaged in manufacturing items such as soap and margarine in their home territories. This applied fully to the UAC, while the powerful Lesieur group processing oils and fats in France had commercial buyers in Africa. However, it is possible to separate the trading operations from the industrial ones. The latter represented the final stage in the long process of exploiting the labor of African peasants—in some ways the most damaging stage.

Peasants worked for large numbers of hours to produce a given cash crop, and the price of the product was the price of those long hours of labor. Since primary produce from Africa has always received low prices, it follows that the buyer and user of the raw material was engaging in massive exploitation of the peasants.

The above generalization can be illustrated with reference to cotton, which is one of the most widely encountered cash crops in Africa. The Ugandan farmer grew cotton which ultimately made its way into an English factory in Lancashire or a British-owned factory in India. The Lancashire factory owner paid his workers as little as possible, but his exploitation of their labor was limited by several factors. His exploitation of the labor of the Ugandan peasant was unlimited because of his power in the colonial state, which insured that Ugandans worked long hours for very little. Besides, the price of the finished cotton shirt was so high that when re-imported into Uganda, cotton in the form of a shirt was beyond the purchasing power of the peasant who grew the cotton.

The differences between the prices of African exports of raw materials and their importation of manufactured goods constituted a form of unequal exchange. Throughout the colonial period, this inequality in exchange got worse. Economists refer to the process as one of deteriorating terms of trade. In 1939, with the same quality of primary goods colonies could buy only 60 per cent of manufactured goods which they bought in the decade 1870–80 before colonial rule. By 1960, the amount of European manufactured goods purchasable by the same quantity of African raw materials had fallen still further. There was no objective economic law which determined that primary produce should be worth so little. Indeed, the developed countries sold certain raw materials like timber and wheat at much higher prices than a colony could command. The explanation is that the unequal exchange was forced upon Africa by the political and military supremacy of the colonizers, just as in the sphere of international relations unequal treaties were forced upon small states in the dependencies, like those in Latin America.

The unequal nature of the trade between the metropole and the colonies was emphasised by the concept of the "protected market," which meant even an inefficient metropolitan producer could find a guaranteed market in the colony where his class had political control. Furthermore, as in the preceding era of pre-colonial trade, European manufacturers built up useful sidelines of goods which would have been substandard in their own markets, especially in textiles. The European farmer also gained in the same way by selling cheap butter, while the Scandinavian fisherman came into his own through the export of salted cod. Africa was not a large market for European products, compared to other continents, but both buying-prices and selling-prices were set by European capitalists. That certainly allowed their manufacturers and traders more easy access to the surplus of wealth produced in Africa than they would have had if Africans were in a position to raise the price of their own exports.

Shipping and Banking Services

Channels for the exploitation of surplus were not exhausted by the trading companies and the industrial concerns. The shipping companies constituted an exploitative channel that cannot be overlooked. The largest shipping companies were those under the flags of the colonizing nations, especially the British. The shippers were virtually a law unto themselves, being very favorably regarded by their home governments as earners of superprofits, as stimulators of industry and trade, as carriers of mail, and as contributors to the navy when war came. African peasants had absolutely no control over the freight rates which were charged, and actually paid more than citizens in other lands. The rate for flour from Liverpool to West Africa was 35 shillings per ton as compared with only 7½ shillings from Liverpool to New York (a roughly equivalent distance). Freight rates normally varied with the volume of cargo carried, but the rate for cocoa was established at 50 shillings per ton when amounts exported were small at the beginning of this century, and the same high figure remained when exports increased. Coffee carried from Kenya to New York in the 1950s earned the shippers 280 shillings per ton ($40 at the rate of exchange then). Theoretically, it was the merchant who paid the shipper the freight charges, but in practical terms it meant that peasant production was bearing all the costs, since the merchants paid out of profits made by buying cheaply from the peasants. Alternatively, white settler planters paid the costs as in Kenya, and then regained their profits through exploitation of rural wage labor.

Shipping companies retained a high profit margin by a practice similar to the "pools" of the commercial firms. They established what were known as "Conference Lines" which allowed two or more shippers to share the freight loads between themselves on the most favorable basis possible. Their returns on investment were so high and their greed so uncontrollable that even the merchants of the colonizing powers protested. From 1929 to

1931, the UAC (backed by Unilever) engaged in an economic war with the West African Lines Conference—comprising the British shipping firm of Elder Dempster, the Holland West Africa Line, and the German West Africa Line. In that instance, the trading monopoly won a victory over the shipping monopoly; but it was a fight between two elephants, and the grass was trampled all the more. At the end of it all, the African peasant was the greatest loser, because both traders and shippers adjusted their differences by lowering prices of primary products as paid to Africans.

In the background of the colonial scene hovered the banks, insurance companies, maritime underwriters, and other financial houses. One can say "in the background" because the peasant never dealt directly with such institutions, and was generally ignorant of their exploiting functions. The peasant or worker had no access to bank loans because he had no "securities" or "collateral." Banks and finance houses dealt only with other capitalists who could prove to the bankers that whatever happened the bank would recover its money and make a profit. In the epoch of imperialism, the bankers became the aristocrats of the capitalist world, so in another sense they were very much in the foreground. The amount of surplus produced by African workers and peasants and passing into the hands of metropolitan bankers is quite phenomenal. They registered a return on capital higher even than the mining companies, and each new direct investment that they made spelled further alienation of the fruits of African labor. Furthermore, all investment in the colonies meant in effect the involvement of the big finance monopolies, since the smallest trading company was ultimately linked to a big banker. The returns on colonial investment were consistently higher than those in investments in the metropoles, so the financiers stood to benefit from sponsoring colonial enterprise.

In the earliest years of colonialism, the banks of Africa were small and relatively independent. This applied to the *Banque de Senegal,* started as early as 1853, and to the Bank of British West Africa which began as an offshoot of the shipping firm of Elder Dempster. However, the great banking houses of Europe, which had carried on remote control of developments ever since the 1880s, soon moved in directly on the colonial banking scene when the volume of capitalist transactions made this worthwhile. The *Banque de Senegal* merged into the *Banque de L'Afrique Occidentale* (BAO) in 1901, acquiring links with the powerful Bank of Indochina, which in turn was a special creation of several powerful metropolitan French bankers. In 1924, the *Banque Commerciale de l'Afrique* (BCA) emerged in the French territories, linked with the *Credit Lyonnais* and the BNCI in France. By that time the Bank of British West Africa had its finance backed by Lloyds Bank, Westminster Bank, the Standard Bank, and the National Provincial Bank—all in England. The other great English banking firm, Barclays, moved directly into Africa. It purchased the Colonial Bank and set it up as Barclays DCO (i.e., Dominion and Colonial).

The Bank of British West Africa (which became the Bank of West Africa in 1957) and Barclays held between them the lion's share of the banking business of British West Africa, just as French West and Equatorial Africa were shared out between the BAO and the BCA. There was also a union of French and British banking capital in West Africa in 1949 with the formation of the British and French West Africa Bank. French and Belgian exploitation also overlapped in the financial sphere, since the *Société Générale* had both Belgian and French capital. It supported banks in French Africa and the Congo. Other weaker colonial powers were served by the international banks such as Barclays, and also used their colonial territories as grazing ground for their own national banks. In Libya, the *Banco di Roma* and the *Banco di Napoli* operated; while in Portuguese territories the most familiar name was that of the *Banco Ultramarino*.

In Southern Africa, the outstanding banking firm was the Standard Bank of South Africa Ltd., started in 1862 in the Cape Colony by the heads of business houses having close connections with London. Its headquarters were placed in London, and it made a fortune out of financing gold and diamond strikes, and through handling the loot of Cecil Rhodes and De Beers. By 1895, the Standard Bank spread into Bechuanaland, Rhodesia, and Mozambique; and it was the second British bank to be established in British East Africa. The actual scale of profits was quite formidable. In a book officially sponsored by the Standard Bank, the writer modestly concluded as follows:

> Little attention has been paid in the text of this book to the financial outcome of the Standard Bank's activities, yet their profitability was an inevitable outcome of survival and was therefore bound to be a primary objective from first to last.

In 1960, the Standard Bank produced a net profit of 1,181,000 pounds and paid a 14 per cent dividend to its shareholders. Most of the latter were in Europe or else were whites in South Africa, while the profit was produced mainly by the black people of South and East Africa. Furthermore, these European banks transferred the reserves of their African branches to the London head office to be invested in the London money market. This was the way in which they most rapidly expatriated African surplus to the metropoles.

The first bank to be set up in East Africa in the 1890s was an offshoot of a British bank operating in India. It later came to be called the National & Grindlays. In neighboring Tanganyika the Germans established the German East African Bank in 1905, but after the First World War the British had a near monopoly of East African banking. Altogether nine foreign banks were in existence in East Africa during the colonial period, out of which the big three were National & Grindlays, the Standard Bank, and Barclays.

East Africa provides an interesting example of how effectively foreign banks served to dispossess Africa of its wealth. Most of the banking and other financial services were rendered to white settlers whose conception of "home" was always Britain. Consequently, when the white settlers felt threatened towards the end of the colonial period, they rushed to send their money home to Britain. For example, when the decision to concede self-government to Kenya was taken by the British in 1960, a sum amounting to over 5½ million dollars was immediately transferred to "safety" in London by whites in Tanganyika. That sum, like all other remittances by colonial banks, represented the exploitation of African land resources and labor.

The Colonial Administration as Economic Exploiter

In addition to private companies, the colonial state also engaged directly in the economic exploitation and impoverishment of Africa. The equivalent of the colonial office in each colonizing country worked hand in hand with their governors in Africa to carry out a number of functions, the principal ones being as follows:

(1) To protect national interests against competition from other capitalists.

(2) To arbitrate the conflicts between their own capitalists.

(3) To guarantee optimum conditions under which private companies could exploit Africans.

The last-mentioned objective was the most crucial. That is why colonial governments were repeatedly speaking about "the maintenance of law and order," by which they meant the maintenance of conditions most favorable to the expansion of capitalism and the plunder of Africa. This led the colonial governments to impose taxes.

One of the main purposes of the colonial taxation system was to provide requisite funds for administering the colony as a field of exploitation. European colonizers insured that Africans paid for the upkeep of the governors and police who oppressed them and served as watchdogs for private capitalists. Indeed, taxes and customs duties were levied in the nineteenth century with the aim of allowing the colonial powers to recover the costs of the armed forces which they dispatched to conquer Africa. In effect, therefore, the colonial governments never put a penny into the colonies. All expenses were met by exploiting the labor and natural resources of the continent; and for all practical purposes the expense of maintaining the colonial government machinery was a form of alienation of the products of African labor. The French colonies were especially victimized in this respect. Particularly since 1921, the local revenue raised from taxation had to meet all expenses as well as build up a reserve.

Having set up the police, army, civil service, and judiciary on African soil, the colonizing powers were then in a position to intervene much more directly in the economic life of the people than had been the case previously. One major problem in Africa from a capitalist viewpoint was how to induce Africans to become laborers or cash-crop farmers. In some areas, such as West Africa, Africans had become so attached to European manufactures during the early period of trade that, on their own initiative, they were prepared to go to great lengths to participate in the colonial money economy. But that was not the universal response. In many instances, Africans did not consider the monetary incentives great enough to justify changing their way of life so as to become laborers or cash-crop farmers. In such cases, the colonial state intervened to use law, taxation, and outright force to make Africans pursue a line favorable to capitalist profits.

When colonial governments seized African lands, they achieved two things simultaneously. They satisfied their own citizens (who wanted mining concessions or farming land) and they created the conditions whereby landless Africans had to work not just to pay taxes but also to survive. In settler areas such as Kenya and Rhodesia the colonial government also prevented Africans from growing cash crops so that their labor would be available directly for the whites. One of the Kenya white settlers, Colonel Grogan, put it bluntly when he said of the Kikuyu: "We have stolen his land. Now we must steal his limbs. Compulsory labor is the corollary of our occupation of the country."

In those parts of the continent where land was still in African hands, colonial governments forced Africans to produce cash crops no matter how low the prices were. The favorite technique was taxation. *Money* taxes were introduced on numerous items—cattle, land, houses, and the people themselves. Money to pay taxes was got by growing cash crops or working on European farms or in their mines. An interesting example of what colonialism was all about was provided in French Equatorial Africa, where French officials banned the Mandja people (now in Congo Brazzaville) from hunting, so that they would engage solely in cotton cultivation. The French enforced the ban although there was little livestock in the area and hunting was the main source of meat in the people's diet.

Finally, when all else failed, colonial powers resorted widely to the physical coercion of labor—backed up of course by legal sanctions, since anything which the colonial government chose to do was "legal." The laws and by-laws by which peasants in British East Africa were required to maintain minimum acreages of cash crops like cotton and groundnuts were in effect forms of coercion by the colonial state, although they are not normally considered under the heading of "forced labor."

The simplest form of forced labor was that which colonial governments exacted to carry out "public works." Labor for a given number of days per year had to be given free for these "public works"—building castles for governors, prisons for Africans, barracks for troops, and bungalows for colonial officials. A great deal of this forced labor went into the construction of roads, railways, and ports to provide the infrastructure for private capitalist investment and to facilitate the export of cash crops. Taking only one example from the British colony of Sierra Leone, one finds that the railway which started at the end of the nineteenth century required forced labor from thousands of peasants driven from the villages. The hard work and appalling conditions led to the death of a large number of those engaged in work on the railway. In the British territories, this kind of forced labor (including juvenile labor) was widespread enough to call forth in 1923 a "Native Authority Ordinance" restricting the use of compulsory labor for porterage, railway and road building. More often than not, means were found of circumventing this legislation. An international Forced Labor Convention was signed by all colonial powers in 1930, but again it was flouted in practice.

The French government had a cunning way of getting free labor by first demanding that African males should enlist as French soldiers and then using them as unpaid laborers. This and other forced labor legislation known as "prestation" was extensively applied in vast areas of French Sudan and French Equatorial Africa. Because cash crops were not well established in those areas, the main method of extracting surplus was by taking the population and making it work in plantation or cash-crop regions nearer the coast. Present-day Upper Volta, Chad, and Congo Brazzaville were huge suppliers of forced labor under colonialism. The French got Africans to start building the Brazzaville to Pointe-Noire railway in 1921, and it was not completed until 1933. Every year of its construction, some ten thousand people were driven to the site—sometimes from more than a thousand kilometers away. At least 25 per cent of the labor force died annually from starvation and disease, the worst period being from 1922 to 1929.

Quite apart from the fact that the "public works" were of direct value to the capitalists, the colonial government also aided private capitalists by providing them with labor recruited by force. This was particularly true in the early years of colonialism, but continued in varying degrees up to the Second World War, and even to the end of colonialism in some places. In British territories, the practice was revived during the economic depression of 1929–33 and during the subsequent war. In Kenya and Tanganyika, forced labor was reintroduced to keep settler plantations functioning during the war. In Nigeria, it was the tin companies which benefited from the forced-labor legislation, allowing them to get away with paying workers 5 pence per day plus rations. For most of the colonial period, the French government performed the same kind of service for the big timber companies who had great concessions of territory in Gabon and Ivory Coast.

The Portuguese and Belgian colonial regimes were the most brazen in directly rounding up Africans to go and work for private capitalists under conditions equivalent to slavery. In Congo, brutal and extensive forced labor started under King Leopold II in the last century. So many Congolese were killed and maimed by Leopold's officials and police that this earned European disapproval even in the midst of the general pattern of colonial outrages. When Leopold handed over the "Congo Free State" to the Belgian government in 1908, he had already made a huge fortune; and the Belgian government hardly relaxed the intensity of exploitation in Congo.

The Portuguese have the worst record of engaging in slavery-like practices, and they too have been repeatedly condemned by international public opinion. One peculiar characteristic of Portuguese colonialism was the provision of forced labor not only for its own citizens but also for capitalists outside the boundaries of Portuguese colonies. Angolans and Mozambicans were exported to the South African mines to work for subsistence, while the capitalists in South Africa paid the Portuguese government a certain sum for each laborer supplied. (The export of Africans to South Africa is still continuing.)

In the above example, the Portuguese colonialists were cooperating with capitalists of other nationalities to maximize the exploitation of African labor. Throughout the colonial period, there were instances of such cooperation, as well as competition between metropolitan powers. Generally speaking, a European power was expected to intervene when the profits of its national bourgeoisie were threatened by the activities of other nations. After all, the whole purpose of establishing colonial governments in

Africa was to provide protection to national monopoly economic interests. Thus, the Belgian government legislated to insure that freight to and from the Congo would be mainly carried by Belgian shipping lines; and the French government placed high taxes on groundnuts brought into France by foreign ships, which was another way of insuring that groundnuts from French Africa would be exported in French ships. In a sense, this meant that Africans were losing their surplus through one straw rather than another. But it also meant that the sum total of exploitation was also greater, because if competition among Europeans were allowed, it would have brought down the cost of services and raised the price paid for agricultural products.

Africans suffered most from exclusive trade with the "mother country" in cases where the "mother country" was backward. African peasants in Portuguese colonies got lower prices for their crops and paid more for imported items. Yet, Britain, the biggest of the colonialists in Africa, was also faced with competition from the more vigorous capitalists of Germany, the U.S.A., and Japan. British merchants and industrialists lobbied their government to erect barriers against competition. For example, Japanese cloth exports to British East Africa rose from 25 million yards in 1927 to 63 million yards in 1933; and this led Walter Runciman, president of the British Board of Trade, to get Parliament to impose heavy tariffs on Japanese goods entering British colonies in Africa. This meant that Africans had to pay higher prices for a staple import, since British cloth was more expensive. From the viewpoint of the African peasant, that amounted to further alienation of the fruits of his labor.

A perfect illustration of the identity of interests between the colonial governments and their bourgeois citizens was provided by the conduct of Produce Marketing Boards in Africa. The origins of the Boards go back to the Gold Coast "cocoa hold-up" of 1937. For several months, cocoa farmers refused to sell their crop unless the price was raised. One apparently favorable result of the "hold-up" was that the British government agreed to set up a Marketing Board to purchase cocoa from the peasants in place of the big business interests like the UAC and Cadbury which had up until then been the buyers. A West African Cocoa Control Board was set up in 1938, but the British government used this as a bush to hide the private capitalists and to allow them to continue making their exorbitant profits.

In theory, a Marketing Board was suppose to pay the peasant a reasonable price for his crop. The Board sold the crop overseas and kept a surplus for the improvement of agriculture and for paying the peasants a stable price if world market prices declined. In practice, the Boards paid peasants a low fixed rate during many years when world prices were rising. None of the benefits went to Africans, but rather to the British government itself and to the private companies, which were used as intermediaries in the buying and selling of the produce. Big companies like the UAC and John Holt were given quotas to fulfill on behalf of the Boards. As agents of the government, they were no longer exposed to direct attack, and their profits were secure.

The idea of the Marketing Boards gained support from top British policy makers because the war came just at that time, and the British government was anxious to take steps to secure certain colonial products in the necessary quantities and at the right times, given the limited number of ships available for commercial purposes during war. They were also anxious to save private capitalists who were adversely affected by events connected with the war. For example, East African sisal became of vital importance to Britain and her war allies after the Japanese cut off supplies of similar hard fibers from the Philippines and Dutch East Indies. Actually, even before fighting broke out, sisal was bought in bulk by the British government to help the non-African plantation owners in East Africa who had lost markets in Germany and other parts of Europe. Similarly, oil seeds (such as palm produce and groundnuts) were bought by a Board from September 1939, in preparation for shortages of butter and marine oils.

With regard to all peasant cash crops, the Produce Marketing Boards made purchases at figures that were way below world market prices. For instance, the West African Produce Board paid Nigerians a bit under 17 pounds for a ton of palm oil in 1946 and sold that through the Ministry of Food for 95 pounds, which was nearer the world market price. Groundnuts which received 15 pounds per ton when bought by the Boards were later sold in Britain at 110 pounds per ton. Furthermore, export duties were levied on the Boards' sales by the colonial administrators, and that was an indirect tax on the peasants. The situation reached a point where many peasants tried to escape from under the Boards. In Sierra Leone in 1952, the price for coffee was so low that growers smuggled their crop into nearby French territories. At about the same time, Nigerian peasants were running away from palm oil into rubber collection or timber felling which did not come under the jurisdiction of the Produce Boards.

If one accepts that the government is always the servant of a particular class, it is perfectly understandable that the colonial governments should have been in collusion with capitalists to siphon off surplus from Africa to Europe. But even if one does not start from that (Marxist) premise, it would be impossible to ignore the evidence of how the colonial administrators worked as committees on behalf of the big capitalists. The governors in the colonies had to listen to the local representatives of the companies and to their principals. Indeed, there were company representatives who wielded influence in several colonies at the same time. Before the First World War, the single most important individual in the whole of British West Africa was Sir Alfred Jones—chairman of Elder Dempster Lines, chairman of the Bank of West Africa, president of the British Cotton-Growing Association. In French West Africa in the late 1940s, the French governor showed himself very anxious to please one Marc Rucart, a man with major interests in several of the French trading companies. Such examples could be cited for each colony throughout its history although in some of them the influence of the white settlers was greater than that of individual metropolitan businessmen.

Company shareholders in Europe not only lobbied Parliament but actually controlled the administration itself. The chairman of the Cocoa Board within the Ministry of Food was none other than John Cadbury, a director of Cadbury Brothers, who were participants in the buying "pool" which exploited West African cocoa farmers. Former employees of Unilever held key positions in the Oils and Fats Division of the Ministry of Food, and continued to receive checks from Unilever! The Oils and Fats Division handed over the allocation of buying quotas for the Produce Boards to the Association of West African Merchants, which was dominated by Unilever's subsidiary, the UAC.

It is no wonder that the Ministry of Food sent a prominent Lebanese businessman a directive that he had to sign an agreement drawn up by the UAC. It is no wonder that the companies had government aid in keeping prices down in Africa and in securing forced labor where necessary. It is no wonder that Unilever then sold soap, margarine, and such commodities at profitable prices within a market assured by the British government.

Of course, the metropolitan governments also insured that a certain proportion of the colonial surplus went directly into the coffers of the state. They all had some forms of direct investment in capitalist enterprises. The Belgian government was an investor in mining, and so too was the Portuguese government through its part-ownership of the Angolan Diamond Company. The French government was always willing to associate itself with the financial sector. When colonial banks were in trouble, they could count on rescue from the French government, and, indeed, a proportion of their shares passed into the hands of the French government. The British colonial government was perhaps the least anxious to become directly involved in everyday business enterprises, but it did run the Eastern Nigerian coal mines—apart from railways.

Marketing Boards helped the colonizing power to get its hands on some immediate cash. One finds that the Cocoa Board sold to the British Ministry of Food at very low prices; and the Ministry in turn sold to British manufacturers, making a profit that was as high as 11 million pounds in some years. More important still, the Board sold to the U.S.A., which was the largest market and one where prices were very high. None of the profits went back to the African farmer, but instead represented British foreign exchange in American dollars.

From 1943, Britain and the U.S.A. engaged in what was known as "reverse lend-lease." This meant that wartime United States loans to Britain were repaid partly by raw materials shipped from British colonies to the U.S.A. Tin and rubber from Malaya were very important in that context, while Africa supplied a wide range of products, both mineral and agricultural. Cocoa was third as a dollar earner after tin and rubber. In 1947, West African cocoa brought over 100 million dollars to the British dollar balance. Besides, having a virtual monopoly of the production of diamonds, (South) Africa was also able to sell to the U.S.A. and earn dollars for Britain. In 1946, Harry F. Oppenheimer told his fellow directors of the De Beers Consolidated Mines that "sales of gem diamonds during the war secured about 300 million American dollars for Great Britain."

It was on this very issue of currency that the colonial government did the most manipulations to insure that Africa's wealth was stashed away in the coffers of the metropolitan state. In the British colonial sphere, coins and notes were first issued through private banks. Then this function was taken over by the West African Currency Board and the East African Currency Board, established in 1912 and 1919 respectively. The currency issued by those Boards in the colonies had to be backed by "sterling reserves," which was money earned by Africa. The manner in which the system worked was as follows. When a colony earned foreign exchange (mainly) through exports, these earnings were held in Britain in pounds sterling. An equivalent amount of local East or West African currency was issued for circulation in the respective colonies, while the sterling was invested in British government stock, thereby earning even more profit for Britain. The commercial banks worked hand in hand with the metropolitan government and the Currency Boards to make the system work. Together they established an intricate financial network which served the common end of enriching Europe at Africa's expense.

The contribution to sterling reserves by any colony was a gift to the British treasury, for which the colony received little interest. By the end of the 1950s, the sterling reserves of a small colony like Sierra Leone had reached 60 million pounds; while in 1955 the British government was holding 210 million derived from the sale of cocoa and minerals from Gold Coast. Egypt and the Sudan were also heavy contributors to Britain. Africa's total contribution to Britain's sterling balances in 1945 was 446 million pounds, which went up to 1,446 million by 1955—more than half the total gold and dollar reserves of Britain and the Commonwealth, which then stood at 2,120 million. Men like Arthur Creech-Jones and Oliver Lyttleton, major figures in British colonial policy-making, admitted that in the early 1950s Britain was living on the dollar earnings of the colonies.

The British government was surpassed by its Belgian counterpart in exacting tribute from its colonies, especially during and after the last war. After Belgium was overrun by the Germans, a government-in-exile was set up in London. The Colonial Secretary of that exiled regime, Mr. Godding, admitted:

> During the war, the Congo was able to finance all the expenditure of the Belgian government in London, including the diplomatic service as well as the cost of our armed forces in Europe and Africa, a total of some 40 million pounds. In fact, thanks to the resources of the Congo, the Belgian government in London had not to borrow a shilling or a dollar, and the Belgian gold reserve could be left intact.

Since the war, surplus of earnings by the Congo in currencies other than the Belgian franc have all accrued to the National Bank of Belgium. Therefore, quite apart from all that the private capitalists looted from Congo, the Belgian government was also a direct beneficiary to the tune of millions of francs per annum.

To discuss French colonialism in this context would be largely to repeat remarks made with reference to the British and Belgians. Guinea was supposedly a "poor" colony, but in 1952 it earned France one billion (old) francs, or about 5.6 million dollars in foreign exchange, based on the sale of bauxite, coffee, and bananas. French financial techniques were slightly different from those of other colonial powers. France tended to use the commercial banks more, rather than set up separate currency boards. France also squeezed more out of Africans by imposing levies for military purposes. The French government dressed Africans in French army uniforms and used them to fight other Africans, to fight other colonized peoples like the Vietnamese, and to fight in European wars. The colonial budgets had to bear the cost of sending these African "French" soldiers to die, but if they returned alive they had to be paid pensions out of African funds.

To sum up briefly, colonialism meant a great intensification of exploitation within Africa—to a level much higher than that previously in existence under communalism or feudal-type African societies. Simultaneously, it meant the export of that surplus in massive proportions, for that was the central purpose of colonialism.

The Strengthening of the Technological and Military Aspects of Capitalism

A Preliminary Examination of the Non-monetary Benefits of Colonialism to Europe

There are still some bourgeois propagandists who assert that colonialism was not a paying concern for Europeans, just as there are those who say that the slave trade was not profitable to Europeans. It is not worthwhile to engage in a direct refutation of such a viewpoint, since it consumes time which could otherwise be more usefully employed. The foregoing section was a statement on the level of actual monetary profits made by colonialist powers out of Africa. But, Africa's contribution to European capitalism was far greater than mere monetary returns. The colonial system permitted the rapid development of technology and skills within the metropolitan sectors of imperialism. It also allowed for the elaboration of the modern organizational techniques of the capitalist firm and of imperialism as a whole. Indeed, colonialism gave capitalism an added lease of life and prolonged its existence in Western Europe, which had been the cradle of capitalism.

At the beginning of the colonial period, science and technology as applied to production already had a firm base inside Europe—a situation which was itself connected to overseas trade, as previously explained. Europe then was entering the age of electricity, of advanced ferrous and non-ferrous metallurgy, and of the proliferation of manufactured chemicals. All of these were carried to great heights during the colonial period. Electrical devices were raised to the qualitatively new level of electronics, incorporating miniaturization of equipment, fantastic progress in telecommunications, and the creation of computers. Chemical industries were producing a wide range of synthetic substitutes for raw materials, and a whole new branch of petrochemicals had come into existence. The combination of metals by metallurgical innovations meant that products could be offered to meet far-reaching demands of heat resistance, lightness, tensile strength. At the end of colonialism (say 1960), Europe was on the verge of another epoch—that of nuclear power.

It is common knowledge that the gap between the output of the metropoles and that of the colonies increased by at least fifteen to twenty times during the epoch of colonialism. More than anything else, it was the advance of scientific technique in the metropoles which was the cause of the great gulf between African and Western European levels of productivity by the end of the colonial period. Therefore, it is essential to understand the role of colonialism itself in bringing about the scientific progress in the metropoles, and its application to industry.

It would be extremely simple-minded to say that colonialism in Africa or anywhere else *caused* Europe to develop its science and technology. The tendency towards technological innovation and renovation was inherent in capitalism itself, because of the drive for profits. However, it would be entirely accurate to say that the colonization of Africa and other parts of the world formed an indispensable link in a chain of events which made possible the technological transformation of the base of European capitalism. Without that link, European capitalism would not have been producing goods and services at the level attained in 1960. In other words, our very yardsticks for measuring developed and underdeveloped nations would have been different.

Profits from African colonialism mingled with profits from every other source to finance scientific research. This was true in the general sense that the affluence of capitalist society in the present century allowed more money and leisure for research. It is also true because the development of capitalism in the imperialist epoch continued the division of labor *inside the capitalist metropoles* to the point where scientific research was a branch of the division of labor, and indeed one of its most important branches. European society moved away from scientific research as an *ad hoc,* personal, and even whimsical affair to a situation where research was given priority by governments, armies, and private capitalists. It was funded and guided. Careful scrutiny reveals that the source of funding and the direction in which research was guided were heavily influenced by the colonial situation. Firstly, it should be recalled that profits made by Europe from Africa represented *investible surpluses*. The profit was not merely an end in itself. Thus, the East and West African Currency Boards invested in the British government stock, while the commercial banks and insurance companies invested in government bonds, mortgages, and industrial shares. These investment funds acquired from the colonies spread to many sectors in the metropoles and benefited industries that had nothing to do with processing of colonial products.

However, it is easier to trace the impact of colonial exploitation on industries directly connected with colonial imports. Such industries had to improvise that kind of machinery which most effectively utilized colonial raw materials. That led for example to machinery for crushing palm kernels and to a process for utilizing the less delicately flavored coffee by turning it into a soluble powder, namely "instant coffee." Merchants and industrialists also considered ways in which colonial raw materials could be modified to meet specifications of European factories in quality and quantity. An example of this type would be the care taken by the Dutch in Java and by the Americans in Liberia to breed and graft new varieties of rubber plants yielding more and being more resistant to disease. Ultimately, the search for better-quality raw materials merged with the search for sources of raw material which would make European capitalism less dependent on colonial areas—and that led to synthetics.

In the sphere of shipping, it can readily be appreciated that certain technological modifications and innovations would be connected with the fact that such a high proportion of shipping was used to tie together colonies and metropoles. Ships had to be refrigerated to carry perishable goods; they had to make special holds for bulky or liquid cargoes such as palm oil; and the transport of petroleum from the Middle East, North Africa, and other parts of the world led to oil tankers as a special class of ships. The design of ships and the nature of their cargoes in turn affected the kind of port installations in the metropoles.

Where connections were remote or even apparently non-existent, it can still be claimed that colonialism was a factor in the European technological revolution. As science blossomed in the present century, its interconnections became numerous and complex. It is impossible to trace the origin of every idea and every invention, but it is well understood by serious historians of science that the growth of the body of scientific knowledge and its application to everyday life is dependent upon a large number of forces operating within the society as a whole, and not just upon the ideas within given branches of science. With the rise of imperialism, one of the most potent forces within metropolitan capitalist societies was precisely that emanating from colonial or semi-colonial areas.

The above considerations apply fully to any discussion of the military aspects of imperialism, the protection of empire being one of the crucial stimulants added to the science of armaments in a society that was already militaristically inclined ever since the feudal era. The new colonial dimension to European military preoccupation was particularly noticeable in the sharp naval rivalry among Britain, Germany, France, and Japan before and during the First World War. That rivalry over colonies and for spheres of capitalist investment produced new types of armed naval vessels, such as destroyers and submarines. By the end of the Second World War, military research had become the most highly organized branch of scientific research, and one that was subsidized by the capitalist states from the profits of international exploitation.

During the inter-war years, Africa's foremost contribution to the evolution of organizational techniques in Europe was to the strengthening of monopoly capital. Before the war of 1914, the Pan-Africanists Duse Mohammed Ali and W. E. B. Du Bois recognized that monopoly capital was the leading element in imperialist expansion. The most thorough and the best-known analysis of this phenomenon was made by the Russian revolutionary leader, Lenin. Lenin was virtually prophetic, because as the colonial age advanced it became more and more obvious that those who stood to benefit most were the monopoly concerns, and especially those involved in finance.

Africa (plus Asia and Latin America) contributed to the elaboration of the strategies by which competition among small companies gave way to domination by a small handful of firms in various economic activities. It was on the India trade routes that shipping companies first started the "Conference Lines" in 1875. This monopoly practice spread rapidly to the South African trade and reached a high pitch in West Africa in the early years of this century. On the commercial side, it was in West Africa that both the French and the English derived considerable experience in pooling and market-sharing; apart from the fact that little companies were steadily being gobbled up by bigger ones from the beginning to the end of colonialism.

It was in Southern Africa that there emerged the most carefully planned structures of interlocking directorates, holding companies, and giant corporations which were multinational both in their capital subscriptions and through the fact that their economic activities were dispersed in many lands. Individual entrepreneurs like Oppenheimer made huge fortunes from the Southern African soil, but Southern Africa was never really in the era of individual and family businesses, characteristic of Europe and America up to the early part of this century. The big mining companies were impersonal professional things. They were organized in terms of personnel, production, marketing, advertising, and they could undertake long-term commitments. At all times, inner productive forces gave capitalism its drive towards expansion and domination. It was the system which expanded. But in addition, one can see in Africa and in Southern Africa in particular the rise of a capitalist superstructure manned by individuals capable of consciously planning the exploitation of resources right into the next century, and aiming at racist domination of the black people of Africa until the end of time.

Ever since the fifteenth century, Europe was in strategic command of world trade and of the legal and organizational aspects of the movement of goods between continents. Europe's power increased with imperialism, because imperialism meant investments, and investments (with or without colonial rule) gave European capitalists control over production within each continent. The amount of benefits to capitalism increased accordingly, since Europe could determine the quantity and quality of different raw material inputs which would need to be brought together in the interests of capitalism as a whole, and of the bourgeois class in particular. For instance, sugar production in the West Indies was joined in the colonial period by cocoa production within Africa, so that both merged into the chocolate industry of Europe and North America. In the metallurgical field, iron ore from Sweden, Brazil, or Sierra Leone could be turned into different types of steel with the addition of manganese from the Gold Coast or chrome from Southern Rhodesia. Such examples could be multiplied almost indefinitely to cover the whole range of capitalist production in the colonial period.

As John Stuart Mill said, the trade between England and the West Indies in the eighteenth century was like the trade between town and country. In the present century, the links are even closer and it is more marked that the town (Europe) is living off the countryside (Africa, Asia, and Latin America). When it said that colonies should exist for the metropoles by producing raw materials and buying manufactured goods, the underlying theory was to introduce an *international division of labor* covering working people everywhere. That is to say, up to that point each society had allocated to its own members particular functions in production— some hunted, some made clothes, some built houses. But with colonialism, the capitalists determined what types of labor the workers should carry on in the world at large. Africans were to dig minerals out of the subsoil, grow agricultural crops, collect natural products, and perform a number of other odds and ends such as bicycle repairing. Inside Europe, North America, and Japan, workers would refine the minerals and the raw materials and make the bicycles.

The international division of labor brought about by imperialism and colonialism insured that there would be the maximum increase in the level of skills in the capitalist nations. It took mainly physical strength to dig the minerals from and to farm the African soil, but the extraction of the metals from the ores and the subsequent manufacture of finished goods in Europe promoted more and more technology and skills there as time went on. Take the iron and steel industry as an example. Modern steel manufacture derives from the Siemens open-hearth system and the Bessemer process, which were both already in existence in the second half of the last century. They both underwent major modifications, transforming steel manufacture from intermittent operations to something requiring huge continuous electrical furnaces. In more recent years, skilled workmen have been replaced by automation and computerization, but altogether the gains in technology and skills were immense, as compared with the years before imperialism got under way.

Iron ore was not one of Africa's major exports in the colonial days and it may therefore appear to be an irrelevant example. However, iron was very significant in the economy of Sierra Leone, Liberia, and North Africa. It can be used to illustrate the trend by which the international division of labor allowed technology and skills to grow in the metropoles. Furthermore, it must be recalled that Africa was an important source of the minerals that went into making steel alloys, notably manganese and chrome. Manganese was essential in the Bessemer process. It was mined in several places in Africa, with the Nouta mine on the Gold Coast having the largest single manganese deposit in the world. American companies owned the Gold Coast and North African mines and used the product in the steel industry of the U.S.A. Chrome from South Africa and Southern Rhodesia also played a similar role in steel metallurgy, being essential for the manufacture of stainless steel.

Columbite was another of the African minerals valuable for the creation of steel alloys. Being highly heat-resistant, one of its principal uses was in making steel for jet engines. First of all, it was the rapid development of European industry and technology which caused columbite to assume value. It had been a discarded by-product of tin mining in Nigeria up to 1952. Then, once it was utilized, it gave further stimulus to European technology in the very sophisticated sphere of airplane engines.

Obviously, according to the international division of labor prevailing under colonialism, it was the American, Canadian, British, and French workers who had access to the skills involved in working with columbite, rather than the Nigerian worker who dug the ore out of the ground. For certain reasons, columbite fell off sharply in demand after a few years, but during that time it had contributed towards making the European metallurgist even more proficient and experienced. In that way, it was helping to promote self-sustained growth and to produce the gap which is evident in any comparison of the developed and underdeveloped countries.

Copper, too, fell neatly into the category under discussion. Unskilled production by Africans was required to get the ore for export, followed by refinement in a European capitalist plant. Copper was Africa's chief mineral export. Being an excellent conductor of electricity, it became an indispensable part of the capitalist electrical industry. It is an essential component of generators, motors, electric locomotives, telephones, telegraphs, light and power lines, motor cars, buildings, ammunition, radios, refrigerators, and a host of other things. A technological era tends to be defined by the principal source of power. Today, we speak of a Nuclear Age, since the potential of nuclear power is shown to be immense. The Industrial Revolution in Europe during the eighteenth and nineteeth centuries was the Age of Steam. In a parallel manner, the colonial epoch was the Age of Electricity. Therefore, the vital copper exports from Congo, Northern Rhodesia, and other parts of Africa were contributing to the leading sector of European technology. From that strategic position, its multiplier effects were innumerable and were of incalculable benefit to capitalist development.

In the context of a discussion of raw materials, special reference must again be made to the military. African minerals played a decisive role both with regard to conventional weapons and with regard to the breakthrough to atomic and nuclear weapons. It was from the Belgian Congo during the Second World War that the U.S.A. began getting the uranium that was a prerequisite to the making of the first atomic bomb. In any case, by the end of the colonial period, industry and the war machine in the colonizing nations had become so interwined and inseparable that any contribution to one was a contribution to the other. Therefore, Africa's massive contribution to what initially appears as peaceful pursuits such as the making of copper wire and steel alloys ultimately took the shape of explosive devices, aircraft carriers, and so on.

It was only after European firearms reached a certain stage of effectiveness in the nineteenth century that it became possible for whites to colonize and dominate the whole world. Similarly, the invention of a massive array of new instruments of destruction in the metropoles was both a psychological and a practical disincentive to colonized peoples seeking to regain power and independence. It will readily be recalled that a basic prop to colonialism in Africa and elsewhere was the "gunboat policy," which was resorted to every time that the local police and armed forces seemed incapable of maintaining the metropolitan law and the colonial order of affairs. From the viewpoint of the colonized, the strengthening of the military apparatus of the European powers through colonial exploitation was doubly detrimental. Not only did it increase the overall technological gap between metropole and colony, but it immeasurably widened the gap in the most sensitive area, which had to do with concepts such as power and independence.

The international division of labor of the colonial period also insured that there would be growth of employment opportunities in Europe, apart from the millions of white settlers and expatriates who earned a livelihood in and from Africa. Agricultural raw materials were processed in such a way as to form by-products, constituting industries in their own right. The number of jobs created in Europe and North America by the import of mineral ores from Africa, Asia, and Latin America can be seen from the massive employment roll of institutions such as steel works, automobile factories, alumina and aluminum plants, copper wire firms. Furthermore, those in turn stimulated the building industry, the transport industry, the munitions industry, and so on. The mining that went on in Africa left holes in the ground, and the pattern of agricultural production left African soils impoverished; but, in Europe, agricultural and mineral imports built a massive industrial complex.

In the earliest phases of human organization, production was scattered and atomized. That is to say, families preserved a separate identity while working for their upkeep. Over time, production became more social and interrelated in character. The making of a pair of shoes in a mature feudal trading economy involved the cattle rearer, a tanner of the leather, and a shoemaker—instead of one peasant killing an animal and making himself a pair of shoes, as under self-sufficient communalism. The extent to which a society achieves this social interdependence in making commodities is an index of its development, through specialization and coordination.

Undoubtedly, European capitalism achieved more and more a social character in its production. It integrated the whole world; and with colonial experience as an important stimulus, it integrated very closely every aspect of its own economy—from agriculture to banking. But *distribution* was not social in character. The fruits of human labor went to a given minority class, which was of the white race and resident in Europe and North America. This is the crux of the dialectical process of development and underdevelopment, as it evolved over the colonial period.

The Example of Unilever as a Major Beneficiary of African Exploitation

Just as it was necessary to follow African surplus through the channels of exploitation such as banks and mining companies, so the non-monetary contribution which Africa made to European capitalism can also be accurately traced by following the careers of the said companies. We offer below a brief outline of the relevant features of the development of a single firm—that of Unilever—in relationship to its exploitation of African resources and people.

In 1885, while Africa was being carved up at the conference table, one William H. Lever started making soap on the Merseyside near Liverpool in England. He called his soap "Sunlight" and in the swamps where his factory stood, the township of Port Sunlight grew up. Within ten years, the firm of Lever was selling 40,000 tons of soap per year in England alone and was building an export business and factories in other parts of Europe, America, and the British colonies. Then came Lifebuoy, Lux, Vim, and within another ten years, Lever was selling 60,000 tons of soap in Britain, and in addition had factories producing and selling in Canada, the U.S.A., South Africa, Switzerland, Germany, and Belgium. However, soap did not grow in any of those countries. The basic item in its manufacture was stearin, obtained from oils and fats. Apart from animal tallow and whale oil, the desirable raw materials all came from the tropics: namely, palm oil, palm-kernel oil, groundnut oil, and copra. West Africa happened to be the world's great palm produce zone and was also a major grower of groundnuts.

In 1887, the Austrian firm of Schicht, which was later to be incorporated in the Unilever combine, built the first palm-kernel crushing mill in Austria, supplied with raw materials by a Liverpool firm of oil merchants. That was not simply coincidence, but part of the logic of imperialism and the opening up of Africa as the raw material reservoir for Europe. As early as 1902, Lever sent out his own "explorers" to Africa, and they came to the decision that the Congo would be the most likely place to get palm produce, because the Belgian government was willing to offer huge concessions of land with innumerable palm trees. Lever obtained the necessary concessions in Congo and brought in machinery to extract oil from palm kernels.

But the main palm-oil experts came from areas on the coast to the north of the Congo. Therefore, in 1910, Lever purchased W. B. McIver, a small Liverpool firm in Nigeria. That was followed by acquisitions of two small companies in Sierra Leone and Liberia. Indeed, Lever (at that time called Lever Bros.) got a foothold in every colony in West Africa. The first major breakthrough occurred when Lever bought the Niger Company in 1920 for 8 million pounds. Then, in 1929, the African and Eastern, the last big rival trading concern, was brought into partnership; and the result of the merger was called the United Africa Company (UAC).

During the 1914–18 war, Lever had begun making margarine, which required the same raw materials as soap; namely, oils and fats. The subsequent years were ones in which such enterprises in Europe were constantly getting bigger through takeovers and mergers. The big names in soap and margarine manufacture on the European continent were two Dutch firms, Jurgens and Van der Bergh, and the Austrian firms of Schicht and Centra. The Dutch companies first achieved a dominant position; and then in 1929 there was a grand merger between their combine and Lever's, who in the meantime had been busy buying off virtually all other competitors. The 1929 merger created Unilever as a single monopoly, divided for the sake of convenience into Unilever Ltd. (registered in Britain) and Unilever N.V. (registered in Holland).

For its massive input of oils and fats, Unilever depended largely on its UAC subsidiary which was formed that very year. The UAC itself never stopped growing. In 1933, it took over the important trading firm of G. B. Ollivant, and in 1936, it bought the Swiss Trading Company on the Gold Coast. By that time, it was not relying simply on wild palms in the Congo, but had organized plantations. The Lever factories in the U.S.A. drew their oil supplies mainly from the Congo, and in 1925 (even before Unilever and the UAC emerged as such) the Lever works in Boston showed a profit of 250,000 pounds.

Unilever flourished in war and in peace. Only in Eastern Europe did the advent of socialism lead to the loss of factories through nationalization. By the end of the colonial period, Unilever was a world force, selling traditional soaps, detergents, margarine, lard, ghee, cooking oil, canned foods, candles, glycerin, oil cake, and toilet preparations such as toothpaste. From where did this giant octopus suck most of its sustenance? Let the answer be provided by the Information Division of Unilever House, London.

> Most striking of all in the post-war development of Unilever, had been the progress of the United Africa Company. In the worst of the depression, the management of Unilever had never ceased to put money into UAC, justifying their action more by general faith in the future of Africa than by particular consideration of UAC's immediate prospects. Their reward has come with the post-war prosperity of the primary producer, which has made Africa a market for all kinds of goods, from frozen peas to motor cars. Unilever's centre of gravity lies in Europe, but far and away its largest member (the UAC) is almost wholly dependent for its livelihood (represented by a turnover of 300 million pounds) on the well-being of West Africa.

In some instances, Lever's African enterprises made losses in the strict cost-accounting sense. It took years before the Congo plantations paid for themselves and made a profit. It also took some time before the purchase of the Niger Company in 1920 was financially justified; while the SCKN in Chad never showed worthwhile monetary profits. But, even in the worst financial years, the subsidiaries comprising the UAC were invaluable assets, in that they allowed the manufacturing side of Unilever to have control over a guaranteed source of essential raw materials. Of course, the UAC itself also provided handsome monetary dividends, but it is the purpose here to draw attention not to the financial gains of UAC and

Unilever but to the way that the exploitation of Africa led to multiple technical and organizational developments in Europe.

Both the soap industry and the margarine industry had their own scientific and technical problems which had to be solved. Scientific advance is most generally a response to real need. Oils for margarine and for cooking purposes had to be deodorized; substitutes had to be sought for natural lard; and, when margarine was faced with competition from cheap butter, the necessity arose to find means of producing new high-grade margarine with added vitamins. In 1916, two Lever experts published in a British scientific journal the results of tests showing the growth of animals fed with vitamin concentrates inside margarine. They kept in touch with Cambridge University scientists who pursued the problem, and by 1927 the vitamin-rich margarine was ready for human consumption.

With regard to soap (and to a lesser extent margarine), it was essential to devise a process for hardening oils into fats—notably whale oil, but also vegetable oils. This process, referred to as "hydrogenation," attracted the attention of scientists in the early years of this century. They were paid and urged on by rival soap companies, including Lever and the other European firms which later merged to form Unilever.

One of the most striking illustrations of the technological ramifications of the processing of colonial raw materials is in the field of detergents. Soap itself is a detergent or "washing agent," but ordinary soaps suffer from several limitations, such as the tendency to decompose in hard water and in acids. Those limitations could only be overcome by "soapless detergents," without the kind of fatty base of previous soaps. When Germany was cut off from colonial supplies of oils and fats in the first imperialist war, German scientists were spurred on to the first experiments in producing detergents out of coal tar. Later on in the 1930s, chemical companies began making similar detergents on a larger scale, especially in the U.S.A. Two of the firms which immediately stepped into detergent research were Unilever and Procter & Gamble, a soap combine with its headquarters in Cincinnati.

It may at first appear strange that though detergents were competitors to ordinary soap, they were nevertheless promoted by soap firms. However, it is the practice of monopoly concerns to move into new fields which supplement or even replace their old business. That is necessary to avoid their entire capital from being tied up in products that go out of fashion. The soap firms could not leave detergents to chemical firms, or else their own hard soap, soap flakes, and soap powders would have suffered, and they would not have been the ones with the new brands on the markets. So great effort was put into the chemistry of detergents by Unilever, retaining to a considerable extent the vegetable oils, but modifying them chemically. That kind of research was not left to chance or to private individuals. By 1960, Unilever had four main laboratories—two in England, one in Holland, and one in the U.S.A. These four, together with other smaller research units, employed over three thousand people, of whom about one-third were qualified scientists and technologists.

The multiplier effects radiating from Unilever and its colonial exploitation can be traced with some accuracy. When palm kernels were crushed, the residue formed a cake which was excellent for livestock. One byproduct of the soap industry was glycerin, which was utilized in the making of explosives. Europeans killed themselves with some of the explosives, but some went into peaceful purposes, such as mining, quarrying, and construction. Several other products were linked to soap through the common base in oils and fats—notably cosmetics, shampoos, perfumes, shaving creams, toothpaste, and dyes. As one writer put it, those by-products "served to broaden the commercial base on which Unilever rested, while making further use of the fund of knowledge already possessed by the oils and fats technologist." Besides, these operations were creating hundreds of thousands of additional jobs for European workers.

The manufacturing of soap and margarine required raw material inputs other than oils and fats. Soap-making consumed large quantities of caustic soda, so that in 1911 Lever bought land in Cheshire suitable for the manufacture of that alkali. Capitalist giants nourished by colonialism and imperialism could afford to do things in a big way. When Lever needed abrasives, the company bought a limestone mine in Bohemia; and when Unilever wanted to assure themselves of supplies of wrapping paper, they bought a paper mill.

Transport was another key problem which stimulated growth at the European end. Within a month of buying the Niger Company in 1920, Lever was engaged in a project for constructing facilities on the Mersey to receive ocean-going ships bringing cargoes from West Africa. The UAC was a pioneer in getting ships constructed to carry palm oil in bulk tanks, and Van der Bergh considered buying a shipyard to build ships for his company some years before the merger. This did not materialize, but Unilever did acquire several ships of their own, including vessels fresh from the shipyards and made to their specifications.

Another linkage of the Unilever industries was that with retail distribution. Their products had to be sold to the housewife, and the Dutch firms that went into Unilever decided that they should own grocery stores to guarantee sales. By 1922, Jurgens had control of a chain of grocery stores in England, appropriately named the "Home and Colonial." Van der Bergh (at the time a rival) was not to be left behind, so he secured majority shares in the chain store owned by Lipton of Lipton's Tea fame. All of these shops passed to Unilever. The grocery store business soon ceased being considered merely as an outlet for soap and margarine, and became an end in itself.

Sometimes, the multiplier effects do not seem connected. On the surface, there was no apparent reason why Lever should set up a huge retail chain called Mac Fisheries to sell fish! There is little in common between soap, sausages, and ice cream—but Lever bought Walls as a sausage firm and later Walls opened an ice cream manufacturing plant. The underlying connection is that capital seeks domination. It grows and spreads and seeks to get hold of everything in sight. The exploitation of Africa gave European monopoly capital full opportunities to indulge in its tendencies for expansion and domination.

Before leaving Unilever, it should be noted in conclusion how a company such as that pointed the way towards change in the capitalist system. The device of the dual structure of Unilever Ltd. and Unilever N.V. was an innovation first utilized when Schicht and Centra of Central Europe merged with the Dutch margarine firms of Jurgens and Van der Bergh, and it was designed to cut down taxation. Unilever comprised two holding companies with the same governing boards and with arrangements to transfer and equalize profits. It was a professional company from its inception. All of the firms involved in the merger had years of experience in organizing staff, production plants, and marketing procedures. Schicht was one of the earliest to work out a system of cost accounting and financial control. Lever had himself been a pioneer of mass advertising in Europe and in the competitive field of the U.S.A. The firm of Unilever inherited and perfected the techniques of mass production and advertising so as to achieve mass consumption.

The significance of the organizational changes are best seen on a long-term basis, by comparing Unilever's sophisticated international organization with the chartered companies of the sixteenth and seventeenth centuries which had difficulties managing accounts. The efficient accounting and business methods which are supposed to characterize capitalist firms did not drop from the sky. They are the result of historical evolution, and in that evolution the exploitation of Africa played a key role—from the era of the chartered companies right through the colonial period.

Contributions of Colonialism to Individual Colonizing Powers

Analysis of the non-monetary benefits of colonialism to the colonizers can of course be carried out most readily within the framework of relations between each colony and its "mother country," apart from the framework of the individual firm, which has just been discussed in some detail. Using the conventional approach of European metropole in relationship to its own colonies, one finds a wide range of positive effects, although the benefits varied in extent from colony to colony. Portugal was the lowliest of the colonizing powers in Africa, and its was nothing in Europe without its colonies: so much so that it came to insist that Angola, Mozambique, and Guinea were integral parts of Portugal, just like any province of the European country named Portugal. France sometimes propounded the same doctrine by which Algeria, Martinique, and Vietnam were all supposedly "overseas France."

Neither Britain nor Belgium put forward any theories of a greater Britain or overseas Belgium; but in practice they were as determined as other colonial powers to insure that sustenance should flow from colony to metropole without hindrance. Few areas of the national life of those Western European countries failed to benefit from the decades of parasitic exploitation of the colonies. One Nigerian, after visiting Brussels in 1960, wrote: "I saw for myself the massive palaces, museums and other public buildings paid for by Congo ivory and rubber."

In recent times, African writers and researchers have also been amazed to find the amount of looted African treasure stacked away in the British Museum; and there are comparable if somewhat smaller collections of African art in Paris, Berlin, and New York. Those are some of the things which, in addition to monetary wealth, help to define the metropoles as developed and "civilized."

Sustenance given by colonies to the colonizers was most obvious and very decisive in the case of contributions by soldiers from among the colonized. Without colonial troops, there would have been no "British forces" fighting on the Asian front in the 1939–45 war, because the ranks of the British forces were filled with Indians and other colonials, including Africans and West Indians. It is a general characteristic of colonialism that the metropole utilized the manpower of the colonies. The Romans had used soldiers of one conquered nationality to conquer other nationalities, as well as to defend Rome against enemies. Britain applied this to Africa from the early nineteenth century, when the West Indian Regiment was sent across the Atlantic to protect British interests in the West African coast. The West Indian Regiment had black men in the ranks, Irish (colonials) as NCOs, and Englishmen as officers. By the end of the nineteenth century, the West Indian Regiment also included lots of Sierra Leoneans.

The most important force in the conquest of West African colonies by the British was the West African Frontier Force—the soldiers being

Africans and the officers English. In 1894, it was joined by the West African Regiment, formed to help suppress the so-called Hut Tax War in Sierra Leone, which was the expression of widespread resistance against the imposition of colonial rule. In East and Central Africa, the King's African Rifles was the unit which tapped African fighting power on behalf of Britain. The African regiments supplemented the metropolitan military apparatus in several ways. Firstly, they were used as emergency forces to put down nationalist uprisings in the various colonies. Secondly, they were used to fight other Europeans inside Africa, notably during the First and Second World Wars. And thirdly, they were carried to European battlefields or to theatres of war outside Africa.

African roles in European military operations were vividly displayed by the East African campaign during the First World War, when Britain and Germany fought for possession of East Africa. At the beginning of the war, the Germans had in Tanganyika a regular force of 216 Europeans and 2,540 African *askari*. During the war, 3,000 Europeans and 11,000 *askari* were enrolled. On the British side, the main force was the K.A.R., comprising mainly East Africans and soldiers from Nyasaland. The battalions of the K.A.R. had by November 1918 over 35,000 men, of whom nine out of ten were Africans.

Quite early in the East African campaign, the British brought in an expeditionary force of Punjabis and Sikhs, as well as regiments of West Africans. Some Sudanese and West Indians were also there. At first, a few white settlers joined the war, because they thought it was a picnic; but within a year the white residents of British East Africa were showing extreme reluctance to join local fighting forces. In effect, therefore, Africans were fighting Africans to see which European power should rule over them. The Germans and the British had only to provide the officers. According to the history books, the "British" won the campaign in East Africa.

France was the colonial power that secured the greatest number of soldiers from Africa. In 1912, conscription of African soldiers into the French army was pursued on a large scale. During the 1914–18 war, 200,000 soldiers were recruited in French West Africa, through the use of methods reminiscent of slave hunting. These "French" soldiers served against the Germans in Togo and Cameroon, as well as in Europe itself. On the European battlefields, an estimated 25,000 "French" Africans lost their lives, and many more returned mutilated, for they were used as cannon fodder in the European capitalist war.

France was so impressed by the military advantages to be gained from colonial rule that when a part of Cameroon was mandated to France by the League of Nations, France insisted on the privilege of using Cameroon African troops for purposes unconnected with the defense of Cameroon. Naturally, France also made the maximum use of African troops in the last world war. Indeed, Africans saved France after the initial losses when France and most of French Africa fell under the Germans and the fascist (Vichy) French. In French Equatorial Africa, it was a black man, Felix Eboue, who proved loyal to the forces led by General de Gaulle, and who mobilized manpower against the French and German fascists. Africa provided the base and much of the manpower for launching the counter-attack which helped General de Gaulle and the Free French to return to power in France.

French use of African troops did not end with the last war. West Africans were sent to Madagascar in 1948, and put down nationalist forces in a most bloody manner. African troops were also employed to fight the people of Indochina up to 1954; and, later still, black African troops and Senegalese in particular were used against the Algerian liberation movement.

No comprehensive studies have as yet been devoted to the role of Africans in the armies of the colonial powers in a variety of contexts. However, the indications are that such studies would reveal a pattern very similar to that discovered by historians who have looked at the role of black soldiers in the white-controlled armies of the U.S.A.; namely, that there was tremendous discrimination against black fighting men, even though black soldiers made great and unacknowledged contributions to important victories won by the white-officered armies of the U.S.A. and the colonial powers. Hints regarding discrimination are to be seen from regulations such as that barring African soldiers in the West African Regiment from wearing shoes and from the fact that there were actually race riots in the European campaigns, just as black troops fighting for the U.S.A. continued to riot right up to the Vietnam campaign.

A number of Africans served as colonial soldiers with pride, because they mistakenly hoped that the army would be an avenue for displaying the courage and dignity of Africans, and, perhaps, in the process, even earning the freedom of the continent, by making Europeans pleased and grateful. That hope was without foundation from the outset, because the colonialists were viciously using African soldiers as pawns to preserve colonialism and capitalism in general. A very striking instance of the above fact was provided when John Chilembwe led an African nationalist uprising in Nyasaland (now Malawi) in 1915. Nyasaland was then a British colony, and although the British were fighting the Germans in East Africa at that time, they immediately dispatched a column of the

K.A.R. to contend against Chilembwe. Furthermore, before the K.A.R. arrived, it was a German lieutenant who organized the resistance of Nyasa white settlers against Chilembwe's bid for freedom. In the light of that evidence, one writer commented:

> While their countrymen in Europe fought the bloodiest war ever known, in Africa Europeans were instinctively white men first—and German and British second, [for] John Chilembwe was part of something that in the end would swamp all their colonial dreams.

The African continent and the African people were used by the colonialists in some curious ways to advance their military strengths and techniques. By chance, North Africa and the Sahara became available as a laboratory for the evolution of techniques of armored warfare in the period when Rommel and Montgomery battled for superiority. And, by design, Ethiopians were used as guinea pigs, upon whom the Italian fascists experimented with poison gas. This followed their brazen invasion in 1935 of that small portion of Africa which still clung to some form of political independence. At that time, the Italians argued that it was absolutely essential that the fruits of colonialism be opened to Italy if it were to take "its place in the sun." Significantly enough, both Britain and France had already seen so much of the sun and products of Africa that they found it difficult to refute Italy's claims.

Britain and France ruled over the greater part of colonial Africa and they also had the largest empires in other parts of the world. The whole existence and development of capitalism in Britain and France between 1885 and 1960 was bound up with colonization, and Africa played a major role. African colonies meant surplus appropriated on a grand scale; they led to innovations and forward leaps in technology and the organization of capitalist enterprise; and they buttressed the capitalist system at home and abroad with fighting men. Sometimes, it appeared that these two principal colonial powers reaped so many colonial benefits that they suffered from "too much of a good thing."

Certainly, in Britain's case, it can be argued that colonialism allowed British industry to lead a soft life, and that, in some decisive spheres of production and marketing, Britain grew lazy. Industrial plants installed in the nineteenth century were not renovated or replaced, and little dynamism was put into selling new lines of goods. In contrast, when deprived of colonies after 1918, Germany was forced to live off its own resources and ingenuity. Nevertheless, while that is an interesting detail of the whole colonial picture, it must be borne in mind that colonialism was one aspect of imperialism. Colonialism was based on alien political rule and was restricted to some parts of the world. Imperialism, however, underlay all colonies, extended all over the world (except where replaced by socialist revolutions), and it allowed the participation of all capitalist nations. Therefore, lack of colonies on the part of any capitalist nation was not a barrier to enjoying the fruits of exploiting the colonial and semi-colonial world, which was the backyard of metropolitan capitalism.

Colonialism as a Prop to Metropolitan Economies and Capitalism as a System

The composition of Unilever should serve as a warning that colonialism was not simply a matter of ties between a given colony and its mother country, but between colonies on the one hand and metropoles on the other. The German capital in Unilever joined the British in exploiting Africa and the Dutch in exploiting the East Indies. The rewards spread through the capitalist system in such a way that even those capitalist nations who were not colonial powers were also beneficiaries of the spoils. Unilever factories established in Switzerland, New Zealand, Canada, and the U.S.A. were participants in the expropriation of Africa's surplus and in using that surplus for their own development.

Germany always had a stake in colonial Africa, even after 1918 when the other capitalist powers deprived Germany of its colonies. German ship-ping revived in the 1920s and played an active role in East, West, and South Africa. German financial houses also had contacts with Africa, the most direct being the Twentsche Bank in East Africa. Dutch shipping companies were involved with the German and British in the West African Conference Line, while the Scandinavian shippers were noted for the hiring out of "tramp" ships which freighted cargo between Africa and Europe outside of the scheduled lines. The old East African Trading Company was supported by Danish capital. The Swiss had no colonies in Africa, but they had substantial capital in SCOA, they played a key role in imperialist banking, and they kept out of the wars fought by other capitalists so that they could still continue to trade with both sides and thereby acquire colonial produce. Then there was Japan—a capitalist/ imperialist power with colonies in Asia and with a keen interest in trade with Africa. Japanese capitalists tried to undersell their European counter-parts, but the trade they conducted with Africa was still unequal and disadvantageous to the Africans.

To fully understand the colonial period, it is necessary to think in terms of the economic partition of Africa. Unlike the political partition of the nineteenth century, the economic partition had no fixed or visible boundaries. It consisted of the proportions in which capitalist powers divided up among themselves the monetary and non-monetary gains from colonial Africa. For instance, Portugal had two large political colonies in Southern Africa, but economically Mozambique and Angola were divided among several capitalist powers, which were invited by the Portuguese government, because Portuguese capitalists were too weak to handle those vast territories.

Congo and South Africa had their own special arrangements of economic partition, both of them being valuable territories. At first, Congo was designated the "Congo Free State" under King Leopold II of Belgium. That meant that it was to have been a free trade zone and an area open to investment by capitalists of all nationalities. In practice, Leopold used administrative devices to monopolize the wealth of the Congo, and that was one of the principal reasons the international capitalist community moved against Leopold in 1908. When Belgium took over the administration of the Congo, it also insured that most of the surplus and other benefits should accrue to Belgium. However, non-Belgian capitalist interests were able to penetrate through investment in mining; and, as the colonial period advanced, the British, French, and Americans cut bigger pieces of the Congo cake.

For a long while, South Africa was the most important raw material reservoir for the whole of imperialism. Britain was the European power which had already been entrenched in South Africa for many years when gold and diamonds were discovered in the nineteenth century, on the eve of the Scramble. Britain had to come to terms with the Boer settlers, whose livelihood then came primarily from the land, and whose main interest was to see to the exploitation and domination of the African population and other groups of non-white immigrants. Therefore, the economic and political partition of Africa gave Britain the lion's share of the mineral wealth, while the Boers retained the political power necessary to institutionalize white racism. As capitalists of other nationalities entered into relations with South Africa through investment and trade, those capitalists agreed to strengthen, and did, the racist/fascist social relations of South Africa.

Economic partition and repartition of Africa was going on all the time, because the proportions of the spoils that went to different capitalist countries kept changing. Special mention must be made of the U.S.A., because its share of the benefits from Africa was constantly increasing throughout the colonial period.

As time went on, the U.S.A. got an ever bigger slice of the unequal trade between the metropoles and colonial Africa. The share of the U.S.A.

in Africa's trade rose from just over 28 million dollars in 1913 to 150 million dollars in 1932 and to 1,200 million dollars in 1948, at which figure it represented nearly 15 per cent of Africa's foreign trade. The share of the U.S.A. in West Africa's trade rose from 38 million dollars in 1938 to 163 million dollars in 1946 and to 517 million dollars by 1954.

However, it was South Africa which was America's best trading partner in Africa, supplying her with gold, diamonds, manganese, and other minerals and buying heavy machinery in turn. Apart from direct U.S.A.-South African trade, most of South Africa's gold was resold in London to American buyers, just as most Gold Coast and Nigerian cocoa was resold to the U.S.A.

Intercontinental trade brought out the need for shipping services and America did not leave those in the hands of capitalists of other nations. James Farrell, President of the United States Steel Export Company, acquired a shipping line to Africa because of his "belief in the future of the Dark Continent." Officials of the UAC had said exactly the same thing, and it is obvious that, like them, Farrell meant the bright future of metropolitan capitalism in exploiting Africa. It is always best when these individuals speak for themselves. Vice-Admiral Cochrane of the United States Navy was a great admirer of Farrell shipping lines. In 1959, he wrote an introduction to a study of Farrell's operations in Africa, in which he said:

> We read of stiff international competition to assure the supply of strategic materials for our current industrial-military economy. Farrell Lines is making American maritime history. It is demonstrating clearly and emphatically that ships wearing the flag of a nation do in fact stimulate the commerce of that nation . . . demonstrating the value of American-flag ocean commerce to the health and wealth of the United States.

United States capitalists did not confine themselves to mere trade with Africa, but they also acquired considerable assets within the colonies. It is common knowledge that Liberia was an American colony in everything but name. The U.S.A. supposedly aided the Liberian government with loans, but used the opportunity to take over Liberian customs revenue, to plunder thousands of square miles of Liberian land, and generally to dictate to the weak government of Liberia. The main investment in Liberia was undertaken by Firestone Rubber Company. Firestone made such huge profits from Liberian rubber that it was the subject of a book sponsored by American capitalists to show how well American business flourished overseas. Between 1940 and 1965, Firestone took 160 million dollars' worth of rubber out of Liberia; while in return the Liberian government received 8 million dollars. In earlier years, the percentage of the value that went to the Liberian government was much smaller, but, at the best of times, the average net profit made by Firestone was three times the Liberian revenue.

And yet the non-monetary benefits to the United States capitalist economy were worth far more than the money returns. Vice-Admiral Cochrane, in the quotation above, went to the heart of the matter when he mentioned strategic raw materials for the functioning of the industrial and military machine of the American imperialists. Firestone acquired its Liberian plantations precisely because Britain and Holland had been raising the price of the rubber which came from their Asian colonies of Malaya and the Dutch East Indies, respectively. In Liberia, the United States rubber industry obtained a source that was reliable in peace and war—one that was cheap and entirely under American control. One of rubber's most immediate connections was with the automobile industry, and so it is not surprising that Harvey Firestone was a great friend and business colleague of Henry Ford. Liberian rubber turned the town of Akron, Ohio, into a powerful rubber tire manufacturing center, and the tires then went over to the even bigger automobile works of Ford in Detroit.

American investment in Africa during the last fifteen years of colonialism was in some ways at the expense of the actual colonizing powers and yet ultimately it was in the interest of Western European capitalism. This paradox is explained by noting that the U.S.A. had become the world's leading capitalist/imperialist power by the outbreak of the Second World War. It possessed the colonies of Puerto Rico and the Philippines, but much more important were its imperialistic investments throughout Latin America and to a lesser extent in Asia and Africa. America's foreign investments in the 1930s drew slightly ahead of those of Britain, which were a long way ahead of the imperialist outlay of France, Germany, and Japan. The 1939–45 war tremendously accelerated the changeover in America's favor.

Europe suffered staggering losses, but no battles were fought on American soil, and so its productive capacity expanded. Therefore, after 1945, American capital moved into Africa, Asia, and Europe itself with new aggressiveness and confidence, due to the fact that other capitalist competitors were still lying on the ground. In 1949, both British and French bankers had no choice but to invite American financiers into the African continent, for the French and British had insufficient capital of their own. The United States-controlled International Bank for Reconstruction and Development became an important vehicle for American influence in Africa and one of the tools for the economic repartition of the continent.

Research by Dr. Kwame Nkrumah revealed that direct private investment by Americans in Africa increased between 1945 and 1958 from 110 million dollars to 789 million dollars, most of its drawn from profits. Official estimates of profits made by United States companies from 1946 to 1959 in Africa are put at 1,234 million dollars. In considering the question of economic partition, what is relevant is the *rate of growth* of United States investments and profits compared to those of Britain, France, Belgium. For instance, the American investment in 1951 was 313 million dollars, which was nearly three times what it was five years earlier, and in the subsequent five years the investment went up two and a half times. Meanwhile, British and French investment increased much more slowly.

However, while the U.S.A. was edging out the other colonialists, they all stood to gain from the advances made within the North American capitalist economy in terms of science, technology, organization, and military power. As pointed out earlier, when an African colony contributed to the European metallurgical industries or to its electrical industry, that contribution passed into other aspects of the society, because the sectors concerned were playing leading roles within the capitalist economy. Similarly, the U.S.A. was a geographical area that was in the forefront of capitalist development. For instance, its technological know-how passed into Western European hands by way of a series of legal devices such as patents.

Furthermore, because the U.S.A. was by then the world's leading capitalist state, it also had to assume active responsibility for maintaining the capitalist imperialist structure in all its economic, political, and military aspects. After the war, the U.S.A. moved into Western Europe and Japan both to establish its own stranglehold and at the same time to give a blood transfusion to capitalism in those areas. A lot of the blood was definitely African. It is not just that America made (relatively) small profits out of Africa in the nineteenth century and in the early twentieth century, but above all it must be recalled that North America was that part of the European capitalist system which had been the most direct beneficiary of the massacre of the American Indians and the enslavement of Africans. The continued exploitation of African peoples within its own boundaries and in the Caribbean and Latin America must also be cited as evidence against American monster imperialism. The U.S.A. was a worthy successor to Britain as the leading force and policeman of the imperialist/colonialist world from 1945 onwards.

Under the Marshall Plan, by which United States capitalism aided Western European capitalism after the last war, it was announced that American experts were exploring Africa from end to end for agricultural and mineral wealth—especially the latter. Marshall Plan money (through the Economic Commission for Africa) went to firms like the Mines de Zellidja, which mined lead and zinc in North Africa; and, at the same time, the money allowed Americans to buy controlling shares in the company. Thus in 1954, Morgan of the U.S.A. shared with Rothschilds of Europe most of the net profit of 1,250 million old francs (8.16 million dollars) made by the Mines de Zellidja in that year. Similarly, the Belgian government received substantial aid from the U.S.A. to implement a ten-year economic program in Congo from 1950 to 1959; and, as the price of the aid, United States monopolies established control over some companies in Congo. The U.S.A. took second place after Belgium in Congo's foreign trade, and United States capitalists had to be granted a range of privileges.

So the paradox continued, whereby United States capitalists intruded and elbowed out French, British, and Belgian capitalists in colonial Africa, while providing the funds without which the Western European nations could not have revived and could not have increased their exploitation of Africa—which is what they did in the period of 1945–60.

Over the last few decades of colonialism, colonial possessions served capitalism as a safety valve in times of crisis. The first major occasion when this was displayed was during the great economic depression of 1929–34. During that period, forced labor was increased in Africa and the prices paid to Africans for their crops were reduced. Workers were paid less and imported goods cost a great deal more. That was a time when workers in the metropolitan countries also suffered terribly; but the colonialists did the best they could to transfer the burdens of the depression away from Europe and on to the colonies.

The great economic depression did not affect the Soviet Union, where socialism caused great development; but the slump spread from one end of the capitalist system to the other. It was a product of the irrationality of the capitalist mode of production. The search for profits caused production to run ahead of people's capacity to purchase, and ultimately both production and employment had to be drastically reduced. Africans had nothing to do with the inherent shortcomings of capitalism; but, when Europeans were in a mess, they had no scruples about intensifying the exploitation of Africa. The economic depression was not a situation from which Britain could benefit at the expense of Sweden or where Belgium could gain at the expense of the U.S.A. They were all drowning, and that was why the benefits of the colonies saved not only the colonizing powers but all capitalist nations.

The second major occasion on which the colonies had to bail out the metropoles was during the last world war. As noted earlier, the African people were required to make huge sacrifices and to supply vital raw materials at little cost to the metropoles. Africa's military importance was also decisive. Not only did Africans fight and die on various battlefields of the war, but the continent held a key strategic position. In November 1942, a third front was opened in Africa (following the European and Asian fronts), and that front was the means to final victory.

Accidents of geography meant that Africa controlled communications in the Mediterranean and in the South Atlantic, and it commanded the two western entrances into the Indian Ocean. As one military analyst put it, "The side that held Africa was on the way to final victory." With the aid of African fighting men and resources, the major colonial powers maintained control of the continent in the face of attacks by the Italians, who had only Libya, Somaliland, and (briefly) Ethiopia. The Germans of course by then had no colonies in Africa, and they had to use what was offered by the Italians and fascist Vichy Frenchmen.

Unlike the First World War, the Second World War was not simply one between capitalist powers. The aggressor states of Italy, Germany, and Japan were fascist. The governments of Portugal, Spain, and South Africa also subscribed to that ideology, although for opportunist reasons both the Portuguese and the South African Boers found it more convenient to be allied with Britain, France, the U.S.A., and the other bourgeois democracies.

Fascism is a deformity of capitalism. It heightens the imperialist tendency towards domination which is inherent in capitalism, and it safeguards the principle of private property. At the same time, fascism immeasurably strengthens the institutional racism already bred by capitalism, whether it be against Jews (as in Hitler's case) or against African peoples (as in the ideology of Portugal's Salazar and the leaders of South Africa). Fascism reverses the political gains of the bourgeois democratic system such as free elections, equality before the law, parliaments; and it also extolls authoritarianism and the reactionary union of the church with the state. In Portugal and Spain, it was the Catholic church—in South Africa, it was the Dutch Reformed church.

Like its progenitor, capitalism, fascism is totally opposed to socialism. Fascist Germany and Italy attacked both the other capitalist states and the Soviet Union, which was still the only socialist state in the world by 1939. The defeat of fascism was therefore a victory for socialism, and at the same time it preserved the other capitalist nations from having to take the historically retrograde step of fascism.

When the last world war ended, Africa's further role was to help Europe reconstruct. In that crisis, the U.S.A. played a major part, as has just been mentioned; but the colonizing nations also had direct recourse to their colonies, in spite of shortage of capital. It is noteworthy that

European capitalism from the late 1940s onwards recognized Africa's potential as a savior of their own war-torn economies, and they openly made statements to that effect.

It was in 1946 that the Ministry of Colonies in the French cabinet was renamed the Ministry of Overseas France and that colonized Africans were euphemistically called "overseas Frenchmen." About that time, a statement from the French Ministry of Education frankly admitted that:

> France would be only a little state of Europe without the seventy-five million overseas Frenchmen whose young force has revealed itself to the world in such a remarkable manner [referring to Africa's role in the war].

Shortly afterwards, when France prepared its Four Year Plan for 1949–52, statements such as the following were to be encountered:

> Morocco will take an active part in the recovery of France by supplying manganese, cobalt and lead ore, canned goods and agricultural produce.

At the end of the last war, both Britain and France set up agencies for the "development" of their colonies. In the British sphere, this was known as the Colonial Development and Welfare (CD&W), while the French fund was known as FIDES. Their principal function was to provide loans, the purpose of which was to help the colonies to help the metropoles. In other words, the crisis of postwar reconstruction required that even greater effort should be made to maximize the resources of colonies.

It was no ordinary postwar crisis which Western Europe faced in the 1940s and 1950s. The bourgeoisie had to rebuild capitalist states at a time when socialism had already proved itself in the Soviet Union, and in a period when the Red Army of the Soviets had aided groups of socialists to come to power in Eastern Europe. This was the greatest challenge ever to be faced by the bourgeoisie because (unlike fascism) socialism threatened the basic capitalist principle of private ownership of the means of production. Furthermore, socialist principles were making their presence felt even in remote corners of the colonies, and the capitalists realized the necessity for cutting the colonies off from socialist thought, as well as using colonial resources to stave off what they termed "the threat of communism."

In the capitalist struggle to keep off the challenge of socialism as a competing mode of production and way of life, Africa played at least two key roles—one being to provide bases for the capitalist militarists, and the other being to provide a wide range of raw materials essential for modern armament industries. The most vital of these raw materials were uranium and other radioactive substances for atomic and later nuclear weapons, including the hydrogen bomb. Almost rivaling uranium in importance were certain rare minerals (like lithium from Rhodesia) needed for the special steels that went into new aircraft rockets, tanks, guns, and bombs.

Colonial powers already had small military establishments in each colony, and right up to the end of the colonial era, it was considered necessary to strengthen those. For instance, in the 1955 French budget there was a special vote of six billion francs (16.8 million dollars) for the improvement of military installations in the colonies, and notably for strategic bases in Dakar and Djibouti. Some time previously, the Belgians had completed a huge air base near Kamina in the Congo.

Adding to the regular bases in long-established colonies, the imperialist powers were able to set up military installations in African territories which fell into their hands during the war. In this context, the U.S.A. was particularly important, because it was already the principal buttress of the capitalist defense system in the form of the North Atlantic Treaty Organization (NATO). Thus, after helping to recapture North Africa from the fascists, the United States was able to build major air-force bases in Morocco and Libya. In Italian Eritrea, the Americans stepped in with modern radar stations; and Ethiopia conceded military bases.

Though nominally independent, Liberia had little option but to accept a massive military presence of Americans, as a logical consequence of America's economic exploitation and domination of Liberia. When the U.S.A. agreed to build a port at Monrovia in 1943, they also obtained the concession that the U.S.A. was to have "the right to establish, use, maintain and control such naval, air and military facilities and installations at the site of the port, and in the general vicinity thereof, as may be desired for the protection of the strategic interests of the U.S.A. in the South Atlantic." Throughout the war, Liberia's Robertsfield airfield had been of considerable value to the U.S.A. and later on it continued to have a military utility. To tie matters up further, the U.S.A. entered into what it called a military assistance pact with Liberia in 1951.

Needless to say, in the 1950s when most Africans were still colonial subjects, they had absolutely no control over the utilization of their soil for militaristic ends. Virtually the whole of North Africa was turned into a sphere of operations for NATO, with bases aimed at the Soviet Union. There could easily have developed a nuclear war without African peoples having any knowledge of the matter. The colonial powers actually held military conferences in African cities like Dakar and Nairobi in the early 1950s, inviting the whites of South Africa and Rhodesia and the government of the U.S.A. Time and time again, the evidence points to this cynical use of Africa to buttress capitalism economically and militarily, and therefore in effect forcing Africa to contribute to its own exploitation.

Apart from saving capitalism in times of crisis, the dependencies had always been prolonging the life of capitalism by taking the edge off the internal contradictions and conflicts which were a part of the capitalist system. The principal contradiction within capitalism from the outset was that between the capitalists and the workers. To keep their system going, the capitalists had constantly to step up the rate of exploitation of their workers. At the same time, European workers were gaining increasing mastery over the means of production in the factories and mines, and they were learning to work collectively in big enterprises and within their own trade union structures. If the bourgeoisie continued to deprive them of the major part of the fruits of their own labor and to oppress them socially and politically, then those two classes were set on a collision path. Ever since the mid-nineteenth century, Marx had predicted class collision would come in the form of revolution in which workers would emerge victorious. The capitalists were terribly afraid of that possibility, knowing full well that they themselves had seized power from the feudal landlord class by means of revolution. However, imperialism introduced a new factor into this situation—one that deferred the confrontation between workers and capitalists in the metropoles.

Only in Russia was there a workers' revolution, and Russia was on the fringe of Europe rather than being one of its metropolitan capitalist centers. That very fact highlighted how much capitalism in places like Britain, France, and Germany had been stabilized by exploiting the colonies and other semi-colonies such as Latin America, where states were independent in name only.

Surplus from Africa was partly used to offer a few more benefits to European workers and served as a bribe to make the latter less revolutionary. The bribe came in the form of increased wages, better working conditions, and expanded social services. The benefits of colonialism were diffused throughout European society in many ways. Most capitalist enterprises offered consumer goods which were mass produced at low prices, and therefore the European housewife got some relief. For instance, instant coffee brought that beverage within the reach of the ordinary worker. Meanwhile, the capitalist still made his fortune by insuring that the Ivory Coast or Colombian grower got no price increase. In that way, colonialism was serving all classes and sectors of Western Europe and other capitalist metropoles.

European workers have paid a great price for the few material benefits which accrued to them as crumbs from the colonial table. The class in power controls the dissemination of information. The capitalists misinformed and miseducated workers in the metropoles to the point where they became allies in colonial exploitation. In accepting to be led like sheep, European workers were perpetuating their own enslavement to the capitalists. They ceased to seek political power and contented themselves with bargaining for small wage increases, which were usually counter-balanced by increased costs of living. They ceased to be creative and allowed bourgeois cultural decadence to overtake them all. They failed to exercise any independent judgment on the great issues of war and peace, and therefore ended up by slaughtering not only colonial peoples but also themselves.

Fascism was a monster born of capitalist parents. Fascism came as the end-product of centuries of capitalist bestiality, exploitation, domination, and racism—mainly exercised outside Europe. It is highly significant that many settlers and colonial officials displayed a leaning towards fascism. Apartheid in South Africa is nothing but fascism. It was gaining roots from the early period of white colonization in the seventeenth century, and particularly after the mining industry brought South Africa fully into the capitalist orbit in the nineteenth century. Another example of the fascist potential of colonialism was seen when France was overrun by Nazi Germany in 1940. The French fascists collaborated with Hitler to establish what was called the Vichy regime in France, and the French white settlers in Africa supported the Vichy regime. A more striking instance to the same effect was the fascist ideology developed by the white settlers in Algeria, who not only opposed independence for Algeria under Algerian rule, but they also strove to bring down the more progressive or liberal governments of metropolitan France.

Inside Europe itself, some specific and highly revealing connections can be found between colonialist behavior and the destruction of the few contributions made by capitalism to human development. For instance, when Colonel Von Lettow returned from leading the German forces in East Africa in World War I, he was promoted to a general in the German army, and Von Lettow was in command of the massacre of German communists in Hamburg in 1918. That was a decisive turning point in German history, for once the most progressive workers had been crushed, the path was clear for the fascist deformation of the future. In brutally suppressing the Maji Maji War in Tanganyika and in attempting genocide against the Herero people of Namibia (South-West Africa), the German ruling class were getting the experience which they later applied against the Jews and against German workers and progressives.

When the fascist dictatorship was inaugurated in Portugal in 1926, it drew inspiration from Portugal's colonial past. After Salazar became the dictator in 1932, he stated that his "New State" in Portugal would be based on the labor of the "inferior peoples," meaning of course Africans. In addition, Portuguese peasants and workers had to submit to police terror, poverty, and dehumanization, so they paid (and are still paying) a high price for fascism at home and colonialism abroad.

Colonialism strengthened the Western European ruling class and capitalism as a whole. Particularly in its later phases, it was evidently giving a new lease of life to a mode of production that was otherwise dying. From every viewpoint other than that of the minority class of capitalists, colonialism was a monstrous institution holding back the liberation of man.

Brief Guide to Reading

Here again, few scholars have treated capitalism and imperialism as an integral system involving the transfer of surplus and other benefits from colonies to metropoles. And, where there is an awareness of the unity of the system, no detailed analysis necessarily follows. In effect, one is faced with the limitations of a metropolitan viewpoint. Thus, European or white American Marxists who expose the rapacious nature of modern capitalism within their own countries have not generally integrated this with the exploitation of Africa, Asia, and Latin America—except for the very recent neo-colonial period.

GEORGE PADMORE, *Africa: How Britain Rules Africa*. London: Wishart Books Ltd., 1936.
KWAME NKRUMAH, *Africa Must Unite*. New York: International Publishers, 1970.
———— *Neo-colonialism, the Highest Stage of Imperialism*.
W. A. HUNTON, *Decision in Africa*. New York: International Publishers, 1957.
    The most vociferous remarks about Africa's contribution to Europe have been made by politically involved Pan-African intellectuals, such as these three.

GROVER CLARK, *The Balance Sheets of Colonialism*. New York: Russell and Russell, 1967.
D. K. FIELDHOUSE, *The Colonial Empires*. New York: Delacorte Press, 1966.
    These two texts proclaim that colonialism was not essentially economic, and that the colonizers did not gain. The second book is recent, and the view is still very much alive.

U.S.S.R. Institute of History, *A History of Africa 1918–1967*.
PIERRE JALÉE, *The Pillage of the Third World*. New York: Monthly Review Press, 1970.
    These (Marxist) texts specifically about Africa and the exploited sector of the capitalist world do make the point that the metropoles were extracting huge colonial surpluses.

CHAPTER
VI

Colonialism as a System For Underdeveloping Africa

· The Supposed Benefits of Colonialism to Africa   · Negative Character of the Social, Political, and Economic Consequences   · Education for Underdevelopment   · Development by Contradiction

THE BLACK MAN CERTAINLY HAS TO PAY DEAR FOR CARRYING THE WHITE
man's burden.

—GEORGE PADMORE
(West Indian) Pan-Africanist, 1936

In the colonial society, education is such that it serves the colonialist. . . .
In a regime of slavery, education was but one institution for forming
slaves.

—Statement of FRELIMO (Mozambique Liberation Front)
Department of Education and Culture, 1968

The Supposed Benefits of Colonialism to Africa

Socio-Economic Services

Faced with the evidence of European exploitation of Africa, many
bourgeois writers would concede at least partially that colonialism was a
system which functioned well in the interests of the metropoles. However,
they would then urge that another issue to be resolved is how much Europeans did for Africans, and that it is necessary to draw up a balance sheet
of colonialism. On that balance sheet, they place both the credits and the
debits, and quite often conclude that the good outweighed the bad. That
particular conclusion can quite easily be challenged, but attention should
also be drawn to the fact that the process of reasoning is itself misleading.
The reasoning has some sentimental persuasiveness. It appeals to the
common sentiment that "after all there must be two sides to a thing." The
argument suggests that, on the one hand, there was exploitation and oppression, but, on the other hand, colonial governments did much for the
benefit of Africans and they developed Africa. It is our contention that
this is completely false. Colonialism had only one hand—it was a one-
armed bandit.

What did colonial governments do in the interest of Africans? Supposedly, they built railroads, schools, hospitals, and the like. The sum total
of these services was amazingly small.

For the first three decades of colonialism, hardly anything was done that
could remotely be termed a service to the African people. It was in fact
only after the last war that social services were built as a matter of policy.
How little they amounted to does not really need illustrating. After all, the

205

statistics which show that Africa today is underdeveloped are the statistics representing the state of affairs at the end of colonialism. For that matter, the figures at the end of the first decade of African independence in spheres such as health, housing, and education are often several times higher than the figures inherited by the newly independent governments. It would be an act of the most brazen fraud to weigh the paltry social amenities provided during the colonial epoch against the exploitation, and to arrive at the conclusion that the good outweighed the bad.

Capitalism did bring social services to European workers—firstly, as a by-product of providing such services for the bourgeoisie and the middle class, and later as a deliberate act of policy. Nothing remotely comparable occurred in Africa. In 1934, long before the coming of the welfare state to Britain, expenditure for social services in the British Isles amounted to 6 pounds 15 shillings per person. In Ghana, the figure was 7 shillings 4 pence per person, and that was high by colonial standards. In Nigeria and Nyasaland, it was less than 1 shilling 9 pence per head. None of the other colonizing powers were doing any better, and some much worse.

The Portuguese stand out because they boasted the most and did the least. Portugal boasted that Angola, Guinea, and Mozambique have been their possessions for five hundred years, during which time a "civilizing mission" has been going on. At the end of five hundred years of shouldering the white man's burden of civilizing "African natives," the Portuguese had not managed to train a single African doctor in Mozambique, and the life expectancy in eastern Angola was less than thirty years. As for Guinea-Bissau, some insight into the situation there is provided by the admission of the Portuguese themselves that Guinea-Bissau was more neglected than Angola and Mozambique!

Furthermore, the limited social services within Africa during colonial times were distributed in a manner that reflected the pattern of domination and exploitation. First of all, white settlers and expatriates wanted the standards of the bourgeoisie or professional classes of the metropoles. They were all the more determined to have luxuries in Africa, because so many of them came from poverty in Europe and could not expect good services in their own homelands. In colonies like Algeria, Kenya, and South Africa, it is well known that whites created an infrastructure to afford themselves leisured and enjoyable lives. It means, therefore, that the total amenities provided in any of those colonies is no guide to what Africans got out of colonialism.

In Algeria, the figure for infant mortality was 39 per 1,000 live births among white settlers; but it jumped to 170 per 1,000 live births in the case of Algerians living in the towns. In practical terms, that meant that the medical, maternity, and sanitation services were all geared towards the well-being of the settlers. Similarly, in South Africa, all social statistics have to be broken down into at least two groups—white and black—if they are to be interpreted correctly. In British East Africa there were three groups: firstly, the Europeans, who got the most; then, the Indians, who took most of what was left; and thirdly, the Africans, who came last in their own country.

In predominantly black countries, it was also true that the bulk of the social services went to whites. The southern part of Nigeria was one of the colonial areas that was supposed to have received the most from a benevolent mother country. Ibadan, one of the most heavily populated cities in Africa, had only about 50 Europeans before the last war. For those chosen few, the British colonial government maintained a segregated hospital service of 11 beds in well-furnished surroundings. There were 34 beds for the half-million blacks. The situation was repeated in other areas, so that altogether the 4,000 Europeans in the country in the 1930s had 12 modern hospitals, while the African population of at least 40 million had 52 hospitals.

The viciousness of the colonial system with respect to the provision of social services was most dramatically brought out in the case of economic activities which made huge profits, and notably in the mining industry. Mining takes serious toll of the health of workers, and it was only recently in the metropoles that miners have had access to the kind of medical and insurance services which could safeguard their lives and health. In colonial Africa, the exploitation of miners was entirely without responsibility. In 1930, scurvy and other epidemics broke out in the Lupa goldfields of Tanganyika. Hundreds of workers died. One should not wonder that they had no facilities which would have saved some lives, because in the first place they were not being paid enough to eat properly.

South Africa's large working class African population was in a sad state. The Tuberculosis Commission of 1912 reported that in the shanty towns,

> Scarcely a single family exists in which at least one member is not suffering or dying from tuberculosis. Hospital services are so inadequate that incurable tuberculosis and other cases are simply sent home to die—and spread the infection. In some areas, a single doctor has to attend to the needs of 40,000 people. The natives must pay for medical treatment. There is no provision for pauper patients. About 65% of the native children die before reaching two years.

That was as early as 1912, when the basis of the South African gold and diamond empire was already laid. After this, the shanty towns increased, the slum conditions grew worse, and the government committed itself to pursuing the odious policy of apartheid, which meant separation of the races so as better to exploit the African people.

Many Africans trekked to towns, because (bad as they were) they offered a little more than the countryside. Modern sanitation, electricity, piped water, paved roads, medical services, and schools were as foreign at the end of the colonal period as they were in the beginning—as far as most of rural Africa was concerned. Yet, it was the countryside that grew the cash crops and provided the labor that kept the system going. The peasants there knew very little of the supposed "credits" on the colonial balance sheet.

Because even the scanty social services were meant only to facilitate exploitation, they were not given to any Africans whose labor was not directly producing surplus for export to the metropoles. That is to say, none of the wealth of exploited Africans could be deployed for the assistance of their brothers outside the money economy.

Multiple examples exist to substantiate the above proposition. The most "wealthy" colonies received greater social services under colonialism. Thus, The Rand in South Africa and Katanga in Congo had to provide for their relatively large working class. For many years, they approached the whole matter indifferently, but in the final analysis, enlightened self-interest made the colonialists realize that more could be gained out of the African worker who maintained basic health and who had some degree of literacy in industrial contexts. This was the same line of reasoning which had previously led the capitalist class in Europe to be somewhat freer in allowing part of the workers' production to go back to keeping the worker alive and well.

In the cash-crop producing countries of Africa, a similar situation existed whereby the tendency was for socio-economic services to decrease in colonies or areas which produced few goods to be shipped abroad. That accounts for the fact that Africans in Gold Coast, Uganda, and Nigeria could be considered as having been "better off" than those in Dahomey, Tanganyika, and Chad.

Within individual countries, considerable regional variations existed, depending on the degree to which different parts of a country were integrated into the capitalist money economy. Thus, the northern part of Kenya or the south of Sudan had little to offer the colonialists, and such a zone was simply ignored by the colonizing power with regard to roads, schools, hospitals, and so on. Often, at the level of the district of a given colony, there would be discrimination in providing social amenities, on the basis of contribution to exportable surplus. For instance, plantations and companies might build hospitals for their workers, because some minimum maintenance of the workers' health was an economic investment. Usually, such a hospital was exclusively for workers of that particular capitalist concern, and those Africans living in the vicinity under subsistence conditions outside the money economy were ignored altogether.

The Arusha Declaration powerfully and simply expressed one of the deepest truths of the colonial experience in Africa when it stated: "We have been oppressed a great deal, we have been exploited a great deal, and we have been disregarded a great deal."

The combination of being oppressed, being exploited, and being disregarded is best illustrated by the pattern of the economic infrastructure of African colonies: notably, their roads and railways. These had a clear geographical distribution according to the extent to which particular regions needed to be opened up to import-export activities. Where exports were not available, roads and railways had no place. The only slight exception is that certain roads and railways were built to move troops and make conquest and oppression easier.

Means of communication were not constructed in the colonial period so that Africans could visit their friends. More important still, they were not laid down to facilitate internal trade in African commodities. There were no roads connecting different colonies and different parts of the same colony in a manner that made sense with regard to Africa's needs and development. All roads and railways led down to the sea. They were built to extract gold or manganese or coffee or cotton. They were built to make business possible for the timber companies, trading companies, and agricultural concession firms, and for white settlers. Any catering to African interests was purely coincidental. Yet in Africa, labor, rather than capital, took the lion's share in getting things done. With the minimum investment of capital, the colonial powers could mobilize thousands upon thousands of workers. Salaries were paid to the police officers and officials, and labor came into existence because of the colonial laws, the threat of force, and the use of force. Take, for instance, the building of railways. In Europe and America, railway building required huge inputs of capital. Great wage bills were incurred during construction, and added bonus payments were made to workers to get the job done as quickly as possible. In most parts of Africa, the Europeans who wanted to see a railroad built offered lashes as the ordinary wage and more lashes for extra effort.

Reference was earlier made to the great cost in African life of the (French) Congo railroad from Brazzaville to Pointe-Noire. Most of the intolerable conditions are explained by the non-availability of capital in the form of equipment. Therefore, sheer manpower had to take the place of earth-moving machinery, cranes, and so on. A comparable situation was provided by the construction of the Embakasi airport of Nairobi. Because it was built during the colonial era (starting in 1953) and with United States loans, it is customary to credit the imperialists for its existence. But it would be much more accurate to say that the people of Kenya built it with their own hands under European supervision.

Embakasi, which initially covered seven square miles and had four runways, was described as "the world's first handmade international airport." Mau Mau suspects numbering several thousand were to be found there "laboring under armed guard at a million-ton excavation job, filling in craters, laying a half million tons of stone with nothing but shovels, stone hammers and their bare hands."

The financial institutions of colonial Africa were even more scandalously neglectful of indigenous African interests than was the case with the European-oriented communications system. The banks did very little lending locally. In British East Africa, credit to Africans was specifically discouraged by the Credit to Natives (Restriction) Ordinance of 1931. Insurance companies catered almost exclusively to the interests of white settlers and capitalist firms. The policy of colonial reserves in metropolitan currencies can also be cited as a "service" inimical to Africans. The Currency Boards and central banks which performed such services denied Africa access to its own funds created by exports. Instead, *the colonial reserves in Britain, France, and Belgium represented African loans to and capital investment in Europe.*

It is necessary to re-evaluate the much glorified notion of "European capital" as having been invested in colonial Africa and Asia. The money available for investment in the capitalist system was itself the consequence of the previous robbery of workers and peasants in Europe and the world at large. In Africa's case, the capital that was invested in nineteenth-century commerce was part of the capital that had been derived from the trade in slaves. The Portuguese government was the first in Europe to ship captives from Africa and the last to let go of slave trading. Much of the profit slipped out of Portuguese hands, and went instead to Britain and Germany; but the Portuguese slave trade nevertheless helped the Portuguese themselves to finance later colonial ventures, such as joint capitalist participation in agricultural and mining companies in Angola and Mozambique.

As indicated earlier, many of the entrepreneurs from the big European port towns who turned to importing African agricultural produce into Europe were formerly carrying on the trade in slaves. The same can be said of many New England firms in the United States. Some of the biggest "names" in the colonial epoch were capitalist concerns whose original capital came from the trade in slaves or from slavery itself. Lloyds, the great insurance underwriting and banking house, falls into this category, having been nourished by profits from the slave territories of the West Indies in the seventeenth and eighteenth centuries; and the ubiquitous Barclays Bank had its antecedents in slave trading. Worms et Compagnie is a French example of the same phenomenon. Back in the eighteenth century, Worms had strong links with the French slave trade, and it grew to become one of the most powerful financial houses dealing with the French empire in Africa and Asia, with particular concentration on Madagascar and the Indian Ocean.

The example of Unilever and the UAC which was highlighted in the previous chapter also reinforces the point that Africa was being exploited by capital produced out of African labor. When Lever Brothers took over the Niger Company in 1929, they became heirs to one of the most notorious exploiters of nineteenth-century Africa. The Niger Company was a chartered company with full governmental and police powers during the years 1885 to 1897. In that period, the company exploited Nigerians ruthlessly. Furthermore, the Niger Company was itself a monopoly that had bought up smaller firms tracing their capital directly to slave trading. Similarly, when the UAC was born out of the merger with the Eastern and African Trading Company, it was associated with some more capital that grew from a family tree rooted in the European slave trade. The capital at the disposal of the big French trading firms CFAO and SCOA can also be traced in the same way.

The process of capital accumulation and reproduction in East Africa lacks the continuity of West Africa. Firstly, Arabs as well as Europeans were participants in the slave trade from East Africa. Secondly, the Germans intervened in 1885, although they had not been previously involved; while the French (who had led the European slave trade in East Africa during the eighteenth and nineteenth centuries) concentrated on colonizing the Indian Ocean islands rather than the East African mainland. Thirdly, German colonialism did not last beyond the 1914–18 war. Even so, on the British side, the capital and profits of the colonizing East Africa Company reappeared in the trading firm of Smith Mackenzie.

The capital that was invested in colonial Africa in later years was a continuation of the nineteenth century, along with new influxes from the metropoles. If one inquired closely into the origins of the supposedly new sources, quite a few would have been connected very closely to previous exploitation of non-European peoples. However, it is not necessary to prove that every firm trading in Africa had a firsthand or secondhand connection with the European slave trade and with earlier exploitation of the continent. It is enough to remember that Europe's greatest source of primary capital accumulation was overseas, and that the profits from African ventures continually outran the capital invested in the colonies.

A conservative bourgeois writer on colonial Africa made the following remarks about the South African gold and diamond industries:

> Apart from the original capital subscribed [in the diamond industry], all capital expenditure was provided for out of profits. The industry also yielded large profits to the international firms which dealt in diamonds. These had a peculiar importance, because a considerable portion of the wealth accumulated by diamond firms was later used in the development of the [gold industry] of the Rand.

Similarly, in Angola the *Diamang* diamond company was an investment that quickly paid for itself, and was then producing capital. The combined profits of that company for the years 1954 and 1955 alone came to the total of invested capital plus 40 per cent. The excess over investment and maintenance costs was of course expatriated to Portugal, Belgium, and the U.S.A., where the shareholders of *Diamang* were resident; and Angola was thereby investing in those countries.

In this sense, the colonies were the generators of the capital rather than the countries into which foreign capital was plowed.

Capital was constantly in motion from metropole to some part of the dependencies, from colonies to other colonies (via the metropoles), from one metropole to another, and from colony to metropole. But because of the superprofits created by non-European peoples ever since slavery, the net flow was from colony to metropole. What was called "profits" in one year came back as "capital" the next. Even progressive writers have created a wrong impression by speaking about capital "exports" from Europe to Africa and about the role of "foreign" capital. What was foreign about the capital in colonial Africa was its ownership and not its initial source.

Apologists for colonialism are quick to say that the money for schools, hospitals, and such services in Africa was provided by the British, French, or Belgian taxpayer, as the case may have been. It defies logic to admit that profits from a given colony in a given year totaled several million dollars and to affirm nevertheless that the few thousand dollars allocated to social services in that colony was the money of European taxpayers! The true situation can accurately be presented in the following terms: African workers and peasants produced for European capitalism goods and services of a certain value. A small proportion of the fruits of their efforts was retained by them in the form of wages, cash payments, and extremely limited social services, such as were essential to the maintenance of colonialism. The rest went to the various beneficiaries of the colonial system.

There can be little dispute over the credibility of the data which are available to amply demonstrate that colonialism for the most part aimed at developing the metropoles, and only allowed certain crumbs to the colonies as incidental by-products of exploitation. British colonial records are full of reports of Royal Commissions investigating this and that; the reports (upon which action was seldom taken) provided the best evidence of the appalling indifference of the colonial regimes to the needs of Africans. In the 1930s, there were riots throughout the West Indies because of the insupportable suffering of the African descendants who were left stranded in those parts after slavery. The Royal Commission investigating the grievances found them so shocking that the full findings were not published during the war, lest they reveal that colonialism was hardly any better than the fascism against which Britain was fighting. It was out of that investigation that the idea of establishing Colonial Development and Welfare (CD&W) was advanced. An act to that effect was passed in 1940, although it was not until 1944 that funds became available for CD&W loans to colonial administrations.

The French also had their counterpart to CD&W in the form of FIDES, set up in 1946. From the earliest days of colonial expansion, there were two kinds of explanations of motives coming out of the metropoles. One was very frank, and appealed to the various Chambers of Commerce in European towns. It said simply that Europeans were in the colonial game because it was damned profitable, and that was that. However, there were other elements who thought it necessary to peddle a line about the welfare of the "uncivilized natives." This was a continuation of earlier justifications of slavery on the ground that it carried the heathen Africans to Christian lands. As colonialism came under heavy criticism during the last decades, more deliberate efforts were made to whitewash it. Both CD&W and FIDES were part of the public relations propaganda of colonialism, striving to mask and deny its viciousness.

Above all, both FIDES and CD&W were born of postwar conditions in Europe, at the time when Western European capitalist nations were desperately falling back on colonies to save them vis-à-vis socialism and even from the competition of the U.S.A. Mr. Bevin, a noted labor leader turned traitor to his class and spokesman for British capitalism, made the observation that "the other two world Powers, the United States and Soviet Russia, have tremendous resources. If Western Europe is to achieve its balance of payments and to get a world equilibrium, it is essential that [African] resources should be developed, and made available." Any close study of the operations of CD&W and FIDES reveals clearly that they had nothing to do with African development but a great deal to do with the welfare of capitalist Europe.

The so-called development funds for Africa went almost exclusively into the building of economic infrastructures and into the provision of certain social services. Of the CD&W grants between 1946 and 1956, less than 1 per cent was allocated to industries. In the case of FIDES from 1949 to 1953, the corresponding figure was less than 0.5 per cent. Agriculture fared very little better, although that was of course the principal activity in which Africans were engaged. The colonial administration of Nigeria set up a Ten Year Plan, with hopes of borrowing heavily from CD&W funds. In that plan, the sum of 1.824 million pounds was voted for agriculture out of a total of 53 million pounds. Most of that agricultural grant was to be consumed by constructing an agricultural school and for providing salaries for British "experts."

Other British colonies drew up Ten Year Plans, which had the same deficiencies as the Nigerian one, and indeed they were all apologies for the true economic plans, being nothing else but a series of disjointed projects drawn up by different government departments as extensions to their then existing activities. Thus, the plans could not be expected to break any new ground; and they completely ignored developmental features such as stimulating internal and intra-African trade.

The high proportion of the "development" funds went into the colonies in the form of loans for ports, railways, electric power plants, water works, engineering workshops, warehouses, which were necessary for more efficient exploitation in the long run. In the short run, such construction works provided outlets for European steel, concrete, electrical machinery, and railroad rolling stock. One-fifth of FIDES funds were spent on prestigious public works in Dakar, which suited French industry and employed large numbers of expatriates. Even the schools built under FIDES funds were of unnecessary high cost per unit, because they had to be of the requisite standard to provide job outlets for white expatriates. Incidentally, loans were "tied" in such a way that the money had to be spent on buying materials manufactured in the relevant metropole.

The "development" funds were raised on the European money market by the governments concerned, and in effect the national metropolitan governments were providing their own bankers and financiers with guaranteed profitable outlets for their capital. In 1956, the French government started a scheme which was a blatant form of promoting their own private capitalists while paying lip service to African development and welfare. The scheme involved the creation of an institution called SDOM (Financial Societies for the Development of Overseas Territories). SDOM was nothing but an association of private capitalists interested primarily in the oil of North Africa, and having large government subventions to achieve their goals.

There were many telltale signs which unmasked the CD&W hoax in the eyes of careful and concerned observers. The Colonial Secretary set up a council to help him in allocation of grants, and it was dominated by really powerful members of the British bourgeoisie, including directors of Barclays Bank. Since the CD&W funds were inadequate even for the hopeless Ten Year Plans of the colonies, the British government then encouraged the colonial administrations to borrow the rest of their finances on the open money market. That was another way of insuring that African labor and resources dispatched surplus to greedy European moneychangers.

Barclays Bank was one of the first to seize the opportunity of lending to colonial regimes to supplement the CD&W grants. That bank set up a special Overseas Development Corporation to "assist" Africa, the chairman of the bank assuring all that "the development of the colonial empire and the well-being of its inhabitants is a matter that concerns every citizen of [Britain]." That was the language of public relations, which fitted in very well with the sordid hypocrisy practiced by white men ever since they started killing and enslaving in the name of civilization and Christianity.

As part of the hypocrisy of colonialism, it became fashionable to speak of how Europe brought Africa into the twentieth century. This assertion has implications in the socio-economic and political spheres, and it can be shown to be false not in some but in all respects.

So often it is said that colonialism modernized Africa by introducing the dynamic features of capitalism, such as private property in land, private ownership of the other means of production, and money relations. Here it is essential to distinguish between *capitalist elements* and *capitalism as a total social system*. Colonialism introduced some elements of capitalism into Africa. In general terms, where communalism came into contact with the money economy, the latter imposed itself. Cash-crop farming and wage labor led away from the extended family as the basis of production and distribution.

One South African saying put forward that "the white man has no kin, his kin is money." That is a profound revelation of the difference between capitalist and pre-capitalist societies; and when capitalism came into contact with the still largely communal African societies, it introduced money relations at the expense of kinship ties. However, colonialism did not transform Africa into a capitalist society comparable to the metropoles. Had it done that, one might have complained of the brutalities and inequalities of capitalism, but it could not then have been said that colonialism failed to advance Africa along the path of human historical development.

Capitalism as a system within the metropoles or epicenters had two dominant classes: firstly, the capitalists or bourgeoisie who owned the factories and banks (the major means for producing and distributing wealth); and secondly, the workers or proletariat who worked in the factories of the said bourgeoisie. Colonialism did not create a capital-owning and factory-owning class among Africans or even inside Africa; nor did it create an urbanized proletariat of any significance (particularly outside South Africa). In other words, capitalism in the form of colonialism failed to perform in Africa the tasks which it had performed in Europe in changing social relations and liberating the forces of production.

It is fairly obvious that capitalists do not set out to create other capitalists, who would be rivals. On the contrary, the tendency of capitalism in Europe from the very beginning was one of competition, elimination, and monopoly. Therefore, when the imperialist stage was reached, the metropolitan capitalists had no intention of allowing rivals to arise in the dependencies. However, in spite of what the metropoles wanted, some local capitalists did emerge in Asia and Latin America. Africa is a significant exception in the sense that, compared with other colonized peoples, far fewer Africans had access even to the middle rungs of the bourgeois ladder in terms of capital for investment.

Part of the explanation for the lack of African capitalists in Africa lies in the arrival of minority groups who had no local family ties which could stand in the way of the ruthless primary accumulation which capitalism requires. Lebanese, Syrian, Greek, and Indian businessmen rose from the ranks of petty traders to become minor and sometimes substantial capitalists. Names like Raccah and Leventis were well known in West Africa, just as names like Madhvani and Visram became well known as capitalists in East Africa.

There were clashes between the middlemen and the European colonialists, but the latter much preferred to encourage the minorities rather than see Africans build themselves up. For instance, in West Africa the businessmen from Sierra Leone were discouraged both in their own colony and in other British possessions where they chose to settle. In East Africa, there was hope among Ugandans in particular that they might acquire cotton gins and perform some capitalist functions connected with cotton growing and other activities. However, when in 1920 a Development Commission was appointed to promote commerce and industry, it favored firstly

Europeans and then Indians. Africans were prohibited by legislation from owning gins.

Taking Africa as a whole, the few African businessmen who were allowed to emerge were at the bottom of the ladder and cannot be considered as "capitalists" in the true sense. They did not own sufficient capital to invest in large-scale farming, trading, mining, or industry. They were dependent both on European-owned capital and on the local capital of minority groups.

That European capitalism should have failed to create African capitalists is perhaps not so striking as its inability to create a working class and to diffuse industrial skills throughout Africa. By its very nature, colonialism was prejudiced against the establishment of industries in Africa, outside of agriculture and the extractive spheres of mining and timber felling. Whenever internal forces seemed to push in the direction of African industrialization, they were deliberately blocked by the colonial governments acting on behalf of the metropolitan industrialists. Groundnut-oil mills were set up in Senegal in 1927 and began exports to France. They were soon placed under restrictions because of protests of oil-millers in France. Similarly in Nigeria, the oil mills set up by Lebanese were discouraged. The oil was still sent to Europe as a raw material for industry, but European industrialists did not then welcome even the simple stage of processing groundnuts into oil on African soil.

Many irrational contradictions arose throughout colonial Africa as a result of the non-industrialization policy: Sudanese and Ugandans grew cotton but imported manufactured cotton goods, Ivory Coast grew cocoa and imported tinned cocoa and chocolate.

The tiny working class of colonial Africa covered jobs such as agricultural labor and domestic service. Most of it was unskilled, in contrast to the accumulating skills of capitalism proper. When it came to projects requiring technical expertise, Europeans did the supervision—standing around in their helmets and white shorts. Of course, in 1885 Africans did not have the technical know-how which had evolved in Europe during the eighteenth and nineteenth centuries. That difference was itself partly due to the kind of relations between Africa and Europe in the pre-colonial period. What is more significant, however, is the incredibly small number of Africans who were able to acquire "modern" skills during the colonial period. In a few places, such as South Africa and the Rhodesias, this was due to specific racial discrimination in employment, so as to keep the best jobs for whites. Yet, even in the absence of whites, lack of skills among Africans was an integral part of the capitalist impact on the continent.

It has already been illustrated how the presence of industry in Europe fostered and multiplied scientific techniques. The reverse side of the coin was presented in Africa: no industry meant no generation of skills. Even in the mining industry, it was arranged that the most valuable labor should be done outside Africa. It is sometimes forgotten that it is labor which adds value to commodities through the transformation of natural products. For instance, although gem diamonds have a value far above their practical usefulness, the value is not simply a question of their being rare. Work had to be done to locate the diamonds. That is the skilled task of a geologist, and the geologists were of course Europeans. Work had to be done to dig the diamonds out, which involves mainly physical labor. Only in that phase were Africans from South Africa, Namibia, Angola, Tanganyika, and Sierra Leone brought into the picture. Subsequently, work had to be done in cutting and polishing the diamonds. A small portion of this was performed by whites in South Africa, and most of it by whites in Brussels and London. It was on the desk of the skilled cutter that the rough diamond became a gem and soared in value. No Africans were allowed to come near that kind of technique in the colonial period.

Much of the dynamism of capitalism lay in the way that growth created more opportunities for further growth. Major industries had by-products, they stimulated local raw-material usage, they expanded transport and the building industry—as was seen in the case of Unilever. In the words of the professional economists, those were the beneficial "backward and forward linkages." Given that the industries using African raw materials were located *outside* Africa, then there could be no beneficial backward and forward linkages *inside* Africa. After the Second World War, Guinea began to export bauxite. In the hands of French and American capitalists, the bauxite became aluminum. In the metropoles, it went into the making of refactory material, electrical conductors, cigarette foil, kitchen utensils, glass, jewel bearings, abrasives, light-weight structures, and aircraft. Guinean bauxite stimulated European shipping and North American hydroelectric power. In Guinea, the colonial bauxite mining left holes in the ground.

With regard to gold, the financial implications in Europe were enormous, and African gold played its part in the development of the monetary system and of industry and agriculture in the metropoles. But, like bauxite and other minerals, gold is an exhaustible resource. Once it is taken out of a country's soil, that is an absolute loss that cannot be replaced. That simple fact is often obscured so long as production continues, as in South Africa; but it is dramatically brought to attention when the minerals have actually disappeared during the colonial epoch. For instance, in the south of Tanganyika, the British mined gold as fast as they could from 1933 onwards at a place called Chunya. By 1953, they had gobbled it all up and exported it abroad. By the end of the colonial period, Chunya was one of the most backward spots in the whole of Tanganyika, which was itself known as the poor Cinderella of East Africa. If that was modernization, and given the price paid in exploitation and oppression, then Africans would have been better off in the bush.

Industrialization does not only mean factories. Agriculture itself has been industrialized in capitalist and socialist countries by the intensive application of scientific principles to irrigation, fertilizers, tools, crop selection, stock breeding. The most decisive failure of colonialism in Africa was its failure to change the technology of agricultural production. The most convincing evidence as to the superficiality of the talk about colonialism having "modernized" Africa is the fact that the vast majority of Africans went into colonialism with a hoe and came out with a hoe. Some capitalist plantations introduced agricultural machinery, and the odd tractor found its way into the hands of African farmers; but the hoe remained the overwhelmingly dominant agricultural implement. Capitalism could revolutionize agriculture in Europe, but it could not do the same for Africa.

In some districts, capitalism brought about technological backwardness in agriculture. On the reserves of Southern Africa, far too many Africans were crowded onto inadequate land, and were forced to engage in intensive farming, using techniques that were suitable only to shifting cultivation. In practice, that was a form of technical retrogression, because the land yielded less and less and became destroyed in the process. Wherever Africans were hampered in their use of their ancestral lands on a wide-ranging shifting basis, the same negative effect was to be found. Besides, some of the new cash crops like groundnuts and cotton were very demanding on the soil. In countries like Senegal, Niger, and Chad, which were already on the edge of the desert, the steady cultivation led to soil impoverishment and encroachment of the desert.

White racist notions are so deep-rooted within capitalist society that the failure of African agriculture to advance was put down to the inherent inferiority of the African. It would be much truer to say that it was due to the white intruders, although the basic explanation is to be found not in the personal ill-will of the colonialists or in their racial origin, but rather in the organized viciousness of the capitalist/colonialist system.

Failure to improve agricultural tools and methods on behalf of African peasants was not a matter of a bad decision by colonial policy-makers. It was an inescapable feature of colonialism as a whole, based on the understanding that the international division of labor aimed at skills in the metropoles and low-level manpower in the dependencies. It was also a result of the considerable use of force (including taxation) in African labor relations. People can be forced to perform simple manual labor, but very little else. This was proven when Africans were used as slaves in the West Indies and America. Slaves damaged tools and carried out sabotage, which could only be controlled by extra supervision and by keeping tools and productive processes very elementary. Slave labor was unsuitable for carrying out industrial activity, so that in the U.S.A. the North went to war in 1861 to end slavery in the South, so as to spread true capitalist relations throughout the land. Following the same line of argument, it becomes clear why the various forms of forced agricultural labor in Africa had to be kept quite simple, and that in turn meant small earnings.

Capitalists under colonialism did not pay enough for an African to maintain himself and family. This can readily be realized by reflecting on the amounts of money earned by African peasants from cash crops. The sale of produce by an African cash-crop farmer rarely brought in 10 pounds per year and often it was less than half that amount. Out of that, a peasant had to pay for tools, seeds, and transport and he had to repay the loan to the middleman before he could call the remainder his own. Peasants producing coffee and cocoa and collecting palm produce tended to earn more than those dealing with cotton and groundnuts, but even the ordinary Akwapim cocoa farmer or Chagga coffee farmer never handled money in quantities sufficient to feed, clothe, and shelter his family. Instead, subsistence farming of yams or bananas continued as a supplement. That was how the peasant managed to eat, and the few shillings earned went to pay taxes and to buy the increasing number of things which could not be obtained without money in the middlemen's shops—salt, cloth, paraffin. If he was extremely lucky, he would have access to zinc sheets, bicycles, radios, and sewing machines, and would be able to pay school fees. It must be made quite clear that those in the last category were extremely few.

One reason why the African peasant got so little for his agricultural crops was that his labor was unskilled. That was not the whole explanation, but it is true that a product such as cotton jumped in value during the time it went through the sophisticated processes of manufacture in Europe. Karl Marx, in clarifying how capitalists appropriated part of the surplus of each worker, used the example of cotton. He explained that the value of the manufactured cotton included the value of the labor that went into growing the raw cotton, plus part of the value of the labor that made the spindles, plus the labor that went into the actual manufacture. From an African viewpoint, the first conclusion to be drawn is that the peasant working on African soil was being exploited by the industrialist who used

African raw material in Europe or America. Secondly, it is necessary to realize that the African contribution of unskilled labor was valued far less than the European contribution of skilled labor.

It has been observed that one hour of work of a cotton peasant in Chad was equivalent to less than one centimeter of cotton cloth, and he needed to work fifty days to earn what was needed to buy three meters of the cloth made from his own cotton in France. Yet, the French textile worker (using modern spindles) ran off three meters of cloth in a matter of minutes! Assuming that the Frenchman was not closer to God (who made the whole world in only six days and rested on the seventh), then there must be factors in the capitalist colonialist system which permitted the great disparity in the relative value of labor in Chad and France. In the first place, the Chad peasant was defrauded through trade so that he sold cheap and bought dear, and therefore received a minute proportion of the value that he created with his labor. This was possible not because of mysterious "market forces" as bourgeois economists would like us to believe, but because of political power being vested entirely in the hands of the colonialists. It was a consequence of monopolistic domination, both economically and politically. Secondly, the quantity of time spent by the Chad peasant was longer because colonialism did not permit him to acquire the tools to shorten the hours required to produce a given quantity of raw cotton.

To a certain extent, it would have been in the interests of the colonial powers to have had better agricultural techniques in Africa, leading to increased volume and quality of production. All colonial regimes sponsored some scientific research into tropical agriculture. However, the research was almost entirely devoted to cash crops, it was limited in scope, and it was more easily adaptable by plantations than by African peasants who had no capital. The pitiable amount devoted to agricultural improvement in Africa during the colonial period contrasts sharply with the increasingly huge sums that were devoted to research in Europe over the same period—with enormous benefits to both industry and agriculture in the metropoles.

Side by side with the ill-founded claims about socio-economic modernization went the claims by colonial apologists that European rule brought political uplift and emancipation. One of the long-standing arguments in this connection is that Africa was in chaos in the nineteenth century, and that "tribes" like the Ngoni and the Yao and Samori's *sofas* were killing left, right, and center. Consequently, Africa was saved by Livingstone and Stanley. For the most part, such wild statements have no place in the works of the present generation of European scholars of Africa, since they are known to have no resemblance to reality. However, some writers still preach that "the Bantu could be saved from the wasting struggles and from their general economic and technical backwardness only by the imposition of stable [European] government."

Another supposed credit of the colonialists is that they developed nationalism in Africa. That is a superficial and mischievous claim, which entirely ignores the numerous states in Africa on the eve of colonization, and the direction of their evolution. Nationalism is a certain form of unity which grows out of historical experience. It is a sense of oneness that emerges from social groups trying to control their environment and to defend their gains against competing groups. The nation-state also imposes order and maintains stability within its own boundaries, usually on behalf of a given class. All of those characteristics were present in nineteenth-century African states, some of which were much larger than the colonies arbitrarily defined by Europeans.

It is true that the present African nationalism took the particular form of adopting the boundaries carved by the imperialists. That was an inevitable consequence of the fact that the struggle to regain African independence was conditioned by the administrative framework of the given colonies. But it would show crass ignorance of the African past to say that colonialism modernized Africa politically through nation-states, especially when the implication is that such a level of political organization and stability would otherwise have been impossible.

One colonialist proposition that has at least an air of plausibility is that capitalism and colonial rule meant greater individual freedom for many Africans. Young men earning wages or individuals farming for cash became independent of the corporate demands of their families. It is debatable to what extent that was a worthwhile phenomenon, but it could be said to be somewhat comparable to the way in which capitalism freed the individual in Europe from the restrictions of feudal society and from such bonds as those imposed by morally self-righteous people. Nevertheless, when any given African did break from what were proving to be onerous extended family obligations, what freedom did he acquire? His choice of alternatives was narrowly dictated by the colonialists, and he was only "free" to participate in the money economy and in the European-oriented cultural sector at the very lowest and uncreative levels.

There is a more sympathetic school of historians of Africa who contend that to see colonialism as completely negative is to underrate the *initiative* of Africans. Africans, they say, moved boldly into the labor market, into cash-crop farming, into commerce in some instances, into the educational field, and into the churches. Yet, those were simply *responses* (albeit vigorous ones) to the options laid open by the colonialists. True historical initiative by a whole people or by individuals requires that they have the power to decide on the *direction* in which they want to move. That latter aspect had to await the decade of the 1960s.

Within any social system, the oppressed find some room to maneuver through their own initiative. For instance, under the slave regime of America and the West Indies, Africans found ways and means of gaining small advantages. They would flatter and "con" the slavemasters, who were so arrogant and bigoted that they were readily fooled. Similarly, under colonialism many Africans played the game to secure what they could. Africans in positions like interpreters, police, and court officials often had their way over the ruling Europeans. However, that should not be mistaken for power or political participation or the exercise of individual freedom. Under slavery, power lay in the hands of the slavemasters: under colonialism, power lay in the hands of the colonialists. The loss of power for the various African states meant a reduction in the freedom of every individual.

Colonialism was a negation of freedom from the viewpoint of the colonized. Even in quantitative terms it could not possibly bring modern political liberation to Africans comparable to the little that had been achieved by capitalism as an improvement of feudalism. In its political aspects, capitalism in the metropoles included constitutions, parliaments, freedom of the press. All of those things were limited in their application to the European working class, but they had existed in some form or fashion in the metropoles ever since the American War of Independence and the French Revolution. But Jules Ferry, a former French colonial minister, explained that the French Revolution was not fought on behalf of the blacks of Africa. Bourgeois liberty, equality, and fraternity was not for colonial subjects. Africans had to make do with bayonets, riot acts, and gunboats.

Negative Character of the Social, Political, and Economic Consequences

The argument so far has been aimed at showing that benefits from colonialism were small and they were not gifts from the colonialists, but rather fruits of African labor and resources for the most part. Indeed, what was called "the development of Africa" by the colonialists was a cynical shorthand expression for "the intensification of colonial exploitation in Africa to develop capitalist Europe." The analysis has gone beyond that to demonstrate that numerous false claims are made purporting to show that Europe developed Africa in the sense of bringing about social order, nationalism, and economic modernization. However, all of that would still not permit the conclusion that colonialism had a negative impact on Africa's development. In offering the view that colonialism was negative, the aim is to draw attention to the way that previous African development was blunted, halted, and turned back. In place of that interruption and blockade, nothing of compensatory value was introduced.

The colonization of Africa lasted for just over seventy years in most parts of the continent. That is an extremely short period within the context of universal historical development. Yet, it was precisely in those years that in other parts of the world the rate of change was greater than ever before. As has been illustrated, capitalist countries revolutionized their technology to enter the nuclear age. Meanwhile, socialism was inaugurated, lifting semi-feudal semi-capitalist Russia to a level of sustained economic growth higher than that ever experienced in a capitalist country. Socialism did the same for China and North Korea—guaranteeing the well-being and independence of the state as well as reorganizing the internal social arrangements in a far more just manner than ever before. It is against those decisive changes that events in Africa have to be measured. To mark time or even to move slowly while others leap ahead is virtually equivalent to going backward. Certainly, in relative terms, Africa's position vis-à-vis its colonizers became more disadvantageous in the political, economic, and military spheres.

The decisiveness of the short period of colonialism and its negative consequences for Africa spring mainly from the fact that Africa lost power. Power is the ultimate determinant in human society, being basic to the relations within any group and between groups. It implies the ability to defend one's interests and if necessary to impose one's will by any means available. In relations between peoples, the question of power determines maneuverability in bargaining, the extent to which one people respect the interests of another, and eventually the extent to which a people survive as a physical and cultural entity. When one society finds itself forced to relinquish power entirely to another society, that in itself is a form of underdevelopment.

During the centuries of pre-colonial trade, some control over social, political, and economic life was retained in Africa, in spite of the disadvantageous commerce with Europeans. That little control over internal matters disappeared under colonialism. Colonialism went much further than trade. It meant a tendency towards direct appropriation by Europeans of the social institutions within Africa. Africans ceased to set indigenous cultural goals and standards, and lost full command of training young members of the society. Those were undoubtedly major steps backward.

The Tunisian, Albert Memmi, puts forward the following proposition:

> The most serious blow suffered by the colonized is being removed from history and from the community. Colonization usurps any free role in either war or peace, every decision contributing to his destiny and that of the world, and all cultural and social responsibility.

Sweeping as that statement may initially appear, it is entirely true. The removal from history follows logically from the loss of power which colonialism represented. The power to act independently is the guarantee to participate actively and *consciously* in history. To be colonized is to be removed from history, except in the most passive sense. A striking illustration of the fact that colonial Africa was a passive object is seen in its attraction for white anthropologists, who came to study "primitive society." Colonialism determined that Africans were no more makers of history than were beetles—objects to be looked at under a microscope and examined for unusual features.

The negative impact of colonialism in political terms was quite dramatic. Overnight, African political states lost their power, independence, and meaning—irrespective of whether they were big empires or small polities. Certain traditional rulers were kept in office, and the formal structure of some kingdoms was partially retained, but the substance of political life was quite different. Political power had passed into the hands of foreign overlords. Of course, numerous African states in previous centuries had passed through the cycle of growth and decline. But colonial rule was different. So long as it lasted, not a single African state could flourish.

To be specific, it must be noted that colonialism crushed by force the surviving feudal states of North Africa; that the French wiped out the large Moslem states of the Western Sudan, as well as Dahomey and kingdoms in Madagascar; that the British eliminated Egypt, the Mahdist Sudan, Asante, Benin, the Yoruba kingdoms, Swaziland, Matabeleland, the Lozi, and the East African lake kingdoms as great states. It should further be noted that a multiplicity of smaller and growing states were removed from the face of Africa by the Belgians, Portuguese, British, French, Germans, Spaniards, and Italians. Finally, those that appeared to survive were nothing but puppet creations. For instance, the Sultan of Morocco retained nominal existence under colonial rule which started in 1912; and the same applied to the Bey of Tunis; but Morocco and Tunisia were just as much under the power of French colonial administrators as neighboring Algeria, where the feudal rulers were removed altogether.

Sometimes, the African rulers who were chosen to serve as agents of foreign colonial rule were quite obviously nothing but puppets. The French and the Portuguese were in the habit of choosing their own African "chiefs"; the British went to Iboland and invented "warrant chiefs"; and all the colonial powers found it convenient to create "superior" or "para-mount" rulers. Very often, the local population hated and despised such colonial stooges. There were traditional rulers such as the Sultan of Sokoto, the Kabaka of Buganda, and the Asantehene of Asante, who retained a great deal of prestige in the eyes of Africans, but they had no power to act outside the narrow boundaries laid down by colonialism, lest they find themselves in the Seychelles Islands as "guests of His Majesty's Government."

One can go so far as to say that colonial rule meant the effective eradication of African political power throughout the continent, since Liberia and Ethiopia could no longer function as independent states within the context of continent-wide colonialism. Liberia in particular had to bow before foreign political, economic, and military pressures in a way that no genuinely independent state could have accepted; and although Ethiopia held firm until 1936, most European capitalist nations were not inclined to treat Ethiopia as a sovereign state, primarily because it was African, and Africans were supposed to be colonial subjects.

The pattern of arrest of African political development has some features which can only be appreciated after careful scrutiny and the taking away of the blinkers which the colonizers put on the eyes of their subjects. An interesting case in point is that of women's role in society. Until today, capitalist society has failed to resolve the inequality between man and woman, which was entrenched in all modes of production prior to socialism. The colonialists in Africa occasionally paid lip service to women's education and emancipation, but objectively there was deterioration in the status of women owing to colonial rule.

A realistic assessment of the role of women in independent pre-colonial Africa shows two contrasting but combined tendencies. In the first place, women were exploited by men through polygamous arrangements designed to capture the labor power of women. As always, exploitation was accompanied by oppression; and there is evidence to the effect that women were sometimes treated like beasts of burden, as for instance in Moslem African societies. Nevertheless, there was a countertendency to insure the dignity of women to greater or lesser degree in all African societies. Mother-right was a prevalent feature of African societies, and particular women held a variety of privileges based on the fact that they were the keys to inheritance.

More important still, some women had real power in the political sense, exercised either through religion or directly within the politico-constitutional apparatus. In Mozambique, the widow of an Nguni king became the priestess in charge of the shrine set up in the burial place of her deceased husband, and the reigning king had to consult her on all important matters. In a few instances, women were actually heads of state. Among the Lovedu of Transvaal, the key figure was the Rain-Queen, combining political and religious functions. The most frequently encountered role of importance played by women was that of "Queen Mother" or "Queen Sister." In practice, that post was filled by a female of royal blood, who might be mother, sister, or aunt of the reigning king in places such as Mali, Asante, and Buganda. Her influence was considerable, and there were occasions when the "Queen Mother" was the real power and the male king a mere puppet.

What happened to African women under colonialism is that the social, religious, constitutional, and political privileges and rights disappeared, while the economic exploitation continued and was often intensified. It was intensified because the division of labor according to sex was frequently disrupted. Traditionally, African men did the heavy labor of felling trees, clearing land, building houses, apart from conducting warfare and hunting. When they were required to leave their farms to seek employment, women remained behind burdened with every task necessary for the survival of themselves, the children, and even the men as far as foodstuffs were concerned. Moreover, since men entered the money sector more easily and in greater numbers than women, women's work became greatly inferior to that of men within the new value system of colonialism: men's work was "modern" and women's was "traditional" and "backward." Therefore, the deterioration in the status of African women was bound up with the consequent loss of the right to set indigenous standards of what work had merit and what did not.

One of the most important manifestations of historical arrest and stagnation in colonial Africa is that which commonly goes under the title of "tribalism." That term, in its common journalistic setting, is understood to mean that Africans have a basic loyalty to tribe rather than nation and that each tribe still *retains* a fundamental hostility towards its neighboring tribes. The examples favored by the capitalist press and bourgeois scholarship are those of Congo and Nigeria. Their accounts suggest that Europeans tried to make a nation out of the Congolese and Nigerian peoples, but they failed, because the various tribes had their age-long hatreds; and, as soon as the colonial power went, the natives *returned* to killing each other. To this phenomenon, Europeans often attach the word "atavism," to carry the notion that Africans were returning to their primitive savagery. Even a cursory survey of the African past shows that such assertions are the exact opposite of the truth.

It is necessary to discuss briefly what comprises a tribe—a term that has been avoided in this analysis, partly because it usually carries derogatory connotations and partly because of its vagueness and the loose ways in which it is employed in the literature on Africa. Following the principle of family living, Africans were organized in groups which had common ancestors. Theoretically, the tribe was the largest group of people claiming descent from a common ancestor at some time in the remote past. Generally, such a group could therefore be said to be of the same ethnic stock, and their language would have a great deal in common. Beyond that, members of a tribe were seldom all members of the same political unit and very seldom indeed did they all share a common social purpose in terms of activities such as trade and warfare. Instead, African states were sometimes based entirely on part of the members of a given ethnic group or (more usually) on an amalgamation of members of different ethnic communities.

All of the large states of nineteenth-century Africa were multi-ethnic, and their expansion was continually making anything like "tribal" loyalty a thing of the past, by substituting in its place national and class ties. However, in all parts of the world, that substitution of national and class ties for purely ethnic ones is a lengthy historical process; and, invariably there remains for long periods certain regional pockets of individuals who have their own narrow, regional loyalties, springing from ties of kinship, language, and culture. In Asia, the feudal states of Vietnam and Burma both achieved a considerable degree of national homogeneity over the centuries before colonial rule. But there were pockets of "tribes" or "minorities" who remained outside the effective sphere of the nation-state and the national economy and culture.

In the first place, colonialism blocked the further evolution of national solidarity, because it destroyed the particular Asian or African states which were the principal agents for achieving the liquidation of fragmented loyalties. In the second place, because ethnic and regional loyalties which go under the name of "tribalism" could not be effectively resolved by the colonial state, they tended to fester and grow in unhealthy forms. Indeed, the colonial powers sometimes saw the value of stimulating the internal tribal jealousies so as to keep the colonized from dealing with their principal contradiction with the European overlords—i.e., the classic technique of divide and rule. Certainly, the Belgians consciously fostered that; and the racist whites in South Africa had by the 1950s worked out a careful plan to "develop" the oppressed African population as Zulu, as Xhosa, and as Sotho so that the march towards broader African national and class solidarities could be stopped and turned back.

The civil war in Nigeria is generally regarded as having been a tribal affair. To accept such a contention would mean extending the definition of tribe to cover Shell Oil and Gulf Oil! But, quite apart from that, it must be pointed out that nowhere in the history of pre-colonial independent Nigeria can anyone point to the massacre of Ibos by Hausas or any incident which suggests that people up to the nineteenth century were fighting each other because of ethnic origin. Of course there were wars, but they had a rational basis in trade rivalry, religious contentions, and the clashes of political expansion. What came to be called tribalism at the beginning of the new epoch of political independence in Nigeria was itself a product of the way that people were brought together under colonialism so as to be exploited. It was a product of administrative devices, of entrenched regional separations, of differential access by particular ethnic groups into the colonial economy and culture.

Both Uganda and Kenya in East Africa are also situations in which a supposedly tribal factor continued to be pre-eminent. There is no doubt that the existence of the Buganda kingdom within independent Uganda posed certain problems. But, even after misapplying the definition of a tribe to the Baganda, it still remains true that the Buganda problem was a colonial problem. It was created by the presence of the missionaries and the British, by the British (Mailo) land settlement in Uganda in 1900, and by the use which Britian made of the Baganda ruling class as "sub-imperialists" within the colony of Uganda.

In Kenya, the pattern of colonialism was different from that in Uganda, because of the presence of white settlers. No African group was allowed any power in the capacity of NCOs for the Colonial Office, since the white settlers themselves filled the role. The white settlers took the best land and then tried to create a new world with African labor. However, the African community which lay outside the immediate white settler sector was regulated along tribal lines. One of the numerous Royal Commissions of British colonialism published a report on Kenya in 1934. A contemporary Kenyan historian commented on the report as follows:

> The Commission's recommendations, which were accepted by the British government, implied that Kenya was to be partitioned into two racial blocks, African and European. And in the African sector, all economic, social and political developments were to be conducted on tribal lines. Racialism thus became institutionalised.

Human activity within small groups connected only by kinship relations (such as the tribe) is a very transient phase through which all continents passed in the phase of communalism. When it ceased to be transient and became institutionalized in Africa, that was because colonialism interrupted African development. That is what is implied in Memmi's reference to Africans being removed from history. Revolutionary African thinkers such as Frantz Fanon and Amilcar Cabral expressed the same sentiments some-what differently when they spoke of colonialism having made Africans into *objects of history*. Colonized Africans, like pre-colonial African chattel slaves, were pushed around into positions which suited European interests and which were damaging to the African continent and its peoples. In continuation, some further socio-economic implications of that situation will be examined.

Pre-colonial trade had started the trend of the disintegration of African economies and their technological impoverishment. Colonial rule speeded up that trend. The story is often told that in order to make a telephone call from Accra in the British colony of the Gold Coast to Abidjan in the adjacent French colony of Ivory Coast it was necessary to be connected first with an operator in London and then with an operator in Paris who could offer a line to Abidjan. That was one reflection of the fact that the Gold Coast economy was integrated into the British economy, and the Ivory Coast economy was integrated into the French economy, while the neighboring African colonies had little or no effective economic relations. The following conclusion reached by the United Nations Economic Commission for Africa in 1959 goes directly to the point.

> The most outstanding characteristic of the transportation systems of Africa is the comparative isolation in which they have developed within the confines of individual countries and territories. This is reflected in the lack of links between countries and territories within the same geographical sub-region.

Some African trade did persist across colonial boundaries. For instance, the centuries' old trade in kola nuts and gold from the forests of West Africa to North Africa never completely ceased. Besides, new forms of African trade developed, notably with regard to supplying foodstuffs to towns or cash-crop areas where there was insufficiency of food. That kind of trade could be entirely within a colony or it could cross colonial boundaries. However, the sum total of energy that went into expansion of inter-African trade was extremely small in comparison with trade that was export-oriented. Since this inter-African trade did not bring benefits to Europeans, it was not encouraged by them, and up to the latter part of the colonial period only 10 per cent of Africa's trade was internal.

It is also worth noting that Africa was denied the opportunity of de-veloping healthy trade links with parts of the world other than Europe and North America. Some trade persisted across the Indian Ocean, but on the whole it is fair to say that the roads in Africa led to the seaports and the sea lanes led to Western Europe and North America. That kind of lop-sidedness is today part of the pattern of underdevelopment and dependence.

The damaging impact of capitalism on African technology is even more clearly measurable in the colonial period than in the earlier centuries. In spite of the slave trade and of the import of European goods, most African handicraft industries still had vitality at the start of the colonial period. They had undergone no technological advance and they had not expanded, but they had survived. The mass production of the more recent phase of capitalism virtually obliterated African industries such as cloth, salt, soap, iron, and even pottery-making.

In North Africa, handicraft industries had made the greatest advances before colonialism, in spheres ranging from brasswork to woolens. As in the towns of feudal Europe, craft workshops flourished in Algerian towns like Oran, Constantine, Algiers, and Tlemcen. But French colonialism destroyed the handicraft industries and threw thousands out of work. The same thing had happened in Europe itself when new machines had thrown artisans out of employment in places like Lancashire and Lyons, but in that instance the new machines became the basis of the prevailing mode of production, and formerly independent artisans returned to factories as proletarians to master different skills and expand the productive capacity of their society. In Africa it was simply destruction without redress. By the time political independence was achieved, surviving craftsmanship had been turned towards attracting tourists rather than meeting the real needs of African people.

Besides, as was true of the European slave trade, the destruction of technology under colonialism must be related to the barriers raised in the path of African initiative. The vast majority of Africans drawn into the colonial money economy were simply providing manual labor, which stimulated perspiration rather than scientific initiative. Africans connected to the trading sector were sometimes successful in a limited way. The resourcefulness of West African market women is well known, but it was put to petty purposes. The problem posed to capitalists and workers in Europe while making insecticide from African pyrethrum was one requiring that resourcefulness be expressed in a technical direction. But the problem posed to an African market woman by the necessity to make a penny more profit on every tin of imported sardines was resolved sometimes by a little more vigor, sometimes by a touch of dishonesty, and sometimes by resort to "juju."

Colonialism induced the African ironworker to abandon the process of extracting iron from the soil and to concentrate instead on working scraps of metal imported from Europe. The only compensation for that interruption would have been the provision of modern techniques in the extraction and processing of iron. However, those techniques were debarred from

Africa, on the basis of the international division of labor under imperialism. As was seen earlier, the non-industrialization of Africa was not left to chance. It was deliberately enforced by stopping the transference to Africa of machinery and skills which would have given competition to European industry in that epoch.

In the period of African development preceding colonialism, some areas moved faster than others and provided the nuclei for growth on a wide regional basis. Northern Nigeria was one of those; and it virtually went to sleep during the colonial period. The British cut it off from the rest of the Moslem world and fossilized the social relations, so that the serfs could not achieve any change at the expense of the ruling aristocracy.

On every continent and within nation-states, some features of growth were always more outstanding than others, and thereby offered a lead to the rest of the society. The towns played that role in late feudal European society, while the electrical industry was an example of a similar impetus for development in metropolitan capitalist society in the first decades of this century. Colonialism provided Africa with no real growth points. For instance, a colonial town in Africa was essentially a center of administration rather than industry. Towns did attract large numbers of Africans, but only to offer them a very unstable life based on unskilled and irregular employment. European towns had slums, but the squalor of towns in underdeveloped countries is a special phenomenon. It was a consequence of the inability of those towns to play the role of expanding the productive base. Fortunately, Africa was never as badly off in this respect as Asia and Latin America.

Instead of speeding up growth, colonial activities such as mining and cash-crop farming speeded up the decay of "traditional" African life. In many parts of the continent, vital aspects of culture were adversely affected, nothing better was substituted, and only a lifeless shell was left. The capitalist forces behind colonialism were interested in little more than the exploitation of labor. Even areas that were not directly involved in the money economy exploited labor. In extracting that labor, they tampered with the factor that was the very buttress of the society, for African "traditional" life when deprived of its customary labor force and patterns of work was no longer "traditional."

During the colonial era, many thinly populated villages appeared in Central and Southern Africa, comprising women, children, and old men. They practiced subsistence agriculture which was not productive enough, and colonialists contrasted them with cash-crop areas, which in comparison were flourishing. However, it was precisely the impact of colonialism which left so many villages deserted and starving, because the able-bodied males had gone off to labor elsewhere. Any district deprived of its effective laboring population could not be expected to develop.

There were several spots within different colonies which were sufficiently far removed from towns and colonial administration that they neither grew cash crops nor supplied labor. In southern Sudan, for instance, there were populations who continued to live a life not dissimilar to that which they had followed in previous centuries. Yet, even for such traditional African societies the scope for development no longer existed. They were isolated by the hold which the colonialists had on the rest of the continent. They could not interact with other parts of Africa. They were subject to increasing encroachment by the money economy and were more and more to be regarded as historical relics. The classic example of this type of obstructed historical development is to be found in the U.S.A., where the indigenous population of Indians who survived slaughter by the whites were placed in reservations and condemned to stagnation. Indian reservations in North America are living museums to be visited by white tourists who purchase curios.

In South Africa and Rhodesia, the policy of establishing "native reserves" was openly followed. Inside a reserve, the major means of production was the land. But the quantity and fertility of the land allocated was entirely inadequate to support the numbers of Africans who were driven in. The reserves were reservoirs of cheap labor, and dumping grounds for those who could not be accommodated within the money economy of the racist southern section of Africa. Further north, there were no areas named as "reserves" except in colonial Kenya and to a very limited extent in Tanganyika. But the money economy was constantly transforming the traditional sector into one which was just as deprived as any reserve.

The money economy of colonialism was a growing sector. That is not to be denied. However, it has already been indicated how limited that growth was, viewed over the continent as a whole. The growth in the so-called modern sector exercised adverse effects on the non-monetary sector. What remains is to emphasize that the character of growth in Africa under colonialism was such that it did not constitute development—i.e., it did not enlarge the capacity of the society to deal with the natural environment, to adjudicate relations between members of the society, and to protect the population from external forces. Such a statement is already implicitly borne out in the inability of capitalism to stimulate skilled labor in colonial Africa. A system which must stand in the way of the accumulation of skills does not develop anything or anybody. It is implicit, too, in the manner in which Africa was cut into economic compartments having no relation one to another, so that, even though the volume of commercial activity within each compartmentalized colony may have increased, there was no development comparable to that which linked together the various states of the U.S.A.

In recent times, economists have been recognizing in colonial and post-colonial Africa a pattern that has been termed "growth without development." That phrase has now appeared as the title of books on Liberia and Ivory Coast. It means that goods and services of a certain type are on the increase. There may be more rubber and coffee exported, there may be more cars imported with the proceeds, and there may be more gasoline stations built to service the cars. But the profit goes abroad, and the economy becomes more and more a dependency of the metropoles. In no African colony was there economic integration, or any provision for making the economy self-sustained and geared to its own local goals. Therefore, there was growth of the so-called enclave import-export sector, but the only things which developed were dependency and underdevelopment.

A further revelation of growth without development under colonialism was the overdependence on one or two exports. The term "monoculture" is used to describe those colonial economies which were centered around a single crop. Liberia (in the agricultural sector) was a monoculture dependent on rubber, Gold Coast on cocoa, Dahomey and southeast Nigeria on palm produce, Sudan on cotton, Tanganyika on sisal, and Uganda on cotton. In Senegal and Gambia, groundnuts accounted for 85 to 90 per cent of money earnings. In effect, two African colonies were told to grow nothing but peanuts!

Every farming people have a staple food, plus a variety of other supplements. Historians, agronomists, and botanists have all contributed to showing the great variety of such foods within the pre-colonial African economy. There were numerous crops which were domesticated within the African continent, there were several wild food species (notably fruits), and Africans had shown no conservatism in adopting useful food plants of Asian or American origin. Diversified agriculture was within the African tradition. Monoculture was a colonialist invention.

Those who justify the colonial division of labor suggest that it was "natural" and respected the relative capacities for specialization of the metropoles and colonies. Europe, North America, and Japan were capable of specializing in industry and Africa in agriculture. Therefore, it was to the "comparative advantage" of one part of the world to manufacture machines while another part engaged in simple hoe-culture of the soil. That kind of arrogant partition of the world was not new. In the fifteenth century, the feudal monarchies of Portugal and Spain wanted the whole world for themselves, and they got the Pope to draw a line around the globe, making the allocations. But Britain, Holland, and France suggested that they were not at all convinced that Adam had left a will which gave the earth to Portugal and Spain. In like manner, it can be questioned whether there is any testament which stated that the river Gambia should inherit groundnut growing while the river Clyde (of Scotland) should become a home of shipbuilding.

There was nothing "natural" about monoculture. It was a consequence of imperialist requirements and machinations, extending into areas that were politically independent in name. Monoculture was a characteristic of regions falling under imperialist domination. Certain countries in Latin America such as Costa Rica and Guatemala were forced by United States capitalist firms to concentrate so heavily on growing bananas that they were contemptuously known as "banana republics." In Africa, this concentration on one or two cash crops for sale abroad had many harmful effects. Sometimes, cash crops were grown to the exclusion of staple foods —thus causing famines. For instance, in Gambia rice farming was popular before the colonial era, but so much of the best land was transferred to groundnuts that rice had to be imported on a large scale to try to counter the fact that famine was becoming endemic. In Asante, concentration on cocoa raised fears of famine in a region previously famous for yams and other foodstuff.

Yet the threat of famine was a small disadvantage compared to the extreme vulnerability and insecurity of monoculture. When the crop was affected by internal factors such as disease, that amounted to an overwhelming disaster, as in the case of Gold Coast cocoa when it was hit by swollen-shoot disease in the 1940s. Besides, at all times, the price fluctuations (which were externally controlled) left the African producer helpless in the face of capitalist maneuvers.

From a capitalist viewpoint, monocultures commended themselves most because they made colonial economies entirely dependent on the metropolitan buyers of their produce. At the end of the European slave trade, only a minority of Africans were sufficiently committed to capitalist exchange and sufficiently dependent upon European imports to wish to continue the relationship with Europe at all costs. Colonialism increased the dependence of Africa on Europe in terms of the numbers of persons brought into the money economy and in terms of the number of aspects of socio-economic life in Africa which derived their existence from the connection with the metropole. The ridiculous situation arose by which European trading firms, mining companies, shipping lines, banks, insurance houses, and plantations all exploited Africa and at the same time caused Africans to feel that without those capitalist services no money or European goods would be forthcoming, and therefore Africa was in debt to its exploiters!

The factor of dependency made its impact felt in every aspect of the life of the colonies, and it can be regarded as the crowning vice among the negative social, political, and economic consequences of colonialism in Africa, being primarily responsible for the *perpetuation* of the colonial relationship into the epoch that is called neo-colonialism.

Finally, attention must be drawn to one of the most important consequences of colonialism on African development, and that is the stunting effect on Africans as a physical species. Colonialism created conditions which led not just to periodic famine but to chronic undernourishment, malnutrition, and deterioration in the physique of the African people. If such a statement sounds wildly extravagant, it is only because bourgeois propaganda has conditioned even Africans to believe that malnutrition and starvation were the *natural* lot of Africans from time immemorial. A black child with a transparent rib cage, huge head, bloated stomach, protruding eyes, and twigs as arms and legs was the favorite poster of the large British charitable operation known as Oxfam. The poster represented a case of *kwashiorkor*—extreme malignant malnutrition. Oxfam called upon the people of Europe to save starving African and Asian children from *kwashiorkor* and such ills. Oxfam never bothered their consciences by telling them that capitalism and colonialism created the 'starvation, suffering, and misery of the child in the first place.

There is an excellent study of the phenomenon of hunger on a world scale by a Brazilian scientist, Josue de Castro. It incorporates considerable data on the food and health conditions among Africans in their independent pre-colonial state or in societies untouched by capitalist pressures; and it then makes comparisons with colonial conditions. The study convincingly indicates that African diet was previously more varied, being based on a more diversified agriculture than was possible under colonialism. In terms of specific nutritional deficiencies, those Africans who suffered most under colonialism were those who were brought most fully into the colonial economy: namely, the urban workers.

For the sake of the doubters, several of De Castro's observations are listed below (occasionally supplemented by other data).

(1) Investigators who have studied the nutritional conditions of "primitive" Africans in tropical Africa are unanimous in stating that they show no clinical signs of dietary deficiency. One of the most striking indications of the superiority of indigenous African diet is the

magnificent condition of the teeth. One researcher among six ethnic groups in Kenya could not find a single case of tooth decay, not a single deformation of dental arch. But when those same people were transplanted and put on the "civilized" diet available under colonialism, their teeth began to decay at once.

(2) In Egypt, the peasants, or fellahin, had always suffered from periodic famines, but under colonialism this deteriorated to become chronic hunger. It was the intervention of the British which upset the balance of the peasants' diet; and comparison with early accounts shows that there was once a much greater variety of legumes and fruits.

(3) The *kwashiorkor* (of the Oxfam posters) is itself noticeable wherever the African's contact with the European was prolonged. A Committee on Nutrition in the Colonial Empire found a noticeable absence of animal fat and protein in the Gambia. The absence of proteins of good quality is one of the principal contributors to *kwashiorkor;* and once again comparison with what Europeans saw in the Gambia ever since the fifteenth century would indicate that a change had come about after the coming of the whites. The Gambia not only grew a variety of food in the early period, but it was stock-raising country where meat was consumed in considerable quantity. Throughout the seventeenth and eighteenth centuries, cattle hides were sold by the thousands to European buyers every year, and the local population ate the meat. How then could they have suffered from an absence of animal fat!

(4) Studies in Equatorial Africa have revealed frequent signs of dietary deficiencies caused by the absence of fresh foods among Africans entering the service of the colonizers. These include beriberi, rickets, and scurvy. Rickets is a typical temperate climate disease, to which lack of sun contributes. But after colonialism had so destroyed the pattern of judicious food consumption in tropical Africa, even the sun was not enough to keep children's bones straight. As for scurvy, that is so closely identified with the English sailor that he was nicknamed "Limey," from eating limes to prevent scurvy while lacking access to fresh food on long sea voyages. However, a scurvy epidemic broke out in the middle of Tanganyika in the colonial epoch—among workers in the goldfields, whose wages and conditions of work did not permit them to get fresh citrus and other nourishment.

(5) In South Africa, white settlement and capitalism transformed African diet from meat and cereal to dependence on mealy-meal

(maize). Pellagra, or "rough skin," was unknown in South Africa until about 1914. Subsequently, it became a scourge among Africans, because it derives from absence of milk and meat.

(6) An official report on Basutoland (now Lesotho) had this to say: "According to residents of long standing, the physique and health of the Basuto today is not what it used to be. Malnutrition is seen in every village, dispensary, school and recruiting office. Mild scurvy and subscorbic conditions are not infrequent; pellagra is becoming more and more frequent and lower resistance to disease increasingly apparent. It is becoming generally accepted, too, that the occurrence of leprosy is associated with faulty diet."

To clinch the argument that colonialism had a deleterious effect on the African as a physical (and hence mental) entity, it is useful to point to those African peoples who until today have managed to maintain their own pattern of existence in so far as food is concerned. The pastoral Masai, Galla, Ankoli, Batutsi, and Somali are all in that category. Their physique is generally so superb, their resistance and endurance so great, that they have become the objects of scientific research to discover why they do so much better than the "well-fed" capitalists who are collapsing from heart disease.

In the light of the prevailing balance-sheet concept of what colonial rule was about, it still remains to take note of European innovations in Africa such as modern medicine, clinical surgery, and immunization. It would be absurd to deny that these were objectively positive features, however limited they were quantitatively. However, they have to be weighed against the numerous setbacks received by Africa in all spheres due to colonialism as well as against the contributions Africa made to Europe. European science met the needs of its own society, and particularly those of the bourgeoisie. The bourgeoisie did not suffer from hunger and starvation. Bourgeois science therefore did not consider those things as needs which had to be met and overcome—not even among their own workers and least of all on behalf of Africans. This is just a specific application of the general principle that the exploitation of Africa was being used to create a greater gap between Africa and capitalist Europe. The exploitation and the comparative disadvantage are the ingredients of underdevelopment.

Education for Underdevelopment

Education is crucial in any type of society for the preservation of the lives of its members and the maintenance of the social structure. Under certain circumstances, education also promotes social change. The greater portion of that education is informal, being acquired by the young from the example and behavior of elders in the society. Under normal circumstances, education grows out of the environment; the learning process being directly related to the pattern of work in the society. Among the Bemba of what was then Northern Rhodesia, children by the age of six could name fifty to sixty species of tree plants without hesitation, but they knew very little about ornamental flowers. The explanation is simply that knowledge of the trees was a necessity in an environment of "cut and burn" agriculture and in a situation where numerous household needs were met by tree products. Flowers, however, were irrelevant to survival.

Indeed, the most crucial aspect of pre-colonial African education was its *relevance* to Africans, in sharp contrast with what was later introduced. The following features of indigenous African education can be considered outstanding: its close links with social life, both in a material and spiritual sense; its collective nature; its many-sidedness; and its progressive development in conformity with the successive stages of physical, emotional, and mental development of the child. There was no separation of education and productive activity or any division between manual and intellectual education. Altogether, through mainly informal means, pre-colonial African education matched the realities of pre-colonial African society and produced well-rounded personalities to fit into that society.

Some aspects of African education were formal: that is to say, there was a specific program and a conscious division between teachers and pupils. Formal education in pre-colonial Africa was also directly connected with the purposes of society, just like informal education. The programs of teaching were restricted to certain periods in the life of every individual, notably the period of initiation or "coming of age." Many African societies had circumcision ceremonies for males or for both sexes, and for some time before the ceremonies a teaching program was arranged. The length of time involved could vary from a few weeks to several years. A famous example of the latter was the initiation school held by the Poro brotherhood in Sierra Leone. Formal education was also available at later stages in life, such as on the occasion of passing from one age-grade to another or of joining a new brotherhood. Specialized functions such as hunting, organizing religious ritual, and the practice of medicine definitely involved formal education within the family or clan. Such educational practices all dated back to communal times in Africa, but they persisted in the more developed African feudal and pre-feudal societies, and they were to be found on the eve of colonialism.

As the mode of production moved towards feudalism in Africa, new features also emerged within the educational pattern. There was, for instance, more formal specialization, because the proportion of formal to informal education increases with technological advance. Apart from hunting and religion, the division of labor made it necessary to create guilds for passing down the techniques of ironworking, leather-making, cloth manufacture, pottery molding, professional trading, and so on. The emphasis on military force also led to formal education in that sphere, as in the case of Dahomey, Rwanda, and Zulu cited earlier. A state structure with a well-defined ruling class always encouraged the use of history as a means of glorifying the class in power. So in the Yoruba state of Ketu in the nineteenth century there existed a school of history, where a master drilled into the memories of his pupils a long list of the kings of Ketu and their achievements. Of course, reliance on memory alone placed severe limits on education of that type, and that is why education was much more advanced in those African countries where the use of writing had come into being.

Along the Nile, in North Africa, in Ethiopia, in the Western Sudan, and along the East African coast, a minority of Africans became literate, producing a situation comparable to that of Asia and Europe before the latter part of the nineteenth century. As in other parts of the world, literacy in Africa was connected with religion, so that in Islamic countries it was a Koranic education and in Christian Ethiopia the education was designed to train priests and monks. Moslem education was particularly extensive at the primary level, and it was also available at the secondary and university levels. In Egypt there was the Al-Azhar University, in Morocco the University of Fez, and in Mali the University of Timbuktu—all testimony to the standard of education achieved in Africa before the colonial intrusion.

The colonizers did not introduce education into Africa: they introduced a new set of formal educational institutions which partly supplemented and partly replaced those which were there before. The colonial system also stimulated values and practices which amounted to new informal education.

The main purpose of the colonial school system was to train Africans to help man the local administration at the lowest ranks and to staff the private capitalist firms owned by Europeans. In effect, that meant selecting a few Africans to participate in the domination and exploitation of the continent as a whole. It was not an educational system that grew out of the African environment or one that was designed to promote the most rational use of material and social resources. It was not an educational system designed to give young people confidence and pride as members of African societies, but one which sought to instill a sense of deference towards all that was European and capitalist. Education in Europe was dominated by the capitalist class. The same class bias was automatically transferred to Africa; and to make matters worse the racism and cultural boastfulness harbored by capitalism were also included in the package of colonial education. Colonial schooling was education for subordination, exploitation, the creation of mental confusion, and the development of underdevelopment.

A European-type school system hardly operated during the first forty years or so of colonialism. In that period, missionaries gave schooling for their own Christianizing purposes, and it was in the 1920s that the colonizing powers carried out a series of investigations into educational possibilities in Africa. Thereafter, colonial education became systematic and measurable, though it approached its maximum dimensions only in the post-Second World War era.

Colonial education was a series of limitations inside other limitations. The first practical limitation was politicio-financial, which means that political policy, rather than the actual availability of money, guided financial expenditure. The metropolitan governments and their African administrations claimed that there was not enough money for education. As late as 1958, the British Colonial Office said of Northern Rhodesia:

> Until more money becomes available for the building of schools, no rapid progress can be expected and the practical prospects of providing full primary education for all children therefore remains fairly remote.

It is amazing that Northern Rhodesia with its immense copper wealth did not have enough money to educate Africans! One cannot be certain whether the colonialists were trying to deceive others or whether they had succeeded in fooling themselves; but probably most of the confused white settlers in the Rhodesias fell into the latter category, for they consistently argued that Africans did not pay as much tax per head as Europeans and therefore Africans could not expect to get education and other services out of taxes paid by white settlers. This is the fundamental failure to perceive that a country's wealth comes not from taxes but from production. African soil and African labor in Northern Rhodesia produced vast wealth, but African children under colonialism had little access to that wealth for their schooling.

As noted earlier, most of Africa's surplus was exported; and, out of the small portion which remained behind as government revenue, the percentage channeled into education was tiny. In every colony, the budget for education was incredibly small, compared to amounts being spent in capitalist Europe itself. In 1935, of the total revenue collected from taxing

Africans in French West Africa, only 4.03 per cent was utilized on education. In the British colony of Nigeria, it was only 3.4 per cent. In Kenya, as late as 1946 only 2.26 per cent of the revenue was spent on African education. By 1960, those percentages had gone up two, three, or four times; but, being so small to begin with, they still remained insignificant.

Since such small sums were spent, it followed that another basic limitation was quantitative, in the sense that very few Africans made it into schools. In the whole of French Equatorial Africa (Chad, Central African Republic, Gabon, and Congo Brazzaville), there were only 22,000 pupils enrolled in 1938—and that represented quite a jump over figures for the preceding five years. In 1938, the French provided education for 77,000 pupils in French West Africa, with a population of at least 15 million. A very illuminating fact that should be noted is that in 1945 there were more than 80,000 students attending independent Islamic schools in French West Africa—a number not far short of those attending French-built schools by that date. In other words, it was only in the final stages of colonialism that the ruling European power began to provide Africans in the former Islamic states of West Africa with educational institutions having an enrollment greater than that of the previous formal education.

Occasionally, in West and North Africa, the French government gave some financial support to the Koranic primary schools and to the *medresas*, or Islamic secondary schools. On the whole, however, the pre-colonial African school system was simply ignored and it tended to decline. In Algeria, the Arab Islamic institutions of learning suffered severely during the French wars of conquest, while others were deliberately suppressed when the French gained the upper hand. Throughout French North Africa, the old established Islamic universities suffered because colonialism deprived them of the economic base which previously gave them support. As with so many other aspects of African life, what the colonialists put in must be weighed against what they halted and what they destroyed in both real and potential terms.

British colonies tended to do on average somewhat better than French ones with regard to educational activities, largely because of missionary initiatives rather than the British government itself. Ghana, Nigeria, and Uganda were fairly well off as far as colonial education went. Of course, that was in a purely relative sense, and the absolute numbers involved were never large. Sierra Leone was better off educationally than French West Africa because the seven out of every hundred children going to school in Sierra Leone before the last war compared favorably with five out of every hundred in French West Africa. As far as the British are concerned, their slightly superior record in some colonies is also offset by the very poor educational facilities offered to Africans in Kenya, Tanganyika, the Central African territories, and South Africa itself, which was for a long time a British responsibility.

One limitation of the educational system of colonial Africa which is obscured by statistical averages is the great variation in opportunity between different regions in the same colony. In many colonies, only Africans living in or near the principal towns had educational opportunities. For instance, in Madagascar the capital town of Tananarive had the most substantial school facilities; in Gambia literacy was high for Bathurst town but low outside; and in Uganda the urbanized region of Buganda practically monopolized education. Generally speaking, the unevenness in educational levels reflected the unevenness of economic exploitation and the different rates at which different parts of a colony entered the money economy. Thus, in Gold Coast, the Northern Territories were neglected educationally, because they did not offer the colonialists any products for export. In Sudan it was the huge southern region which was in a similar position. Inside Tanganyika, a map showing the major cotton and coffee areas virtually coincides with a map showing areas in which colonial education was available. It means that those whom the colonialists could not readily exploit were not offered even the crumbs of education.

The closer one scrutinizes the educational contribution of colonialism even in purely quantitative terms the more it shrinks into insignificance. It must be noted, for instance, that there was an extremely high rate of "dropouts." A large percentage of those enrolled never finished school. In big capitalist countries like the U.S.A., there are many dropouts at the college and university level; in colonial Africa, the dropouts were occurring at the primary level, at a rate as high as 50 per cent. For every student who completed primary school, one fell by the wayside. The dropouts were from primary schools because there was hardly any other type of school— this absence of secondary, technical, and university education being yet another of the stumbling blocks.

Africans were being educated inside colonial schools to become junior clerks and messengers. Too much learning would have been both superfluous and dangerous for clerks and messengers. Therefore, secondary education was rare and other forms of higher education were virtually nonexistent throughout most of the colonial epoch. That which was provided went mainly to non-Africans. As late as 1959, Uganda spent about 11 pounds per African pupil, 38 pounds per Indian, and 186 pounds on each European child—the difference being due largely to the availability of secondary education for the children of the capitalists and the middlemen. In Kenya, the discrimination was worse and the number of European children involved was high. In 1960, more than 11,000 European children were attending school in Kenya, and 3,000 of those were receiving secondary education. The settler colony of Algeria displayed similar characteristics. Only 20 per cent of the secondary pupils in 1954 were denoted as "Moslems," which meant in effect "Algerian" as distinct from European. Other minorities also did better than the indigenous population. For instance, the Jews in North Africa and especially in Tunisia played the middlemen roles, and their children were all educated right up to secondary standards.

African countries without a big white settler population also had racist educational structures with regard to opportunities at all levels and especially opportunities for higher education. In Senegal in 1946, the high school had 723 pupils, of whom 174 were Africans. Later on, a university was set up in Dakar (to serve the whole of French West Africa); and yet in the 1950s, on the eve of independence, more than half of the university students were French.

The Portuguese have not been discussed so far, because there is scarcely any education to be discussed in their colonial territories. For many years, the statistical data were never made available, and when published towards the end of the colonial period the figures were often inflated. What is undeniable is that the African child growing up in Portuguese colonial territories stood one chance out of a hundred of getting instruction beyond grade 2 or grade 3. The secondary schools that came into existence were for Europeans and Indians, the latter drawn mainly from Goa. The colonial powers with small territories in Africa were Spain and Italy. Like Portugal, they were also backward from a European capitalist viewpoint, and they provided their colonial subjects with a tiny amount of primary education and no secondary education.

Belgium was in a somewhat special category as far as colonial education was concerned. Although small, Belgium was a relatively developed and industrialized country, and it ruled one of the richest areas of Africa: namely, the Congo. By colonial standards, the people of Congo and Rwanda-Urundi had fair access to primary education, but schooling beyond that was almost impossible to obtain. This was the consequence of a deliberate policy pursued by the Belgian government and the Catholic church. The African "native" was to be gradually civilized. To give him secondary education was like asking a young child to chew meat when he should be eating porridge. Furthermore, the Belgians were so interested in the welfare of the African masses that they argued that no highly educated African would be able to serve his own people! Consequently, it was only in 1948 that a Belgian commission recommended the establishment of secondary schools for Africans in the colonies. It is not at all surprising that, at the time of regaining political independence, the Congo had only 16 graduates out of a population of more than 13 million.

Educators often refer to "the educational pyramid," comprising primary education as the base and going upwards through secondary, teacher-training, higher technical, and university facilities—the last named being so small that it could be represented as the point at the top of the pyramid. Throughout Africa, the primary base was narrow and yet the pyramid sloped shallowly because so few of the primary students could continue beyond that level. Only in certain British colonies was the pyramid really completed by significant higher and university education. West Africa had Achimota and Yaba Colleges, apart from Fourah Bay which was at university level. Ibadan and the University of Ghana also came into existence some years before the end of the colonial regime. In the Sudan, there was Gordon College, which evolved into the University of Khartoum, and in East Africa there was Makerere University.

The following data for the year 1958 could be used to illustrate the educational pyramid in Southern Rhodesia, where African education was not well favored. Total kindergarten enrollment was 227,000. In the primary schools 77,000 entered grade 1, and 10,000 made it to grade 6. Secondary education began with 3,000 pupils, of whom only 13 made it to grade 12. In that year, there were no African graduates from the recently established University College in Salisbury, but by 1960 there were three.

The final word on the quantity of education provided by Europe to Africa can be said in the form of the statistics at the beginning of the rule of the new African states. Some scholars have worked out a statistical index on education whereby educational facilities are evaluated in numbers from 0 to 100, moving from the poorest to the most advanced. On that index, most African countries are below 10. The developed exploiter countries and the socialist states are usually above 80. A UNESCO publication on education in *black independent Africa* said:

> Of this population (of around 170 million), a little more than 25 million are of school age and of these nearly 13 million have no opportunity of going to school—and of the "privileged" 12 million less than half complete their primary education. Only three out of every 100 children see the inside of a secondary school while not even two of every thousand have a chance of receiving some sort of higher education in Africa itself. The overall estimated illiteracy rate of 80 to 85 per cent is nearly twice that of the average world figure.

The imperialist whites use the above evidence to snigger at Africans for being "illiterate natives" and they would argue that illiteracy is part of "the vicious circle of poverty." Yet, the same people boast proudly that they have educated Africa. It is difficult to see how they can have it both ways. If independent Africa is still without the benefits of modern education (as it is), then seventy-five years of colonial exploitation undoubtedly have something to do with the state of affairs; and the absurdity is so much the greater when one contemplates how much Africa produced in that period and how much of that went to develop all aspects of European capitalist society, including their educational institutions. Cecil Rhodes could afford to leave a legacy of lavish scholarships to white students for study at Oxford University, having made a fortune from exploiting Africa and Africans.

Those Africans who had access to education were faced with certain qualitative problems. The quality was poor by prevailing European standards. The books, the methods of teaching, and the discipline were all brought to Africa in the nineteenth century; and, on the whole, colonial schools remained sublimely indifferent to the twentieth century. New ideas that were incorporated in the capitalist metropoles never reached the colonies. In particular, the fantastic changes in science did not reach African classrooms, for there were few schools where science subjects were taught. Similarly, the evolution of higher technical education did not have any counterpart in colonial Africa.

There were numerous absurdities in the transplantation of a version of European education into Africa. When the Bemba children mentioned above went to school, they had no program of instruction relating to the plant life with which they would otherwise have familiarized themselves. Instead, they were taught about flowers—and about European roses at that. Dr. Kofi Busia some years ago made the following admission:

> At the end of my first year at secondary school (Mfantsipim, Cape Coast, Ghana), I went home to Wenchi for the Christmas vacation. I had not been home for four years, and on that visit, I became painfully aware of my isolation. I understood our community far less than the boys of my own age who had never been to school. Over the years, as I went through college and university, I felt increasingly that the education I received taught me more and more about Europe and less and less about my own society.

Eventually, Busia knew so little about African society that he proposed that independent Africans should "dialogue" with the fascist/racist white minority that maintains apartheid in South Africa.

Some of the contradictions between the content of colonial education and the reality of Africa were really incongruous. On a hot afternoon in some tropical African school, a class of black shining faces would listen to their geography lesson on the seasons of the year—spring, summer, autumn, and winter. They would learn about the Alps and the river Rhine but nothing about the Atlas Mountains of North Africa or the river Zambezi. If those students were in a British colony, they would dutifully write that "we defeated the Spanish Armada in 1588"—at a time when Hawkins was stealing Africans and being knighted by Queen Elizabeth I for so doing. If they were in a French colony, they would learn that "the Gauls, our ancestors, had blue eyes," and they would be convinced that "Napoleon was our greatest general"—the same Napoleon who reinstituted slavery in the Caribbean island of Guadeloupe, and was only prevented from doing the same in Haiti because his forces were defeated by an even greater strategist and tactician, the African Toussaint L'Ouverture.

To some extent Europeans thoughtlessly applied their own curricula without reference to African conditions; but very often they deliberately did so with intent to confuse and mystify. As late as 1949, a Principal Education Officer in Tanganyika carefully outlined that the Africans of that colony should be bombarded in primary school with propaganda about the British royal family. "The theme of the [British] king as father should be stressed throughout the syllabus and mentioned in every lesson," he said. He further urged that African children should be shown numerous pictures of the English princesses and their ponies at Sandringham and Windsor Castle.

Whatever little was discussed about the African past in colonial schools was about European activities in Africa. That trend is now sufficiently reversed to allow the present generation of African pupils to smile at the thought that Europeans "discovered" Mount Kenya or the river Niger. But in the colonial period, the paradox was that whoever had an opportunity to be educationally misguided could count himself lucky, because that misguidance was a means of personal advance within the structure created by European capitalists in and for Africa.

The French, Portuguese, and Belgians made it clear that education at any level was designed "to civilize the African native," and of course only a civilized native could hope to gain worthwhile employment and recognition from the colonialists. According to the French, an African, after receiving French education, stood a chance of becoming an *assimilée*—one who could be assimilated or incorporated into the superior French culture. The Portuguese used the word *assimilado*, which means exactly the same; and Portuguese colonial law distinguished sharply between a native and an *assimilado*. The latter was sometimes called a *civilisado* because of being able to read and write Portuguese. That sort of African was rewarded with certain privileges. One great irony was that in Portugal up to 1960, nearly half the population was illiterate, and therefore if they had been put to the same test, they would have been judged uncivilized! Meanwhile, the Belgians were parading around with the same system. They called their "educated Bantu" in Congo the *évolués* ("those who have evolved" from savagery to civilization, thanks to the Belgians).

Somehow, the British avoided hard and fast legal distinctions between the educated and uneducated African, but they encouraged cultural imitation all the same. Governor Cameron of Tanganyika in the 1920s was known as a "progressive" governor. But when he was attacked for trying to preserve the African personality in the educational system, he denied the charge and declared that his intention was that the African should cease to think as an African and instead should become "a fair-minded Englishman." Students who came out of Livingstonia or Blantyre Mission in Malawi were known as black Scotsmen, because of the effort of Scottish missionaries. In Sierra Leone, the white cultural influence went back to the eighteenth century, and Sierra Leone Creoles stood out even from the rest of miseducated black people. The Creoles were not satisfied with an English Christian name or even with one European surname: they had to choose two European surnames and connect them with a hyphen. Of course, in practical terms, the education with all its warped values meant that the educated handful went as far as colonialism would allow Africans to go in the civil service or in the employ of private capitalist firms.

During the colonial epoch and afterwards, criticism was justly leveled at the colonial educational system for failing to produce more secondary school pupils and more university graduates. And yet, it can be said that among those who had the most education were to be found the most alienated Africans on the continent. Those were the ones who evolved and were assimilated. At each further stage of education, they were battered by and succumbed to the values of the white capitalist system; and, after being given salaries, they could then afford to sustain a style of life imported from outside. Access to knives and forks, three-piece suits, and pianos then further transformed their mentality. There is a famous West Indian calypsonian who in satirizing his colonial school days, remarked that had he been a bright student he would have learned more and turned out to be a fool. Unfortunately, the colonial school system educated far too many fools and clowns, fascinated by the ideas and way of life of the European capitalist class. Some reached a point of total estrangement from African conditions and the African way of life, and like Blaise Diagne of Senegal they chirped happily that they were and would always be "European."

There is no getting away from the conclusion reached by the African educationalist Abdou Moumini that "colonial education corrupted the thinking and sensibilities of the African and filled him with abnormal complexes." It followed that those who were Europeanized were to that extent de-Africanized, as a consequence of the colonial education and the general atmosphere of colonial life. Many examples are cited in present-day Africa of the insulting treatment of aspects of African culture in the colonial period, based on cultural imperialism and white racism. What is seldom commented upon is the fact that many Africans were the victims of fascism at the hands of the Portuguese and Spanish, at the hands of the Italians and the Vichy French regime for a brief period in the late 1930s and the early 1940s, and at the hands of the British and Boers in South Africa throughout this century. The fascist colonial powers were retarded capitalist states, where the government police machinery united with the Catholic church and the capitalists to suppress Portuguese and Spanish workers and peasants and to keep them ignorant. Understandably, the fascist colonialists wanted to do the same to African working people, and in addition they vented their racism on Africans, just as Hitler had done on the Jews.

Like most colonial administrations, that of the Italians in Libya disregarded the culture of the Africans. However, after the fascist Mussolini came to power, the disregard gave way to active hostility, especially in relation to the Arabic language and the Moslem religion. The Portuguese and Spanish had always shown contempt for African language and religion. Schools of kindergarten and primary level for Africans in Portuguese colonies were nothing but agencies for the spread of the Portuguese language. Most schools were controlled by the Catholic church, as a reflection of the unity of church and state in fascist Portugal. In the little-known Spanish colony of Guinea (Rio Muni), the small amount of education given to Africans was based on eliminating the use of local languages by the pupils and on instilling in their hearts "the holy fear of God." Schools in colonial Africa were usually blessed with the names of saints or bestowed with the names of rulers, explorers, and governors from the colonizing power. In Spanish Guinea, that practice was followed, resulting in the fact that Rio Muni children had to pass by the José Antonio school— the equivalent of saying the Adolf Hitler school if the region were German, for the school was named in honor of José Antonio, the founder of the Spanish fascist party.

Another aspect of the colonial educational and cultural patterns which needs investigation is the manner in which European racism and contempt was expressed not only by hostility to African culture but by paternalism and by praise of negative and static social features. There were many colonialists who wished to preserve in perpetuity everything that was African, if it appeared quaint or intriguing to them. Such persons merely succeeded in cutting African life off from the potentially beneficial aspects of the international world. An excellent example is the kind of work done in Gabon by Albert Schweitzer, who was in charge of a dirty unhygienic hospital with dogs, cats, goats, and chickens running around, under the guise of fitting into the African culture and environment.

As late as 1959, a friend and colleague of Albert Schweitzer defended his unsterile hospital in the following terms:

> Now to the domestic animals at the Hospital. People have been shocked by the informality with which animals and people mix, and although it is perhaps not always defensible on hygienic grounds, the mixture adds considerably to the charm of the place.

The writer was a dental surgeon from New York, who would obviously have had a fit if a goat or chicken had wandered into his New York surgery. He knew full well that at Schweitzer's hospital "the goats, dogs and cats visit hospital wards teeming with microbial life of the most horrifying varieties," but he defended their habitation with Africans because that was part of the culture and charm that had to be preserved!

In the educational sphere, the Belgians carried out a language policy which might appeal to contemporary nationalists, for they insisted that primary education should be in one of the five main African languages of the territory. However, in practice, they used that apparently progressive decision to seal off one Congolese ethnic group from another and to cut the educated off from a wider world of knowledge, because the missionaries translated into the local languages only that which they thought desirable. The policy of mock respect for African culture reached its highest expression in South Africa in the notorious Bantu Education Act of 1953, which sought to promote the differences between Zulu, Sotho, Xhosa, Venda, and so on—differences which were part of an early stage of development and which would have been transcended if there were no European intervention or if under white rule specific steps were not taken to maintain the anachronistic "tribal" entities.

Not all colonial educators and administrators were consciously taking up the position that the African should be educated the better to be enslaved. On the contrary, most of them thought that they were doing Africans a great favor; and there were a few who were enlightened enough to realize that there was scope for devising a school program which was less divorced from African reality. In 1928, even the French education minister was shocked to learn that Africans were taught that the Gauls, their ancestors, had blue eyes. From the 1920s, both Britain and France produced colonial educators and education commissions which urged greater relevance of teaching programs in Africa. They also put forward suggestions such as the use of local languages in primary schools, more education for girls, and an end to the white-collar orientation of schooling. However, the seemingly progressive nature of those recommendations could not change the fact that colonial education was an instrument to serve the European capitalist class in its exploitation of Africa. Whatever colonial educators thought or did could not change that basic fact.

To recommend that African girls should go to school is more than just an educational policy. It has tremendous social implications, and it presupposes that the society will usefully employ the educated woman. Metropolitan capitalist society itself had failed to liberate women, to offer them equal educational opportunities, or to provide them with responsible jobs at equal rates of pay with men. That being the case, it was wishful thinking to imagine that the colonial educational system would take any serious interest in African women, especially since the colonialists would have had to transform the consciousness on that matter which was characteristic of feudal and pre-feudal societies. Nowhere did the cash-crop economy or the export of basic ores make provision for educated women. As in the capitalist metropoles it was assumed that the civil service was for men. Therefore, the extremely limited employment sector in the colonies had nothing to offer educated women, and modern education remained a luxury with which few African women came into contact.

Another progressive suggestion made by some colonial educationists was for more agricultural and technical schooling. But, genuine technical education was ruled out, because the fundamental purpose of the colonial economy did not permit the development of industry and skills within Africa. Only in rare cases, such as in the Congo, was there an objective necessity for technically trained Africans. In the later stages of colonial rule in Congo, mineral exploitation had developed to such a point that there was practical need for extensive rudimentary technical skills among African workers. A few Katangese and other Congolese also received technical training of a secondary equivalent. Significantly enough, in such cases, the private companies took the initiative, since their profits were at stake, and the technical schools were extensions of their production processes. However, for the most part, whatever skilled jobs needed to be done within the restricted field of mining and industry in Africa were met by the importation of Europeans.

Agriculture was not carried on as a scientific industry, as in Scandinavia or New Zealand, where whites were farming on an intensive capitalist basis. As noted earlier, the production of cash crops in Africa was stimulated by the minimum expenditure on the part of Europeans and with no infusion of new technology. Therefore, when educational advisers suggested agricultural education relevant to African needs, this meant no addition to African knowledge. In many colonial schools, agriculture became an apology for a subject. It was part of the drudgery of the institution. The teachers received no agricultural education, and, therefore, they could not teach anything scientific. Children acquired nothing but distaste for the heavy labor of *shamba* work, and in fact it was used as a form of punishment.

Early educational commissions also accorded high priority to religious and moral flavoring of instruction—something that was disappearing in Europe itself. The role of the Christian church in the educational process obviously needs special attention. The Christian missionaries were as much part of the colonizing forces as were the explorers, traders, and soldiers. There may be room for arguing whether in a given colony the missionaries brought the other colonialist forces or vice versa, but there is no doubting the fact that missionaries were agents of colonialism in the practical sense, whether or not they saw themselves in that light. The imperialist adventurer Sir Henry Johnston disliked missionaries, but he conceded in praise of them that "each mission station is an exercise in colonisation."

In Europe, the church had long held a monopoly over schooling from feudal times right into the capitalist era. By the late nineteenth century, that situation was changing in Europe; but, as far as the European colonizers were concerned, the church was free to handle the colonial educational system in Africa. The strengths and weaknesses of that schooling were very much to be attributed to the church.

Both inside and outside church and school, the personnel of the church were instrumental in setting values during the colonial epoch. They taught an ethic of human relations that in itself could appeal to the finer instincts of Africans, just as it had previously stirred other Europeans. Of course, there was a huge gap between European conduct and the Christian principles with which they were associated; and, on the part of the Africans, it was also true that motives for accepting Christianity often had nothing to do with the content of the religion. Indeed, the church as a source of education was probably more attractive to many converts than the church as a dispenser of religion.

Whatever the church taught in any capacity may be considered as a contribution to formal and informal education in colonial Africa, and its teachings must be placed within a social context. The church's role was primarily to preserve the social relations of colonialism, as an extension of the role it played in preserving the social relations of capitalism in Europe. Therefore, the Christian church stressed humility, docility, and acceptance. Ever since the days of slavery in the West Indies, the church had been brought in on condition that it should not excite the African slaves with doctrines of equality before God. In those days, they taught slaves to sing that all things were bright and beautiful, and that the slavemaster in his castle was to be accepted as God's work just like the slave living in a miserable hovel and working twenty hours per day under the whip. Similarly, in colonial Africa, churches could be relied upon to preach turning the other cheek in the face of exploitation, and they drove home the message that everything would be right in the next world. Only the Dutch Reformed church of South Africa was openly racist, but all others were racist in so far as their European personnel were no different from other whites who had imbibed racism and cultural imperialism as a consequence of the previous centuries of contact between Europeans and the rest of the world.

In serving colonialism, the church often took up the role of arbiter of what was culturally correct. African ancestral beliefs were equated with the devil (who was black anyway), and it took a very long time before some European churchmen accepted prevailing African beliefs as constituting religion rather than mere witchcraft and magic. However, in its hostility towards African cultural and religious manifestations, the Christian church did perform certain progressive tasks. Practices such as killing twins and trial by ordeal were frowned upon by the European missionaries, and those were reflections of superstitious ideas rooted in an early stage of African development, when something like the birth of twins could not be scientifically explained, and, therefore, gave rise to religious fear.

It is to be noted that in West Africa long before the colonial Scramble, many outcasts in society and persons who suffered from religious and social prejudices were the first converts of the Christian church. What was supported by one section of the population was opposed by another, and in the present century the cultural imperialism of the church excited great opposition. Prevailing African customs such as polygamy were attacked without reference to their socio-economic function. On the question of monogamy the Christian missionaries were introducing not a religious principle but rather a facet of European capitalist society. For their propaganda to have been successful, European activity had to work a transformation in the extended family patterns of African societies. That was very slow in occurring, and, in the meanwhile, many Africans accepted the religious aspects while rejecting the cultural appendages and the European missionaries themselves.

Much has been written about the trend in colonial Africa known as the Independent church movement. It was a trend in which thousands of African Christians participated by breaking away from European churches (especially Protestant churches), and setting up their own places of worship under Christian African leadership. The motives were varied. Some Independent churches were highly nationalistic, like that established by John Chilembwe, who led an armed nationalist uprising in Nyasaland (Malawi) in 1917. Others developed as a response of those Africans aspiring to be priests or pastors to the discrimination practiced against them by white missionaries. One constant factor was disgust with the way that Europeans forced Africans to identify as Europeans. Revolting against that concept, one Zulu Independent church put the question to the local population: "Are you a Jew or a Zulu? Were you there when they crucified their Lord?" Nevertheless, many Africans came to accept the dehumanizing principle of alienation from self. African identification with Europeans (be they Gentile or Jew) was a pillar of the informal education of the colonial epoch.

In the final analysis, perhaps the most important principle of colonial education was that of capitalist individualism. Like many aspects of the superstructure of beliefs in a society, it had both its negative and positive sides, viewed historically. The European bourgeoisie were progressive when they defended the individual from the excessive control of the father in the family and against the collective regulations of the church and feudal society. However, the capitalist system then went on to champion and protect the rights of the individual property owners against the rights of the mass of exploited workers and peasants. When capitalism had its impact on Africa in the colonial period, the idea of individualism was already in its reactionary phase. It was no longer serving to liberate the majority but rather to enslave the majority for the benefit of a few.

When individualism was applied to land, it meant that the notions of private ownership and the transfer of land through sale became prevalent in some parts of the continent. Much more widespread was the new understanding that individual labor should benefit the person concerned and not some wider collective, such as the clan or ethnic group. Thus, the practice of collective labor and egalitarian social distribution gave way to accumulative tendencies. Superficially, it appeared that individualism brought progress. Some individuals owned large coffee, cocoa, or cotton *shambas,* and others rose to some prominence in the colonial administration through education. As individuals, they had improved their lot, and they became models of achievement within the society. Any model of achievement is an educational model, which directs the thoughts and actions of young and old in the society. The model of personal achievement under colonialism was really a model for the falling apart and the underdevelopment of African society taken as a whole.

It is a common myth within capitalist thought that the individual through drive and hard work can become a capitalist. In the U.S.A., it is usual to refer to an individual like John D. Rockefeller, Sr., as someone who rose "from rags to riches." To complete the moral of the Rockefeller success story, it would be necessary to fill in the details on all the millions of people who had to be exploited in order for one man to become a multimillionaire. The acquisition of wealth is not due to hard work alone, or the Africans working as slaves in America and the West Indies would have been the wealthiest group in the world. The individualism of the capitalist must be seen against the hard and unrewarded work of the masses.

The idea of individualism was more destructive in colonial Africa than it was in metropolitan capitalist society. In the latter, it could be said that the rise of the bourgeois class indirectly benefited the working classes, through promoting technology and raising the standard of living. But, in Africa, colonialism did not bring those benefits—it merely intensified the rate of exploitation of African labor and continued to export the surplus. In Europe, individualism led to entrepreneurship and adventurism of the type which spearheaded Europe's conquest of the rest of the world. In Africa, both the formal school system and the informal value system of colonialism destroyed social solidarity and promoted the worst form of alienated individualism without social responsibility. That delayed the political process through which the society tried to regain its independence.

Up to this point, it has consistently been held that development is rooted in the material environment, in the techniques of production, and in the social relations deriving from people's work. There are what are known as "conspiracy theories of history" by which the happenings of whole epochs are presented as being the secret scheming of one group or another. Such an approach is not to be recommended in the study of Africa's relations with Europe. However, with regard to colonial educational policy, one comes closest to finding the elements of conscious planning by a group of Europeans to control the destiny of millions of Africans over a considerable period of time extending into the future. The planning of colonial education for the subjugation of Africa was most fully displayed by the French, because French politicians and administrators had the habit of openly expressing their thoughts on Africa. Therefore, the words of the French colonialists themselves will be cited here to illustrate how the colonial educational system did not leave vital political matters to chance, but was consciously carrying out policies hostile to the regaining of freedom by African peoples.

Ever since the period of the imperialist Scramble for Africa, French leaders realized that it was imperative to start some schools in the parts of Africa claimed by France, so that French language and culture might be accepted by some Africans, who would then identify with France rather than Britain or Portugal or some other European rival. This was particularly true in disputed frontier zones. Eugène Etienne, a French minister at the start of the colonial era, stated that the extension of the French language was necessary as "a measure of national defense." As early as 1884, there was set up the *Alliance Française* as an instrument of educational and cultural imperialism, recognized and supported by the French government. The reports of the *Alliance Française* show clearly that they thought of themselves as an arm of French imperialism, fighting so that France could entrench itself. For example, the *Alliance Française* wrote of French schools in Upper Guinea in the late nineteenth century:

> They have to combat the redoubtable influence of the English schools of Sierra Leone in this region. The struggle between the two languages becomes more intense as one moves to the south, invaded by English natives and by their Methodist pastors.

As seen earlier in the case of Portugal and Spain, the spread of the language of the European colonizing power was considered of major importance. Belgium on the other hand encouraged local languages as a means of division and retardation. Only in Tanganyika, under German rule, was there a positive reaction to the potentialities of Swahili as a teaching language, so that there was a further impetus to that language, which had already spread by trade, political relations, and personal contacts.

Apart from language, the pillar of cultural imperialism in most colonies was religion. The church never played as important a role in French colonies as it did in other parts of Africa colonized by predominantly Catholic countries, and the Protestant churches in British colonies also had a much more vital role than the church in French Africa. The explanation is that the French bourgeois revolution of the eighteenth century was more thoroughly anti-clerical than any other bourgeois revolution, and the Catholic church was completely separated from government in France by 1905, after many years of poor relations. Nevertheless, when the French saw that mission schools were helping England to entrench itself in Africa, the French government asked the aid of their own Catholic church to secure national interests.

From the viewpoint of the colonizers, once the frontiers of a colony were firmly decided, the major problem remained that of securing African compliance in carrying out policies favorable to the metropoles. There was always the possible use of force for that purpose, but naked force was best kept in reserve, rather than utilized for everyday affairs. Only education could lay the basis for a smooth-functioning colonial administration. In the first place, there was the elementary language problem of Europeans communicating with Africans. Most of the time, Europeans used translators to pass on orders, but it was known that African translators seized the opportunity to promote themselves and to modify or even sabotage orders. There was a saying in French colonial Africa that "translation is equal to treason," and the only way to avoid that was to teach the mass of the people French.

Then there was the practical aspect of educating Africans to be better workers, just as in Europe the workers received education so that they would be more efficient and produce extra surplus for the capitalists. In colonial Africa, the European bourgeoisie realized that some education would maximize the value of labor. Albert Sarraut, a French Colonial Minister, stressed in 1914 what he termed "the economic utility of educating the [African] masses." Several years earlier the French had made a specific statement to the same effect on Madagascar. An ordinance of 1899 indicated that the purpose of schooling was

> . . . to make the young Malagasy faithful and obedient subjects of France and to offer an education which would be industrial, agricultural and commercial, so as to ensure that the settlers and various public services of the colony can meet their personnel requirements.

In practice, it was not necessary to educate the masses because only a minority of the African population entered the colonial economy in such a way that their performance could be enhanced by education. Indeed, the French concentrated on selecting a small minority, who would be thoroughly subjected to French cultural imperialism, and who would aid France in administering its vast African colonial possessions. William Ponty, an early Governor-General of French West Africa, spoke in terms of forming "an elite of young people destined to aid our own efforts." In 1919, Henry Simon (then Colonial Minister) outlined a program for secondary education in Africa with a view to "making the best indigenous elements into complete Frenchmen."

The best expressions of the political implications of French colonial educational policy came in the 1930s; and, by that time, some action was also matching the words. Brevié, the Governor-General of French West Africa in 1930, urged the extension of the higher levels of primary schooling for Africans "to help us in our work of colonization." Brevié was encouraged by the fact that by then there had appeared "a native elite, of whose zeal for a thorough and exclusive French culture signs are already visible." So with the support of the Inspector-General of education, that governor went on to outline plans for African students to attend secondary school, so as to become colonial cadres. Any socio-political system needs its cadres. That was the role played by the youngest age-grades in Shaka's armies and it was the role played by the Komsomol or Young Communists in the Soviet Union. Being a cadre involved not just training for a practical job but also political orientation to serve as a leading element in the system. The French and other colonialists understood this very well. This is how Brevié expressed it:

> It is in no wise merely a matter of turning out batches of apprentices, clerks and officials according to the fluctuating needs of the moment. The role of these native cadres is much wider.

Only in North Africa, with its heavy white settler population, did the French find it unnecessary to encourage a local elite to run affairs under the direction of the metropolis and the governor; although even in Algeria there emerged a number of subjects called the *Beni Oui Oui*—literally the "Yes, Yes men," who always assented to carrying out French instructions in opposition to the interests of most of their brothers. Another far-sighted aspect of French political policy in the education sphere is the manner in which they forced the sons of chiefs to acquire education. It was a deliberate attempt to capture the loyalty of those persons who had previously held political power in independent Africa, and it was an attempt at continuity with the pre-colonial phase. As the French themselves put it, by educating the sons of traditional rulers, "a bond is thus established between the native cadres formed by us and those that the native community recognizes."

In 1935, a team of British educationalists visited French Africa, and they admitted with a mixture of jealousy and admiration that France had succeeded in creating an elite of Africans in the image of Frenchmen—an elite that was helping to perpetuate French colonial rule. To greater or lesser extent, all colonial powers produced similar cadres to manage and buttress their colonial empires in Africa and elsewhere.

After the Second World War, it became obvious that colonial rule could not forever be maintained in the same form in Africa; Asia already having broken loose and Africa being restless. When the awareness that the end was in sight became generalized, the metropolitan powers turned to their colonial cadres and handed to them the reins of policy in politically independent Africa. It should be emphasized that the choice that Africa should be free was not made by the colonial powers but by the people of Africa. Nevertheless, the changeover from colonialism to what is known as neo-colonialism did have the element of conspiracy in it. In 1960, the then British Prime Minister, Harold Macmillan, made the oft-quoted statement that "a wind of change was blowing across Africa." That was the bourgeois way of expressing what Chinese Premier Chou En-Lai was soon to assert: namely, that "Africa was ripe for Revolution." In order to delay or hijack the African revolution, the colonizing powers turned to a group which they had already created for a different purpose—the elite of colonially educated Africans, from among whom were selected wherever possible those who were most suitable for elevation to political leadership, and the administration and military apparatus were left in the hands of similar trustworthy cadres.

There were a few farsighted Europeans who all along saw that the colonial educational system would serve them if and when political independence was regained in Africa. For instance, Pierre Foncin, a founder of the *Alliance Française,* stated at the beginning of this century that "it is necessary to attach the colonies to the metropole by a very solid psychological bond, against the day when their progressive emancipation ends in a form of federation as is probable—that they be and they remain French in language, thought and spirit." Yet, it was the British who firsh appreciated that they should bow to the inevitable and grant African independence. While the French introduced a few African representatives into their own Parliament in France so as to try and keep African territories tied to France, the British began to prepare to hand over to certain selected Africans.

In the metropolitan capitalist countries, there were (and still are) elite schools which provided the bulk of the political and other leadership. The English public schools of Eton, Harrow, Rugby, and Winchester are well known as training grounds of the British ruling class, and by many authorities they are considered more important that the universities to which the students of such secondary schools invariably go. In France at the secondary level, it was, and still is, usual to find that students emerging from places like the Lycée Louis le Grand and the École Normal Superieure Rue d'Ulm are the future cabinet ministers and top executives of that country. In the U.S.A., in spite of the myth that everyone can reach the top, a high proportion of the ruling class went to exclusive schools like the private boys' schools of Groton, St. Paul's, St. Mark's, and Philips Exeter.

Under African conditions, anyone who went to school in the colonial period virtually entered the elite, because the numbers enjoying that privilege even at the primary level were so small. In addition, within each colony there tended to be at least one secondary school or higher institute which played the role of furnishing the politico-administrative personnel of Africa in the era of political independence. The names of cabinet ministers and permanent secretaries of individual African countries can be found on the school rolls of Gordon College (Sudan), Alliance High School (Kenya), King's College Budo (Uganda), Tabora Secondary School (Tanzania), Livingstonia (Malawi), William Ponty (Senegal), Sierra Leone Grammar School, Mfantsipim (Ghana), the Lycée Gallieni (Madagascar), and a few others. Besides, there were Makerere, Fourah Bay, and Achimota, as long standing university or near-university institutions.

In retrospect, it is now very clear that one of the most significant aspects of the colonial educational system was that provided by the armed forces and police. Colonial armies such as the King's African Rifles, the French Free Army, and the Congolese Force Publique produced sergeants who later became the majors and generals of independent Africa, and in several instances the heads of states. Policemen also achieved similar rapid promotion, although their political position has been rather weaker than the military proper. Like their civilian counterparts, the future police and military elite were at one time trained to be simply low-level assistants to the colonial overlords; but once independence was in sight they were judged by the colonizers to have the requisite qualities of colonial cadres— fit to be part of the ruling class of neo-colonial Africa. In a few instances, the colonial powers towards the latter part of the colonial period rushed to train a few Africans at the metropolitan higher institutions of scientific violence, notably Sandhurst Military Academy and Hendon Police School in Britain and St. Cyr Military Academy in France. Those few who were selected for such training became the cream of the military elite, corresponding to those African civilians who went to university either in Africa or abroad.

Most of what emerged from the colonial educational system was not unique. Educational systems are designed to function as props to a given society, and the educated in the young age groups automatically carry over their values when their turn comes to make decisions in the society. In Africa, the colonialists were training low-level administrators, teachers, NCOs, railroad booking clerks, for the preservation of colonial relations; and it is not surprising that such individuals would carry over colonial values into the period after independence was regained. The colonialists meanwhile took action wherever possible to insure that persons most favorable to their position continued to man African administrations and assumed new political and state police powers. Such a presentation of events would be termed one-sided by many Europeans and Africans, too. In a sense, that is true, and the one-sidedness is deliberate. It is a presentation of what the colonial educational system achieved *in terms of what it set itself to achieve*. The other side of the matter is not the good with which colonial educators can be credited, but rather the good that emerged in spite of the efforts and intentions of the colonizers and because of the struggles of African people.

Development by Contradiction

The only positive development in colonialism was when it ended. It is the purpose of this section to sketch briefly how that development came about, with particular reference to the role of the educated sector.

In contrast to a subjective interpretation of what was good about colonialism on the one hand and what was bad on the other hand, there is the approach which follows closely the aims and achievements of the colonizers and the *counter* aims and achievements of the African people. Sometimes, Africans were restricted merely to manipulating colonial institutions as best they could; but, in addition, certain fundamental contradictions arose within colonial society, and they could only be resolved by Africans' regaining their sovereignty as a people.

Analysis based on the perception of contradictions is characteristic of Marxism. Thus, Soviet historians approach the disintegration of colonialism within the following framework:

> Colonialism fettered the development of the enslaved peoples. To facilitate colonial exploitation, the imperialists deliberately hampered economic and cultural progress in the colonies, preserved and restored obsolete forms of social relations, and fomented discord between nationalities and tribes. However, the drive for super profits dictated development of the extractive industry, plantations and capitalist farms, and the building of ports, railways and roads in the colonies. In consequence, social changes took place in the colonies, irrespective of the will of the colonialists. New social forces emerged—an industrial and agricultural proletariat, a national bourgeoisie and intelligentsia.

Among the different segments of the African population within the so-called modern sector produced by capitalist activity, the cash-crop peasantry was the largest. African cash-crop farmers had profound grievances against the colonialist, centering on the low price for African products and sometimes on land alienation. Agricultural wage earners and urban workers had definitely lost their land, and were resisting wage slavery. They did so by organizing as the European proletariat had been doing since its formation; and, by virtue of compact organization, African workers made their presence felt much more strongly than their limited numbers might otherwise have warranted. In the end, the numerical preponderance of peasants and of those who had one foot in the "subsistence" sector was registered in the mass parties. But, while peasants depended upon sporadic revolts and boycotts to express their grievances, wage earners were engaged in a more continuous process of bargaining, petitioning, striking.

The smallest of the social groupings was that of the educated elite or intelligentsia. As noted earlier, the number of Africans receiving education in the colonial period was so small that anyone who went to school was privileged and belonged to an elite. There were only a few lawyers and doctors, concentrated mainly in North and West Africa. Generally speaking, the intelligentsia were students, clerks, and teachers. The group of the educated also overlapped with that of organized labor leadership, with the traditional African ruling stratum, with ex-servicemen and police, and with traders and independent craftsmen.

Altogether, the educated played a role in African independence struggles far out of proportion to their numbers, because they took it upon themselves and were called upon to articulate the interests of all Africans. They were also required to provide the political organization that would combine all the contradictions of colonialism and focus on the main contradiction, which was that between the colony and the metropole.

The contradiction between the educated and the colonialists was not the most profound. Ultimately, it was possible for the colonizers to withdraw and to satisfy the aspirations of most of the African intelligentsia, without in any way relieving the peasant and worker majority, who were the most exploited and the most oppressed. However, while the differences lasted between the colonizers and the African educated, they were decisive.

It has already been argued at some length that colonial education reached a limited number of Africans, that it was restricted to elementary levels, and that its pedagogical and ideological content was such as to serve the interests of Europe rather than Africa. Even so, the numbers enrolled would have been much smaller, were it not for efforts on the part of Africans themselves. The secondary school opportunities would have been narrower, and the ideological content would have been more negative, if the activities of the African masses were not in constant contradiction to the aims of European colonizers. Above all, education for continued enslavement never quite fulfilled its purpose; and, instead, different levels of contradiction arose—leading to independence, and in some cases heralding a new socialist epoch by the end of colonialism.

If there is anything glorious about the history of African colonial education, it lies not in the crumbs which were dropped by European exploiters, but in the tremendous vigor displayed by Africans in mastering the principles of the system that had mastered them. In most colonies, there was an initial period of indifference towards school education, but once it was understood that schooling represented one of the few avenues of advance within colonial society, it became a question of Africans clamoring and *pushing the colonialists much further than they intended to go.*

When Africans took great pains to enter the cash-crop economy, that generally suited European capitalist ends. But, African initiatives in the sphere of education were producing results antagonistic to at least some of the purposes of colonial exploitation.

Education in French colonial Africa has been referred to several times from the viewpoint of French policy. French administrators also commented on African efforts to go beyond the limited number of cadres that the French had in mind, and whom the French were prepared to subsidize out of African taxes. In 1930, the Governor-General of French West Africa reported:

> Each new school that is opened is immediately filled to overflowing. Everywhere, natives in their multitude are clamoring to be educated. Here, a Chief wants a school of his own, so he builds it; or again, some village or other may offer to bear the cost of fitting out a school. At certain places on the Ivory Coast, the villagers pay the teachers out of their own pockets. Our pupils often come from distances of 20 to 50 kilometers.

African enthusiasm in seeking more and higher education was not confined to any part of the continent; although in some parts it was manifested at an earlier date and more intensely. For instance, the Gold Coast and Sierra Leone had a tradition of European education going back to the seventeenth century. Therefore, it was not at all surprising that in 1824 the *Times Educational Supplement* commented that there was a universal demand for better and more education on the Gold Coast. It was the Gold Coast which produced J. E. K. Aggrey, that distinguished African educator and nationalist; and he fired the imagination of Africans well beyond the Gold Coast, in so far as formal education was concerned.

There was a definite correlation between the degree of colonial exploitation and the amount of social services provided. That applied to education in particular, so that urban, mining, and cash-crop areas had a virtual monopoly of schools. That was partly due to the capitalist policy of enhancing the labor power of workers, but it was also the consequence of efforts made by Africans inside the cash economy. They made demands on the colonial administration, and they also went through a great deal of sacrifice and self-denial to get more school places. Thus, one finds that

Ibos who were earning income from palm oil deployed a significant proportion of their small earnings into building schools, usually in association with the church. Incidentally, it should be noted here that what were called church or mission schools were often entirely financed by Africans. They paid church dues, they made donations for the church harvest, they sometimes contributed to a special education fund, and they often paid school fees. That pattern was widespread in Iboland, and it was not uncommon in other parts of colonial Africa. The existence of schools should be traced through the church back to palm oil and the people's labor. Indeed, it must not be forgotten that missionaries, administrators, white settlers—the whole lot—were living off African labor and resources.

In the cash-crop areas of British Africa, it also became the practice to try and use the agricultural produce boards and similar institutions to finance education. After all, the agricultural boards were supposed to have been established in the interest of peasant producers. They concentrated on exporting surplus in the form of dollar reserves for Britain; but, towards the end of colonial rule in the self-government epoch, it was too much of a scandal to avoid giving Africans some small part of the benefits of their labor, and so the produce boards were prevailed upon to make some funds available for education. For example, in 1953 the Uganda Legislative Council voted to spend about 11 million pounds from the Cotton Price Stabilization Fund on welfare schemes, with agricultural education receiving a big slice.

Among those Africans who did somewhat better than their brothers financially, some philanthropy was expressed in terms of helping African children go to school. The historical records of African education under colonial rule reveal certain tidbits, such as the fact that the first secondary school was established in Somalia in 1949 not by the colonial administration or on the initiative of the church but by a Somali trader. Of course, it is still expected in Africa that anyone who is already educated and is earning a salary should in turn help to educate at least one more member of his extended family. That is precisely because his extended family and his village community often made sacrifices to allow him to be educated in the first place. That was as true in Mauritania as it was in the reserves of South Africa, and no African would have any difficulty in supplying his own examples to that effect.

There are now available a number of biographies of Africans who gained prominence in the colonial period, usually in the movement for the regaining of African independence. It invariably emerges from reading such biographies how much of a *struggle* it was to be educated in colonial times. The same conclusion can be reached through reading the modern

African novel, because the novelist (while writing what is called fiction) is concerned with capturing reality. Apologists for colonialism talk as though education were a big meal handed down to Africans on a platter. It was not. The educational crumbs dropped were so small that individuals scrambled for them; they saved incredibly from small earnings and sent their children to school; and African children walked miles to and from school, and thought nothing of it.

But, apart from physical and financial sacrifices, Africans in some colonies had to wage a political battle to have the principle of African education accepted. The colonies in question were those with white settler populations.

In Kenya, white settlers made it clear that as far as they were concerned, an uneducated African was better than an educated one, and that one with the rudiments of education was at least preferable to one with more than a few years of schooling. The Beecher report on education in Kenya (produced in 1949) was heavily influenced by white settlers, and it stated frankly:

> Illiterates with the right attitude to manual employment are preferable to products of the schools who are not readily disposed to enter manual employment.

Because the white settlers were close to the center of political power in the colonial system, they were able to apply their principles to education in Kenya; and very little education went to Africans. In effect, that meant an exception to the rule that more social facilities followed heightened exploitation; but, the Kikuyu (who were the most exploited in Kenya) did not accept the situation passively. One line of approach was to bombard the colonial government with demands, even though Africans were in a far less favorable position to do so than white settlers. The demands were partially successful. The Beecher report grudgingly conceded a few schools to Africans at the primary and secondary level, by suggesting places for 40 per cent of African children at junior primary, 10 per cent at senior primary or intermediate, and 1 per cent at secondary level. But, by 1960, the number of primary schools was double what the whites considered should have been achieved by that date, and the number of secondary institutions was three times what the white settlers had succeeded in recommending.

Besides, where the government was reluctant to build schools or to subsidize missionaries to do so with African taxes, there was an even greater incentive to handle educational matters directly. In Kenya, there was a spate of what came to be called Independent schools, comparable to the

Independent churches, and, in fact, springing from Independent churches for the most part. The Independent schools in Kenya formed two major associations: namely, the Kikuyu Independent Schools Association and the Kikuyu Karinga Education Association, formed in 1929.

In practice, just as the European Christian missions used schools to attract converts, so the Independent churches attached great importance to schooling. John Chilembwe made striking efforts in that respect, aided by brothers recruited from among African descendants in the U.S.A.

The Moslem religion was also a stimulator of educational advance during the colonial period. In North Africa, Moslems often found it necessary to channel their efforts into schools other than those built by the colonialists. The Society of Reformist Ulema in Algeria started a large primary school program in 1936. By 1955, its primary schools catered to 45,000 Algerian children; and, from 1947, the Society also ran a large secondary school. Similarly, in Tunisia, popular initiative financed modern Koranic primary schools, providing places for 35,000 children—equivalent to one out of four going to primary school.

In Morocco, the Moslem schools that were established by popular effort possessed the unusual feature of aiming at women's emancipation by having a high percentage of girls—far higher than government schools. The French colonial administration deliberately kept mention of such schools out of their official reports, and they tried to keep their existence hidden from visitors.

Another striking example of African self-help with regard to education was the project sponsored by the Graduates' General Congress in Sudan. Founded by students, merchants, and civil servants in 1937, the Graduates' Congress embarked on a program of school building. Within four years, a hundred schools were opened with the help of voluntary contributions. A smaller but equally exciting experiment was that of the Bugabo United Schoolboys Association, founded by two schoolboys in Mwanza, Tanganyika, in 1947. It was aimed at adult education and in a short time attracted over a thousand people of all ages. The organizers set up a camp where they housed and fed those who turned up, while imparting to them the rudiments of literacy.

When Kikuyu peasants or Ga market women or Kabyle shepherds saved to build schools and educate their children, that was not entirely in accordance with the objective of the colonialists, who wanted cash-crop payments and other money in circulation to return as profits to the metropoles through the purchase of consumer goods. In such small ways, therefore, Africans were establishing an order of priorities different from that of the colonialists. This intensified in the later years of colonialism, when education came to be seen as having political significance in the era of self-government.

Having received higher education in colonial Africa in the post-Second World War era, a French African could reach as far as the French Assembly in Paris, while an English colonial subject might reach the local Legislative Assembly as an elected or nominated member. Those openings were absolutely devoid of power, and they were opportunities that only the merest handful could achieve; but they were stimulants, nonetheless, giving Africans the notion that considerable vertical mobility would accompany education. In French Equatorial Africa in the late 1940s, it was the African Governor, Felix Eboue, who spearheaded the demands for more education for Africans, and he was successful to some extent in forcing the hand of his masters in the French Overseas Ministry. In that same period and subsequently, it was also African effort in the Legislative Councils that kept the question of education to the fore. The British had handpicked a few educated Africans and some "chiefs" to advise the Governor in the Legislative Assembly. Generally, they were decorative like the plumes of the Governor's helmet; but, on the issue of education, no African could possibly avoid at least voicing some dissatisfaction with the poor state of affairs.

Ultimately, from a purely quantitative viewpoint, Africans pushed the colonialists and the British in particular to grant more education than was allowed for within the colonial system, and that was an important and explosive contradiction that helped Africans regain political independence.

It has been observed that British colonies tended to create an educated sector that was larger than that which the colonial economy could absorb. The explanation for that lies in the efforts of African people, although it is true that the French were more rigorous in rejecting African demands, and keeping to their schedule of training only a cadre elite to serve French interests. As it was, in a colony such as Gold Coast, African efforts to achieve education undoubtedly went beyond the numbers required to service the economy. Gold Coast was one of the first colonies to experience the "crisis of primary school leavers" or the "secondary school bottleneck." That is to say, among those leaving primary schools, many were frustrated because they could not find places in secondary schools, nor could they find jobs in keeping with the values they had obtained in school and in keeping with the internal stratification of African society caused by capitalism.

It is sometimes said that Kwame Nkrumah organized the illiterates in the Convention People's Party. That was a charge contemptuously made by other conservative educated Ghanaians, who thought that Nkrumah was going too far too fast. In reality, the shock troops in Nkrumah's youth brigade were not illiterate. They had been to primary school, and could read the manifestos and the literature of the African nationalist revolution. But, they were extremely disaffected because (among other things) they were relative latecomers on the educational scene in Gold Coast, and there was no room in the restricted African establishment of the cocoa monoculture.

Colonial powers aimed at giving a certain amount of education to keep colonialism functioning; Africans by various means required more education at the lower level than their "allowance," and this was one of the factors which brought about deep crisis, and forced the British to consider the idea of withdrawing their colonial apparatus from Gold Coast. The timetable for independence was also speeded up against the will of the British. As is well known, the regaining of independence in Ghana was not just a local affair, but one that was highly significant for Africa as a whole; and it therefore highlights the importance of at least one of the educational contradictions in bringing about political independence in Africa.

The Gold Coast colony was not the only one in which there appeared the problem of bottleneck, because of the shallowness of the educational pyramid. In the area that was once the colonial Federation of the Rhodesias and Nyasaland, educators in the 1950s were commenting on the primary school leavers crisis. They claimed to have had a surplus of sixth-grade leavers. A set of colonies that was educating an insignificant number of African school children had a surplus of primary school leavers! All it meant was that colonialism was so bankrupt and had so underdeveloped Africa that it had no use for more than a handful of educated. Furthermore, the colonialists had assured every struggling African that, if he endured missionary education, he would be given a white-collar job and a passport to civilization; but, on leaving school, African youth found the promises to be false. One sixth-grade leaver in the Central African Federation wrote the following letter to a magazine in 1960:

> After I had passed Standard 6, I spent the whole year at home because I could not get a place anywhere to further my education. At the beginning of this year I went to look for work but failed to get it again, from January until now. If I had known that my education would have been useless, I would have told my father not to waste his money in educating me from the beginning to Standard 6.

It would be fairly reasonable to assume that the writer of that letter opposed the white settler Central African Federation. Whether or not he consciously rationalized the matter, he was bound to act as a product of the deep contradictory forces within colonialism—forces which had produced the discrepancy between promise and fulfillment, in terms of his own personal life.

Occasionally, the frustrated school leavers might vent their sentiments in a non-constructive manner. For instance, the problem of the bottleneck in education and employment arose in Ivory Coast by 1958; and, in a context of confused African leadership, the youth of Ivory Coast decided that their enemy was the group of Dahomeans and Senegalese who were employed in Ivory Coast. However, on the whole, the situation of frustration aided Africans to perceive more clearly that the enemy was the colonial power, and it therefore added another platform to the movement for regaining African independence.

Africans clashed with the colonial structure not just over the quantity of education, but also over the quality. One of the key topics for disagreement was colonial agricultural education, to which reference has already been made. The colonialists seemed surprised that a continent of agriculturalists should reject education which was supposedly intended to raise the level of their agriculture. Indeed, some Africans came out against agricultural education and other reforms to "Africanize" curricula, for what appears to have been selfish elitist reasons. For instance, one Guinean demanded that there should not be a single change from the teaching program as used in metropolitan France. "We want a metropolitan curriculum and the same diplomas as in France, for we are as French as the French of the metropoles," he declared. In Tanganyika, during German days, there were also protests against changing the formal and literary educational program, as it had been introduced body and soul from Europe. A prominent Tanganyikan African, Martin Kayamba, asserted that "those who think that literary education is unsuitable for Africans ignore the fact of its importance and indispensability to any sort of education, and therefore deny the Africans the very means of progress."

Statements such as the above have to be seen in their correct context to understand that the African response was perfectly justified. The colonialist value system assigned a low value to manual activity and a high value to white-collar bureaucratic work. Even more important, the colonial economy offered discriminating compensation to those who had literary or "bookish" education, as opposed to those with manual skills. It was extremely difficult to convince any sane African that education which would send him to dig the soil to get 100 shillings at the end of the year was more appropriate than education which qualified him to work in the civil service for 100 shillings per month. When Europeans preached that brand of wisdom, Africans were suspicious.

Africans were very suspicious about taxes in the colonial era. They never wanted to be counted, nor did they want their chickens to be counted, because bitter experience had shown them that that was how the colonialists assessed taxes. Similarly, on educational issues, there was no confidence in colonial plans to provide different versions of education, because such plans almost invariably meant an even more inferior education, and one that was more blatantly intended to be education for underdevelopment. The most extreme example of a colonial education system designed to train Africans to fill their "natural" role of manual laborers was that in South Africa, after the introduction of the Bantu Education Act in 1953. However, the earlier attempts by the British and French to set up what they called "farm schools" or "initiation schools" were along the same lines as have since been ruthlessly pursued by the racists in South Africa. The non-literary education had the superficial appearance of being more relevant to Africa, but it was really inferior education for a people who were supposedly inferior in order to make them accept their own exploitation and oppression. As Abdou Moumini put it, "colonial education was 'cut-rate' education." It offered by European standards low-quality substitutes to suit what was described as the limited intellectual capacity of Africans. In French colonial Africa, the diplomas were seldom equal to those in the metropoles at comparable levels, and in British East Africa one official asked educators to bear in mind the gap between themselves and the "grubby savages" whom Britain was attempting to civilize. It is in this context that agricultural education in particular revealed itself as an exercise in deception.

Consequently, the struggle against agricultural or rural schools was one of the most bitter struggles waged by African nationalists, and helped heighten consciousness at all levels of African society, with regard to the fundamentally exploitative and racist nature of colonialism. In French West Africa, for example, the farm schools were determinedly opposed after the last war, and the French colonial government had to abolish them. In Tanganyika and Nyasa, the confrontation between the colonialists and the African people was much bigger, because opposition to agricultural education was associated with opposition to colonial agricultural innovations (such as terracing) which were forced upon people without consultation and without taking into account the varying conditions in different localities.

In East Africa the British made a few determined efforts to introduce what they considered as relevant agricultural education. One pilot scheme was at Nyakato in Tanganyika, which involved transforming a secondary school into an agricultural school in 1930. It lasted for nine years with tutors recruited from Britain and South Africa, but in the end the attempt failed because of protest by students and the population of the region. Although the school claimed to be offering new agricultural skills, it was readily recognized that it was part of a program defining the "correct attitudes" and "natural place" which Europeans thought fit for the natives.

In the 1940s, as Africans sought to change features of the educational system, they naturally had to demand a voice in councils that formulated educational policy. That was in itself a revolutionary demand, because colonial people are supposed to be ruled, not to participate in decision-making. Besides, on the issue of educational policy-making, Africans not only alarmed the administrators, but they trod on the corns of the missionaries, who generally felt that they inherited education at the partition of Africa. All of those clashes were pointing in the direction of freedom for colonial peoples, because in the background there was always the question of political power.

It would be erroneous to suggest that educated Africans foresightedly moved with the intention of regaining African independence. There would have been very few indeed who, as early as 1939, would have joined Chief Essien of Calabar in asserting:

> Without education it will be impossible for us to get to our destination, which is Nigeria's economic independence and Nigeria's political independence.

However, education (both formal and informal) was a powerful force which transformed the situation in postwar Africa in such a way as to bring political independence to most of colonized Africa within two decades.

There were also a few Europeans who foresaw what were called the "dangers" of giving Africans a modern education: namely, the possibility of its leading towards freedom. Certainly, Europeans were not at all happy with any schools which were of the European type, but which were not under direct colonialist control. For example, the Independent schools of Kenya were disliked by white settlers in that colony and by other Europeans outside Kenya. One Catholic mission report from nearby Tanganyika in 1933 warned against allowing Tanganyika Africans to set up schools controlled by themselves. It noted that: "Independent schools are causing difficulties in Kenya. Such schools may easily become hotbeds of sedition."

When the Mau Mau war for land and liberation broke out in Kenya, one of the first things the British government did was to close the 149 schools of the Kikuyu Independent Schools Association, 21 schools of the Kikuyu Karinga Education Association, and 14 other Independent schools. They were considered "training grounds for rebellion"—a term which essentially captures the fear expressed in the Catholic mission report just cited. Europeans knew well enough that if they did not control the minds of Africans, they would soon cease to control the people physically and politically.

Similarly, in North Africa, the French colonial power and the white *colons,* or settlers, did not take kindly to the self-help schools of the colonized Algerians and Tunisians. The purpose of the schools set up by the Society of Reformist Ulema in Algeria was that they should be modern and scientific, but at the same time present learning in the context of Arab and Algerian culture. Pupils at the Ulema schools began their lessons by singing together: "Arabic is my language, Algeria is my country, Islam is my religion." It was no wonder, therefore, that the colonialists victimized pupils and parents, and took repressive measures on the grounds that those schools were also hotbeds of sedition.

The missionaries asked for control of schools, because that was one of their drawing cards for the church itself and because they considered themselves as experts on the side of cultural imperialism (which they called "civilizing"). However, there were other Europeans both within and without the colonies who were absolutely opposed to schools—be they Christian, Independent, government, or Islamic. Starting from a racist position, they asserted that offering education to Africans was like throwing pearls before swine. Some of the most violent expressions of racism were directed against educated Africans. Starting from the time of individuals like Lord Lugard and through to the days of the last colonial administrators like Sir Alan Burns, many colonialists demonstrated hostility to educated Africans. Educated Africans made colonialists extremely uneasy, because they did not conform to the image which Europeans liked to harbor of the "unspoiled African savage."

But, if one goes to the heart of the matter, it can be discerned that the white racists did not seriously believe that Africans could not master knowledge then in the possession of Europeans. On the contrary, the evidence of educated Africans was before their eyes; and the white settlers especially feared that, given an opportunity, far too many Africans would master white bourgeois knowledge too thoroughly. Such Africans would, therefore, refuse to work as agricultural laborers for 12 shillings per month; they would compete with Europeans in semi-skilled categories; and above all they would want to govern themselves.

In the records of colonialism, it is not uncommon to encounter the following type of remark: "What need is there to educate the natives? You will give them the weapons to destroy you!"

In one sense, those Europeans were simply dreamers, because giving education to Africans was not an option which could have been avoided; it was an objective necessity to keep colonialism functioning. P. E. Mitchell, who later became Governor of Uganda, remarked in 1928 that *"regret it as he may,* no Director of Education can resist the demand for clerks, carpenters, shoemakers and so on—trained in European methods to meet European needs. These men are not being trained to fit into any place in the life of their own people, but to meet the economic needs of a foreign race." At the same time, the available education was also a consequence of the irrepressible actions of the African people, who hoped to move forward within the alien system. So, those Europeans who were absolutely opposed to giving education to Africans did not understand the contradictions of their own colonial society. But in another sense they were defending the interests of colonialism. Firstly, however much the colonialists tried, they could not succeed in shaping the minds of *all* Africans whom they educated in schools. The exceptions were the ones who were going to prove most dangerous to colonialism, capitalism, and imperialism. And secondly, the most timid and the most brainwashed of educated Africans harbored some form of disagreement with the colonialists; and, in the pursuit of their own group or individual interests, the educated elite helped to expose and undermine the structure of colonial rule.

Keeping the above distinction in mind, one can consider both those contradictions which arose between the colonizers and the African educated as a whole, and those which arose between the colonizers and particular individuals among the African educated.

As already noted, insufficient educational facilities and inadequate jobs were the complaints raised by the lower echelons of those who were educated in Africa during the colonial period. Those who went to secondary school or institutions of higher learning found little access to remunerative and responsible posts, because they were destined to fill the lower ranks of the civil and business administration. After working for twenty years, an African in the civil service would have been extremely lucky to have become "head clerk," or in the police to have become a sergeant. Meanwhile, to add insult to injury, any European doing the same job as an African got higher pay; and whites who were less qualified and experienced were placed above Africans, who did the jobs their superiors were paid to do. In the colonial civil service to be a European was enough. It did not matter whether the white person was ignorant and stupid, he would be assured of drawing a fat salary and enjoying wide privileges. The Guinea-Bissau leader, Amilcar Cabral, gave an example of that type.

> I was an agronomist working under a European who everybody knew was one of the biggest idiots in Guinea; I could have taught him his job with my eyes shut but he was the boss; this is something which counts a lot, this is the confrontation which really matters.

Questions such as salaries, promotions, leave, allowances, were ones which were of paramount interest to most African civil servant associations and Welfare or "Improvement" Associations. There should be no illusions concerning the factor of self-interest. But, their complaints were justified in terms of the discrepancy between their living standards and those of white expatriates or settlers, as well as in terms of the ideology of the very bourgeoisie who had colonized Africa. The educational process had equipped a few Africans with a grasp of the international community and of bourgeois democracy, and there was a most unsatisfactory credibility gap between the ideals of bourgeois democracy and the existence of colonialism as a system which negated freedom. Inevitably, the educated started gravitating in the direction of claims for national independence, just as educated Indians had done much earlier on the Indian subcontinent.

According to official Spanish sources, it is said that the school system in Spanish Guinea achieved all that the colonizers expected of it. It produced the required Africans who loved Spaniards more than the Spaniards loved themselves, but it produced no opponents of the colonial regime. It is difficult to believe the truth of such an assertion; and the Spanish took good care that no one from outside got wind of what things were like in the small Spanish colonies in Africa. However, if it were true that the colonial educational system in Spanish Guinea created only whitewashed Africans according to plan, then that would represent an outstanding exception to the general rule. Wherever adequate evidence is available, it shows that the cultural imperialism of colonial education was successful in large measure, but was never entirely successful. It produced *according to plan* many "loyal Kikuyu," "Capicornists," "Anglophiles," "Francophiles"; but it also produced *in spite of itself* those Africans whom the colonialists called upstarts, malcontents, agitators, communists, terrorists.

From the viewpoint of the colonialists, trouble often started with African students before they had completed studies. The Sudan, for example, has a history of nationalist student protests; and Madagascar was outstanding in that respect. From the early years of this century, a politicized student movement was growing in Madagascar, in spite of specific steps taken by two French governors. By 1816, Malagasy students had organized the Vy Vato society, seeking to kick out the French. When the Vy Vato was discovered, students were brutally suppressed. However, as so often happens, students gained inspiration from the martyrdom of their fellows, and they resurfaced at a later date on the nationalist scene.

Students who were taken to universities in the metropoles were the most favored and the most pampered of the Africans selected by the white colonial overlords to become Europeanized; and yet they were among the first to argue vocally and logically that the liberty, equality, and fraternity about which they were taught should apply to Africa. African students in France in the postwar years were placed carefully within the ranks of the then conservative French national student body, but they soon rebelled and formed the Federation of Students of Black Africa (FEANF), which became affiliated to the communist International Union of Students. In Britain, African students formed a variety of ethnic and nationalist organizations, and participated in the Pan-African movement. After all, most of them were sent there to study the British Constitution and Constitutional Law, and (for what it is worth) the word "freedom" appears in those contexts rather often!

The fascists who ruled Africans at some points during the colonial epoch tried to avoid bourgeois democratic ideals altogether. For example, while the Italian fascists were in charge of Somalia between 1922 and 1941, they took away from history textbooks all reference to Mazzini and Garibaldi, two key leaders of the democratic wing of the Italian nationalist movement of the nineteenth century. Yet, the clerks and NCOs who received that education nevertheless went into the Somali Youth League and fought for independence at the head of popular forces.

The fact of the matter is that it was not really necessary to get the idea of freedom from a European book. What the educated African extracted from European schooling was a particular formulation of the concept of political freedom. But, it did not take much to elicit a response from their own instinctive tendency for freedom; and, as has just been noted in the Somali instance, that universal tendency to seek freedom manifested itself among Africans even when the most careful steps were taken to extinguish it.

There was no sector of colonial life in which educated Africans appeared and remained wholly loyal to the colonialists. Teachers were supposed to have been steeped in the culture of domination, so as to pass it on to other Africans; but, in the end, many of them stood in the vanguard of the national independence movements. African priests and pastors were supposed to have been the loyal servants of God and his European lieutenants, but the church gave birth in Nyasaland to John Chilembwe, as early as the First World War. Shortly afterwards, in Congo, when Simon Kimbangu started his Independent church, he actually threatened the colonialists that he would introduce Bolshevism!

It is particularly interesting to notice that the colonialists could not be sure of the loyalty of their African troops. It has already been argued that the army and police were educational and socializing institutions to perpetuate colonialist and capitalist power and values. How successfully they served that function can be seen in the number of veterans of Burma and Indochina who returned to the continent to carry out loyally the policies of Britain and France, respectively. Colonel Bokassa of the Central African Republic and Colonel Lamizana of Upper Volta provide two outstanding examples, both of them having graduated from fighting the Vietnamese to a point where they are prepared to dialogue with the fascist apartheid state of South Africa. However, returned soldiers also played a very positive role in the national independence struggles after both wars. And, occasionally, towards the end of colonial rule, African troops and police mutinied, as in Nyasaland in 1959.

African trade unionists also went to "school" under colonialism. To begin with, the organization and activity of the small wage-earning sector in Africa bothered the colonialists a great deal. Their initial desire was to crush worker dissent, and (when that appeared unlikely to succeed) to coopt it and guide it along "acceptable" channels.

The British Trade Union Council sponsored a number of African trade unions, and tried to get them to accept a rigid separation between industrial matters (such as wages and working hours) and political matters. But, the TUC was in that context acting on behalf of the British bourgeoisie, and they did not succeed in holding back the working class in Africa. African workers were able to appreciate that there was no difference between the private employers and the colonial administration. Indeed, the colonial administration was itself one of the biggest employers, against whom workers had many charges. Consequently, in the 1940s and 1950s, it was common to have strikes that were specifically connected with the struggle for independence, notably in Gold Coast, Nigeria, and Sudan.

The contradiction between French workers and African workers in French colonies emerged in a very acute form. The French trade union movement (and notably the Communist Union, the CGT) insisted that Africans should not have separate unions, but should be members of French labor unions—just like any other French workers. That arrangement gave support to the juridical political fiction that places like Dahomey and Comoro Islands were not colonies, but merely the overseas section of France. Sekou Toure of Guinea was one of the first to break with the patronage of French trade unions and to establish an independent African trade union. In so doing, Sekou Toure made it clear that the principal contradiction of the colonial situation was that between colonized peoples on the one hand and the colonizing nation on the other. So long as African workers remain colonized, they had to think of themselves firstly as *African* workers, rather than members of an international proletariat. That interpretation, which was entirely in accordance with reality, led to the trade union movement taking on a highly politicized and nationalist role in French West Africa. It was an achievement which defeated the chauvinism of white French workers as well as the class interests of the French bourgeoisie.

The attitude of the white metropolitan working class towards their African counterparts was influenced by the prevailing racist values of capitalist society. Indeed, the racist factor heightened the principal contradiction between the colonizers and the colonized. Discriminatory racist methods and measures were found in every colony—with varying degrees of openness or hypocrisy. Sometimes, white racism was vicious and at other times it was paternalist. Nor did it necessarily reflect Europe's desire to exploit Africans economically. In Southern Rhodesia, racial discrimination was very much tied up with the white settlers' maintaining their jobs and the stolen land; but when some semi-literate white inspector insulted an educated Sierra Leonean, that may be referred to as "gratuitous." Racism in such a context actually jeopardized economic exploitation, and it was merely the manifestation of prejudices that had grown over the centuries.

The racial contradiction extended far beyond the shores of Africa, because of the historical antecedence of the slave trade. It is not in the least surprising that Pan-African ideas should have been most forcefully expressed by West Indians like Garvey and Padmore and North Americans like W. E. B. Du Bois and Alpheus Hunton. Those individuals had all been educated within the international capitalist structure of exploitation on the basis of class and race. Having realized that their inferior status in the societies of America was conditioned by the fact of being black and the weakness of Africa, the Pan-Africanists were forced to deal with the central problem of Europe's exploitation and oppression of the African continent. Needless to say, the metropolitan powers could never have foreseen that their humiliation of millions of Africans in the New World would ultimately rebound and help Africa to emancipate itself.

The process by which Africa produced thirty-odd sovereign states was an extremely complex one, characterized by an interplay of forces and calculations on the part of various groups of Africans, on the part of the colonial powers, and on the part of interest groups inside the metropoles. African independence was affected by international events such as the Second World War, the rise of the Soviet Union, the independence of India and China, the people's liberation movement in Indochina, and the Bandung Conference. On the African continent itself, the "domino theory" operated, so that the re-emergence of Egypt under Nasser, the early independence of Ghana, Sudan, and Guinea, and the nationalist wars in Kenya and Algeria all helped to knock down the colonies which remained standing. However, it must be stressed that the move for the regaining of independence was *initiated* by the African people; and, to whatever extent that objective was realized, the motor force of the people must be taken into account.

In a conference held by the French in Brazzaville in 1948 (and chaired by General de Gaulle), it was explicitly stated that "the establishment, *even in the distant future,* of self-government in the colonies is to be avoided." As is well known, the French eventually considered the idea of conceding independence to African peoples after being taught a salutary lesson by the Algerian people. Moreover, when Guinea chose independence in 1958 rather than accept being permanently a footstool for France, the French administrators literally went crazy and behaved like wild pigs before sailing from Guinea. They just could not cope with the idea of African independence.

Apart from the Portuguese, the Belgians were the colonialists who were the most reluctant in withdrawing in the face of African nationalism. In 1955, a Belgian professor suggested independence for the Congo in thirty years, and he was regarded as a radical! Of course, Congo turned out to be one of the places where imperialism was successful in hijacking the African revolution. But, the order of events must still be considered. Firstly, it was the intensity of the Congolese and African demands that made independence thinkable, as far as the Belgians were concerned; and, secondly, it was precisely the strength and potential of the nationalist movement under Lumumba which forced the imperialists to resort to murder and invasion.

The British make much of the fact that they conceded the idea of self-government immediately after the last war; but self-government was a long cry from independence, and the notion of training people for independence was nothing but a political gimmick. Lady Margery Perham, a true voice of patronizing colonialism, admitted that the Colonial Office's timetable for independence had to be scrapped in the face of the mobilized African people. For that matter, even African leaders never hoped to achieve national sovereignty as rapidly as they did, until the mass parties began to roll like boulders down a hillside.

The fact that this analysis has been focused on the role of the educated Africans in the independence movements is not intended to detract from the vital activity of the broad African masses, including the sacrifice of life and limb. In brief, it is enough to say that the African people as a collective had upset the plans of the colonialist, and had surged forward to freedom. Such a position may seem to be a mere revival of a certain rosy and romantic view of African independence which was popular in the early 1960s, but, on the contrary, it is fully cognizant of the shabby reality of neo-colonial Africa. It needs to be affirmed (from a revolutionary, socialist, and people-centered perspective) that even "flag independence" represented a positive development out of colonialism.

Securing the attributes of sovereignty is but one stage in the process of regaining African independence. By 1885, when Africa was politically and juridically partitioned, the peoples and polities had already lost a great deal of freedom. In its relations with the external world, Africa had lost a considerable amount of control over its own economy, ever since the fifteenth century. However, the loss of political sovereignty at the time of the Scramble was decisive. By the same reasoning, it is clear that the regaining of political sovereignty by the 1960s constitutes an inescapable first step in regaining maximum freedom to choose and to develop in all spheres.

Furthermore, the period of nationalist revolution gave rise to certain minority ideological trends, which represent the roots of future African development. Most African leaders of the intelligentsia and even of the labor movement were frankly capitalist, and shared fully the ideology of their bourgeois masters. Houphouet-Boigny was at one time called a "communist" by the French colonizers! He defended himself vigorously against the false charge in 1948:

> We have good relations with the [French] Communist Party, that is true. But it is obvious that that does not mean that we ourselves are communists. Can it be said that I, Houphouet-Boigny—a traditional chief, a doctor of medicine, a big property owner, a catholic—can it be said that I am a communist?

Houphouet-Boigny's reasoning applied to so many more African leaders of the independence epoch. The exceptions were those who either completely rejected the world-view of capitalism or at least stuck honestly to those idealistic tenets of bourgeois ideology such as individual freedom—and, through experience, they could come to realize that the ideals remained myths in a society based on the exploitation of man by man. Clearly, all leaders of the non-conformist type had developed in direct contradiction to the aims of formal and informal colonial education; and their differences with the colonizers were too profound to have been resolved merely by "flag independence."

African independence was greeted with pomp, ceremony, and a resurgence of traditional African music and dance. "A new day has dawned," "we are on the threshold of a new era," "we have now entered into the political kingdom"—those were the phrases of the day, and they were repeated until they became clichés. But, all the to-ing and fro-ing from

Contonou to Paris and from London to Lusaka and all the lowering and raising of flags cannot be said to have been devoid of meaning. Withdrawal of the directly controlled military and juridical apparatus of the colonizers was essential before any new alternatives could be posed with regard to political organization, social structure, economic development.

The above issues were raised most seriously by the minority of African leaders who had individually embarked on a non-capitalist path of development in their mode of thought; and the problems were considered within the context of inequalities and contradictions not just between Africa and Europe but also *inside* Africa, as a reflection of four centuries of slavery and one century of colonialism. As far as the mass of peasants and workers were concerned, the removal of overt foreign rule actually cleared the way towards a more fundamental appreciation of exploitation and imperialism. Even in territories such as Cameroon, where the imperialists brutally crushed peasants and workers and installed their own tried and tested puppet, advance had been made insofar as the masses had already participated in trying to determine their own destiny. That is the element of *conscious activity* that signifies the ability to make history, by grappling with the heritage of objective material conditions and social relations.

Brief Guide to Reading

Colonial rule generated a great deal of written material which can serve as one of the bases for historical reconstruction. Even the non-specialist in African history would be well advised to look at some original sources, such as the data compiled by Lord Hailey. Approached with care, several of the anthropological texts also yield information and insights with regard to detailed changes in African social structures.

Above all, however, the generations who suffered under colonialism are still living repositories of the continent's history. The collective knowledge of the African people derived from experience is the most authentic basis of the history of the colonial period. Unfortunately, much of the experience is not yet written down, but glimpses can be got from biographies of prominent Africans such as Nnamdi Azikiwe, Kwame Nkrumah, Oginga Odinga, and Kenneth Kaunda, as well as from the political writings of these and other leaders—notably Mwalimu Nyerere and Sekou Toure. The books by Padmore and Hunton mentioned in the literature for Chapter 5 are even more relevant in this context.

JACK WODDIS, *Africa, the Roots of Revolt*. London: Lawrence and Wishant, 1960.

———— *Africa, the Lion Awakes.*
GANN, L. H., and DUIGNAN, PETER, *The Burden of Empire.* New York: Praeger, 1967.
The first author and his works are well known for supporting the African anti-colonial stand. The second example is a colonialist interpretation which offers a contrast.

SLOAN and KITCHEN, *The Educated African.*
ABDOU MOUMINI, *Education in Africa.* New York: Praeger, 1968.
For data, the first book is useful. From the viewpoint of analysis, Moumini's book is superb.

FRANTZ FANON, *Black Skins, White Masks.* New York: Grove Press, 1967.
———— *The Wretched of the Earth.* New York: Grove Press, 1963.
———— *Towards the African Revolution.* New York: Monthly Review Press, 1967.
These studies are unique in revealing the psychological aspects of enslavement and colonization as far as Africans are concerned, whether in the Americas or on the African continent. Fanon does not have any equal in analyzing the last stages of African colonialism and the advent of neo-colonialism.

POSTSCRIPT

by A. M. BABU

Are there short cuts to economic development for the underdevelopment economies? This question has occupied the attention of many interested parties during the last decade. These include university lecturers, international economists, the United Nations and its agencies, the O.A.U., planning agencies, economic ministers. Many international conferences under various sponsorship have been held during the decade and volumes of resolutions, guidelines, learning documents, and theses have been published. The end result has been negative. The developing countries continue to remain underdeveloped, only getting worse in relation to the developed countries.

By and large the question still remains unanswered. Are we going to repeat the same exercise all over again during this decade? From the look of it, it appears that we are. Already the UN has launched the Second Economic Decade with the same zeal and fanfare as they did with the first. The same appeal has gone out to the developed countries to be charitable and contribute "one per cent of their national income" for helping the developing countries, as if the population of the world can continue to condone poverty so that the rich can be charitable! If past experience is anything to go by, the seventies will experience the same disappointments which climaxed the end of the sixties.

What, we may ask, has gone wrong? Is it something inherent in the very nature of underdevelopment that makes development such an impossible task? Among the many prescriptions that have been offered—e.g., cultural, social, psychological, even economic—none has produced any encouraging results. In fact nearly all of them have had negative results, and made bad situations worse. Are we to continue with the same experiments at the expense of the people, who, let's face it, have borne the whole burden of these experiments throughout the last decade? This is the question to which all the developing countries, especially those in Africa, must address themselves. And the sooner the better, because there is very little time left before our economies become permanently distorted and probably too damaged for any meaningful reconstruction in the future.

Dr. Walter Rodney, in this very instructive book, provides a very refreshing opening for discussions which may well lead to finding the right solution. He is raising the most basic and fundamental questions regarding the nature of underdevelopment and economic backwardness. Unlike many works of this nature, which to all intents and purposes have approached the problem with a sort of metaphysical outlook (garbed, it is true, in scientific terminology), Dr. Rodney follows the method of historical materialism, which in effect says: "To know the present we must look into the past and to know the future we must look into the past and the present." This is a scientific approach. We can at least be sure that the conclusions will not be marred by subjective distortions.

It is clear, especially after reading Rodney's exposition, that throughout the last decade we have been posing the wrong questions regarding economic backwardness. We did not "look into the past to know the present." We were told, and accepted, that our poverty was *caused* by our poverty in the now famous theory of the "vicious circle of poverty" and we went around in circles seeking ways and means of breaking that circle. Had we asked the fundamental questions which Dr. Rodney raises in this work we would not have exposed our economies to the ruthless plunder brought about by "foreign investments" which the exponents of the vicious circle theory urged us to do. For, it is clear, foreign investment is *the cause,* and not a solution, to our economic backwardness.

Are we not underdeveloped now because we have been colonized in the past? There is no other explanation to the fact that practically the whole of the underdeveloped world has been colonized either directly or indirectly by the Western powers. And what is colonialism if it is not a system of "foreign investments" by the metropolitan powers? If it has contributed to our underdevelopment in the past, is it not likely to contribute to our underdevelopment now, even if the political reins are in our hands? Put in this way the question of underdevelopment is immediately rendered more intelligible, even to the uninitiated. And this is how Dr. Rodney is directing us to pose our questions.

The inevitable conclusion is that foreign investment does not only help to undermine our economies by extracting enormous profits, but it does more serious damage to the economies by distorting them into lopsidedness, and if the process is not arrested in time, the distortion could be permanent. As long as we continue, as we have done for centuries, to produce for the so-called world market which was founded on the hard rock of slavery and colonialism, our economies will remain colonial. Any development will be entirely incidental, leaving the vast majority of the population wholly uninvolved in the economic activity. The more we invest in export branches in order to capture the "world market" the more we divert *away* from investing for people's development and, consequently, the less effective our development effort.

And since this type of investment does not contribute much towards the development of a material and technical base internally, our economies are rendered always responsive only to what the Western world is prepared to buy and sell, and hardly responsive to our internal development needs. That is why, although most of our development plans make elaborate resource allocations for "rural projects," invariably most of these resources find their way back to the urban projects and consequently accentuate the urban-rural disparities. Slums, unemployment, social maladjustment, and, finally, political instability are our most outstanding characteristics.

Almost without exception, all the ex-colonial countries have ignored the cardinal development demand; namely, that, to be really effective, the development process must begin by transforming the economy from its colonial, externally responsive structure, to one which is internally responsive. Where we went wrong is when we followed blindly the assumptions handed down to us by our exploiters. These assumptions can be stated briefly as follows: Growth in underdeveloped countries is hampered by inadequate growth in exports and inadequate financial resources and is made worse by "population explosion" in these countries. And the solution is prescribed as follows: Step up exports, increase aid and loans from the developed countries, and arrest growth in population.

Throughout the last decade our efforts have been to follow religiously the above prescription, and even if our own experience continues to disprove it, we still adhere to it even more fanatically! The greatest need appears to be a process of mental de-colonization, since neither common sense nor sound economics, not even our own experience, is with us in this.

Experiences of other countries that have chosen a different path, a path of economic reconstruction, is most instructive here. Take North Korea or Albania. Both these countries were underdeveloped as late as the fifties. The reason they have been able to register most outstanding economic progress is that they have decided to opt out of production for the so-called world market and have diverted their resources toward the development of a material and technological base internally.

The Pearson Commission's Report—*Partners in Development*—has been hailed, even by the developing countries, as ushering in a new era, a sort of turning point, in international cooperation for development. Even if its recommendations were to be adopted and implemented *in toto* it is doubtful if it would make any impact on the ever widening gap between the developed and the developing countries. This is because it has avoided tackling the most fundamental question, namely, "Can development take place when our production strategy is influenced by the demands of the world market which is determined almost exclusively by the pattern of production and consumption within capitalist Europe and America?" In other words, in distorting our economies to fit in with the demands of the world market, the demands of which are not always compatible with the demands of our own development, are we not, in the process, depriving our economies of the capacity for a self-sustaining growth which is a precondition to development?

By posing the question in this style, it is possible to see through the smokescreen of international do-gooders and begin to understand the real cause of our underdevelopment. It is, of course, too much to expect Pearson or people of his liberal inclination to pose the question in this way, since their training and outlook consider this way of putting the question to be almost morally sinful and economically subversive.

However, as leaders of the developing countries, we are obliged to adopt this style of posing the question since we have taken upon ourselves the responsibility for steering a development course whose success or failure will affect, one way or another, the well-being of hundreds of million of the people who comprise more than two-thirds of the human race. For too long we have left their fate to be determined by the kind of production which is not based on the satisfaction of their wants but rather on serving external interests as expressed by the accepted laws of supply and demand of the so-called world market. We have twisted their education in such a way that the "skills" we direct them to develop are geared towards serving the same ends of the world market rather than towards development of an internal material base, with the result that technologically, and in relation to the developed world, we move backward rather than forward. We have tamely accepted the so-called international division of labor on behalf of our masses, and in doing so we have condemned them to specialize in primary commodities whose production is conducive neither to the development of technological skills nor to the invention of advanced machinery, both of which are the preconditions to real economic development.

The significance of Dr. Rodney's book is that it is addressed, quite appropriately, to the masses and not to the leaders and one hopes that it will be instrumental in arousing some mass action by the people. In the absence of committed leadership, many African countries have fallen prey to military exploitation, to the extent that today the generals constitute the majority at the African summit. This is as it should be, because when the political leadership loses the sense of internal direction, when, in bewilderment, it gives up its efforts to find solutions to people's problems and begins to accumulate wealth for its own individual use, political leadership tends to get increasingly "commandist" in its state operations. Logic and rationale become subversive. And when politicians become commandists, they too become redundant, because who is better fitted to giving command than the army?

With very few exceptions it is sad to have to admit that Africa is ill served by the current conglomeration of what passes for leaders throughout the continent. When Asia and Latin America produce giants, like Mao, Ho, Ché, who inspire and excite the imagination not only of their compatriots within their borders, but of the rest of the world, including the developed world, Africa has produced only one Nyerere and maintained him in power, while we have murdered Lumumba and have locked up or exiled leaders like Ben Bella and Nkrumah in response to the wishes of the imperialists—our donors, our moneylenders, our patrons, our masters, our trading partners.

With all due respect, it is difficult to imagine, apart from one or two honorable exceptions, any of the present leaders who is capable of standing up for the genuine rights of his people, knowing that these rights are of necessity directly opposed to the interests of imperialism. And yet such a stand is necessary if we are to really fulfill our obligation as leaders; otherwise, we have no right to impose our leadership on the people. While most of the leaders on the continent have no sense of urgency in solving the problems of people's misery, since they don't bear the brunt of their misery, the masses, who do, cannot wait. That is why one hopes that Dr. Rodney's book will be read by as many people as possible because it has come at a time when it is most needed, for action.

After reading the harrowing account of the brutalities of slavery, of subjugation, of deprivation and humiliation, when whole civilizations were crushed in order to serve the imperialist interests of the West; when settled societies were disintegrated by force of imperialist arms so that the plantation owners of the "new world" could get their uprooted, and therefore permanent, labor force to build what is now the most advanced capitalist economy, it becomes absolutely clear that the only way out of our current impasse is through a revolutionary path—a complete break with the system which is responsible for all our past and present misery.

Our future course must be guided dialectically. If by looking into the past we have known the present, to know the future we must look into the past and the present. Our action must be related to our concrete experience and we must not give way to metaphysical hopes and wishes—hoping and wishing that the monster who has been after us throughout our history will some day change into a lamb; he won't. As Engels puts it: "Freedom does not consist in the dream of independence from natural laws, but in the knowledge of these laws . . . freedom of the will, therefore, means nothing but the capacity to make decisions with knowledge of the subject." We know the subject only too well, and he is a monster. Do we have the capacity to make a decision—now that Dr. Rodney has provided us with the knowledge of the subject? The people must answer.

Dar es Salaam, Tanzania
December 1971

INDEX